Palgrave Histories of Policing, Punishment and Justice

Series Editor
David G. Barrie, University of Western Australia, Crawley, Australia

Since the 1960s, studies of police, punishment and the courts have been an integral and popular part of historical scholarship, and have followed in the historical trajectory of a more expansive criminal justice apparatus around the world. This international book series aims to examine and debate some of the most pressing issues and problems in the field, and to stimulate new directions in research. It will showcase the work of both emerging and leading scholars of the social, cultural and institutional histories of police, punishment and the judicial sphere, and welcomes work grounded in various disciplines including criminology, sociology, history, law, legal history and political science.

More information about this series at
http://www.palgrave.com/gp/series/15080

Robyn Blewer

Child Witnesses in Twentieth Century Australian Courtrooms

palgrave
macmillan

Robyn Blewer
Griffith University
Brisbane, QLD, Australia

Palgrave Histories of Policing, Punishment and Justice
ISBN 978-3-030-69790-7 ISBN 978-3-030-69791-4 (eBook)
https://doi.org/10.1007/978-3-030-69791-4

Cover illustration: f8 archive/Alamy Stock Photo

This Palgrave Macmillan imprint is published by the registered company Springer Nature Switzerland AG
The registered company address is: Gewerbestrasse 11, 6330 Cham, Switzerland

Preface

I believed her. She was only about eight years old, but I thought she was more impressive than many of the adult witnesses I'd observed in court. By then, I'd watched many children give evidence. I'd watched them cry, some silently, some with great anguish that could be felt through the CCTV screen they appeared on. I watched them re-live their trauma and be traumatised anew as they were accused of lying or imagining things or simply forgetting what had really happened. I thought about how brave this girl was to have endured the abuse, then walked past the room where the offender was sleeping to tell her parents what had happened, to have dealt with the various interviews with police and health professionals, and the pre-recording of her evidence where she appeared composed and truthful even in the face of a difficult cross-examination. It was part of my job as a Judge's Associate to take the jury's verdict at the end of the trial. "How do you find the accused? Guilty, or not guilty?" "Not guilty." *Not* guilty. I was stunned. I'd sat through the same trial they had. This was not the outcome I expected. Judging by his reaction, I don't think it was the outcome the accused expected either. After completing the remaining formalities, I sat back down. I thought again about that little girl. Someone would now have to tell her the jury didn't believe her. Did they fall back on old misconceptions? Children lie. Children fantasise. Or maybe they did believe her, but they gave *him* the benefit of their doubt. Everyone had played their part properly and done their job as required, including the jury. Justice was served. I just wasn't sure I agreed with that idea of justice.

I couldn't help but think, was this the best our criminal justice system could do for these children? How had we gotten to this point, in the early twentieth century? If this was the best, then how awful must the process of giving evidence been for children in the past? What had changed? Who'd fought for these children in the past? How had they managed to change things?

I'd spent the previous twelve months as an Associate to a patient, knowledgeable, experienced and very well-respected judge. "You won't change things as a lawyer, a barrister or even a judge," he said. He wasn't saying members of our profession don't contribute to improving the trial process. They do every day. There wouldn't be any justice without them. By and large, though, they play in the system. They don't change it. The judge told me if I wanted to change things, I had to go back to university. I had to do research, get my research published and change things that way.

Eight years later, the opportunity to do that research arose. As part of my role with the Australian Research Council Laureate Project, *The Prosecution Project*, I contributed to the work of digitising Australian criminal court records from the early nineteenth century onwards and set about trying to answer some of the questions I'd had about what the past was like for child witnesses. I want to acknowledge my colleagues in this project: Professor Mark Finnane, Dr. Yorick Smaal, Dr. Andy Kaladelfos, Dr. Alana Piper, Dr. Lisa Durnian and Mel Davies. I could not have asked for a better team to work with. In particular, I thank Professor Finnane for taking a chance on a commercial litigation lawyer with a Master of Criminology who had no experience researching history but told him she "really liked history."

Thanks to my family and friends who have also supported me through this process, especially Paul, Eleanor, India and Lucas.

For the children in this book, and those giving evidence in court around Australia every day, you are heard.

Brisbane, Australia Robyn Blewer

Contents

1 **Introduction** 1

2 **Child Witnesses and the Common Law** 13

3 **"*Those Troublesome Men in Blue*": Police** 33

4 **"*If the Law Doesn't Get You, the Lord Will*": Competency and Capacity** 63

5 **"*And the Kiddie Was at Home*": The Courtroom Environment** 107

6 **"*What the Nipper Said Was True*": Examination** 139

7 **"*Trying to Bend the Law to Fit*": Corroboration** 171

8 **"*The Law Which Professed to Protect … Served to Crush*": Indigenous Child Witnesses** 209

9 **"*Changes in Law Were Full of Danger*": Conclusion** 241

Index 253

Abbreviations

ALRC	Australian Law Reform Commission
CCTV	Closed Circuit Television
CJ	Chief Justice
CWA	Country Women's Association
DCJ	District Court Judge
ICARE	Interviewing Children and Recording Evidence Program
J	Justice
KC	King's Counsel
PACT	Protect All Children Today Inc. (Qld)
QC	Queen's Counsel
SCAN	Suspected Child Abuse and Neglect
SPCC	Society for the Prevention of Cruelty to Children

List of Tables

Table 4.1	Pre-twentieth-century legislation permitting receipt of unsworn testimony of child witnesses	70
Table 4.2	Summary of statutory reforms to the competency of child witnesses	98
Table 5.1	Summary of legislative reforms for support of child witnesses from 1975	129
Table 7.1	Reforming corroboration rules and requirements	201

1
Introduction

The dingo *did* kill the baby.

We know this because after a Supreme Court trial, a Federal Court appeal, a High Court appeal and three coronial inquests, a fourth coronial inquest told us.[1] How else do we know Azaria Chamberlain was killed by a dingo? Because six-year-old Aidan said so. Shortly after he watched the animal take his baby sister from the tent they shared on that fateful night in 1980, Aidan told a woman who was helping search for the baby that "the dog had got his baby in its tummy." A few hours later, he told a different woman that a dog had taken the baby (*Chamberlain v. The Queen (No.2)* (1984) 153 CLR 521, 546). Two years later, in 1982, Aidan's mother, Lindy Chamberlain, was convicted of murdering her nine-week-old daughter, Azaria. Aidan was not called to give evidence at his mother's trial (*Chamberlain v. The Queen (No.2)* (1984) 153 CLR 521) and Lindy Chamberlain spent four years in prison for a murder she did not commit. In 2012, thirty-two years after Azaria died, the fourth coronial inquest into the matter found that a dingo had, in fact, killed the baby girl (*Inquest into the death of Azaria Chantel Loren Chamberlain*

R. Blewer, *Child Witnesses in Twentieth Century Australian Courtrooms*, Palgrave Histories of Policing, Punishment and Justice,
https://doi.org/10.1007/978-3-030-69791-4_1

2012, 11). The case, including Lindy's exoneration in 1988, has become the stuff of legal history legend in Australia, and, following Meryl Streep's portrayal of Chamberlain in the film *Evil Angels* (1988), is well known around the globe. It is impossible to say for sure, but had the law been more open to listening to young Aidan, this miscarriage of justice may never have occurred.

Over half a century before Aidan witnessed the dingo take his sister from the tent, nine-year-old Alice was running through the streets of inner-city Melbourne, crying hysterically. It was 2 am on Sunday 2 December 1923. Her feet were bare. She was dressed only in her night-gown. Bursting through the doors of the Carlton Police Station, she told the officer on duty that a man was "cutting her mother's neck with a knife" (*Weekly Times* 1923, 11). Within hours, the man, her mother's boyfriend Charles Johnson, was charged with murder. Just eight weeks later, Alice appeared as the chief prosecution witness at Johnson's trial. Stepping into the witness box in Melbourne's Supreme Court, she burst into tears (*The Argus* 1924, 31). Alice nevertheless managed to recount the events of the night she had witnessed her mother's horrific murder. The defendant tried to cut her mother's throat but found the knife too blunt. He had then picked up a sharper knife and kept cutting. Alice's testimony and additional medical evidence proved the defendant had done more than just cut her mother's throat. In front of the nine-year-old child, Johnson had virtually severed the woman's head from her body. Johnson couldn't remember committing the offence as he had been high on cocaine at the time. He was found guilty and sentenced to death (*The Argus* 1924, 31).

It has been assumed that prior to the late twentieth century, children rarely appeared in common law courts because of the legal and procedural barriers that prevented them from giving evidence (*R v Brasier* (1779) 168 E.R 202; Goodman 1982, 9; McGough 1994, 1–2). This is not the case, though. For many crimes to be prosecuted, the criminal justice system needed the evidence of children. The unfortunate reality is that children always have been—and continue to be—called upon to participate in this most adult, combative, adversarial process. This book draws on cases involving more than 250 children who gave evidence in criminal courts in Australia during the twentieth century. It considers the impact that the law—and law reforms—had on cases like Lindy Chamberlain's, or on children just like Alice.

Until recently, it was largely assumed the law and society generally were either indifferent towards children and child victims of crime, or simply did not trust them to be truthful (Australian Law Reform Commission and Australian Human Rights and Equal Opportunity Commission 1997; McGough 1994, 1–3). The testimony of witnesses at the Royal Commission into Institutional Responses to Child Sexual Abuse brought the issue of believing children's reports of abuse into the public spotlight (Royal Commission into Institutional Responses to Child Sexual Abuse 2017). The cases in this book demonstrate that, while child witnesses were a challenge for the criminal justice system throughout the twentieth century, those involved in the process were not necessarily indifferent towards them. The development of evidence law towards the end of the nineteenth and throughout the twentieth centuries, though, resulted in the construction of impossibly high barriers for children giving evidence in court. While many of these reforms drew on assumptions about children and childhood, the structural framework of rules of evidence also played a significant part in the difficulties courts have had in receiving the testimony of child witnesses. Would they be a credible witness? (Ceci and Bruck 1993, 403) Was their evidence corroborated? (Lyon and LaMagna 2007, 1029, 1031; Backhouse 2001, 297, 310–311) How would they cope in the courtroom environment, and with cross-examination? What about the long-term psychological effects giving evidence in court might have on the child? (Goodman 1984, 5; Cashmore and Horsky 1987, 66; McGough 1994, 3; Zajac et al. 2012, 181, 182; Saywitz and Nathanson 1993, 613, 614).

Child witnesses presented a challenge for the legal system in various forms. The cases in this book reveal a process that was aware of these challenges and often prepared to respond to them, where possible, by modifying ordinary courtroom practices. There were three ways in which such adaptations were executed. First, court processes were more pragmatic and flexible than they are today. This allowed for informal modifications, for example, to courtroom procedures to help children who appeared upset (*The Advertiser* 1923, 12; *The Argus* 1932, 1). Second, changes to the law were implemented through the incremental development of common law principles including, for example, those relevant to questions of competency and corroboration. Finally, legislation introduced throughout the century, particularly between 1975 and 2000, heralded new approaches to child witness testimony. These comprehensive reforms were implemented via legislative reforms, which removed a substantial degree of the discretion judicial officers had previously enjoyed, addressed the distinction between sworn and unsworn testimony, abolished rules requiring corroboration and facilitated the adoption of technological innovations allowing courts to receive the testimony of child witnesses in ways courts a century beforehand could never have imagined.

Just as modern understanding of these historical processes is beset by assumptions about the law's approach to child witnesses, so too were historical processes beset by assumptions about children. These assumptions permeated the law, psychological research and society throughout much of the twentieth century. In 1911, for example, Belgian child psychologist Julien Varendonck was giving evidence in a murder trial where two children were the key prosecution witnesses. "When," he asked, "are we going to give up, in all civilised nations, listening to children in courts of law?" (Goodman 1982, 9)

The legal system did not heed Varendonck's suggestions, perhaps realising, as it always had, that if the justice system was to have any appearance or chance of delivering justice, it would have to continue to hear the evidence of children. In spite of this awareness, the criminal justice system continued to make assumptions about the behaviour and psychology of children in assessing their testimony. Towards the end of the 1960s and into the 1970s, researchers took a renewed interest in child victims of crime as a result of medical "discoveries" like "battered child syndrome" and "failure to thrive" diagnoses (Scott and Swain 2002, 112; Fogarty 2008, 52, 58). This medical interest in child victims expanded considerably in the 1980s to include concerns about the abuse, particularly sexual abuse, of children. This in turn led to greater interest from researchers, the legal profession and the public in the prosecution of offences involving the testimony of children (McGough 1994, 10; Scott and Swain 2002, 122). In 1984, American psychologist Gail Goodman rephrased Varendonck's question, conversely asking "*when should* we listen to children's testimony in a court of law?" (Goodman 1984, 10).

Examining child witness law, policy and procedure in criminal courts throughout Australia during the twentieth century and into the twenty-first, this book traces the journey such children took through the criminal justice system. It considers how children engaged with police officers; how courts assessed a child's capacity for truthfulness; the procedure when children appeared in court; how lawyers, barristers and defendants examined and cross-examined children; and how judges received the testimony of children and advised juries on how such evidence should be received. Simply put, this book reconsiders both Varendonck and Goodman's questions, instead asking *when did* we listen to children's testimony in Australian criminal courts of law during the twentieth century?

The Structure of the Book

The book is divided into four parts.

Part One—Introduction

For those unfamiliar with the Australian or English legal systems, Chapter 2 provides a background to the child witness in the context of the English common law tradition. Some of the procedures and procedural reforms discussed in this book reflect complicated intersections between different sources of Australian and English law. Chapter 2 provides some background to the legal system that is discussed throughout the remainder of the book. It also traces the various social, legal and scientific attitudes towards child witnesses that were prevalent across the twentieth century. It considers the wider psychological and cultural understanding of children and childhood. Despite a long history of and fascination with child witnesses, there was little academic research or writing on the topic for most of the twentieth century. Methodological issues dogged early research conducted by psychologists and there was very little legal academic writing on the topic. This changed in the mid-1960s, when researchers and the medical and legal professions began to take a greater interest in the abuse of children.

Part Two—Getting into Court

The second part of the book begins the process of tracing the child witness's journey through the criminal justice system. It examines the hurdles children had to overcome before their evidence could be received in court. Chapter 3 explores the role of police in detecting, investigating and preparing cases involving child witnesses. Police are often described as the gatekeepers of the criminal justice process (Jordan 2015, 84, 96; New Zealand Law Commission 2015, 135; Victorian Law Reform Commission 2004, 103; Cooper 2005, 456, 461). They are the first contact a child has with the criminal justice system and they play a crucial role in gathering evidence from child witnesses. From their initial investigations through to determining whether charges should be laid and often attending court themselves, police have always played a substantial role in getting a child witness into court.

The decision to charge a suspect and proceed with a prosecution did not necessarily mean a child would be heard in court. They still had to prove themselves capable of giving evidence—in particular, capable of swearing an oath, or in some instances, "sufficiently intelligent" (to use the legal terminology of the time) to understand the need to tell the truth in court. Chapter 4 thus explores how a child's competency and capacity to give evidence were assessed. While children today are generally, though not always, presumed to be competent witnesses unless proven otherwise, in the past the law presumed they were *in*competent. Legislative reforms in the 1980s and 1990s removed this presumption in most states, thus removing a significant barrier to child witnesses being able to give evidence.

Chapter 5 considers the nature of the courtroom environment. The experience of being in such a place, with the austere architecture—rows of chairs, elevated benches and the like—may well be intimidating for even trained professionals. And yet, for most of the twentieth century, to have their evidence heard, child witnesses had to be able to give their testimony in crowded courtrooms, in full view of the court and in close proximity to the defendant. Contrary to contemporary assumptions, however, there was a significant degree of support shown to children throughout the twentieth century. The focus of this chapter is the implementation of various supportive measures to help child witnesses. Distressed or quietly spoken children might be seated next to the judge—in one instance, even on his knee. Some children held toys. Some sat with support people and the public was often excluded from the room while a child was giving evidence. Efforts at supporting children could attract controversy if this meant possibly compromising common law principles like open justice or the fairness of the trial. In those circumstances, principle took precedence over the interests of the children. This chapter demonstrates the extent to which children giving evidence in the first three-quarters of the twentieth century had more agency and power in the courtroom than they do now, notwithstanding modern advancements in technology and procedural reforms.

Part Three—Giving Evidence

The third part of this book considers elements of trial procedure that impacted specifically on the testimony of children. Chapter 6 considers the primacy of oral testimony in the adversarial trial. For the better part of the twentieth century, the only way children could give their evidence was by standing in the courtroom and answering questions from the prosecutor and defence counsel—and, if necessary, from defendants directly. The reforms of the late twentieth century led to substantial changes to the examination of children. A child's evidence-in-chief, for example, could be received in the form of their video-recorded police interview. Defendants were precluded from cross-examining children themselves. This chapter suggests this is a case of the more things change, the more they stay the same. By the end of the twentieth century, a significant body of research demonstrated cross-examination, in particular, could be harmful to children. Nevertheless, the legal system remained committed to it as the preferred way of testing a child's evidence—and ascertaining the truth.

Even though a child might have proven their competency to give evidence and been able to stand—somewhere—in the courtroom, and withstood the pressure of examination and cross-examination, the law still placed strict limits on how such testimony could be used to convict a defendant. Chapter 7 focusses on the various contexts in which the testimony of children needed to be corroborated as a means of overcoming the perceived risks of unreliable testimony being admitted in court. Children who had demonstrated their competency to swear an oath had their credibility questioned yet again through the common law practice of judges warning juries of the danger of convicting a defendant in the absence of evidence corroborating a child witness's testimony.

Part 4—Reflections and Conclusions

The purpose of collecting the cases for this book was primarily to find examples of the application of relevant legal principles and processes, like competency tests, examination and cross-examination of children, and the impact of corroboration rules. Other than being a child under eighteen years of age, particular types of witnesses were not sought out. Similarly, the choice was made not to select or exclude cases on the basis of offence type, gender, age group and the like. But during the course of conducting this research, only one of the 250 children in the original sample was Indigenous. This was interesting, yet not surprising, knowing what we know today of the continued mistreatment of Indigenous children in Australian criminal justice systems. To a large extent, it seems that offences where Indigenous children were witnesses or victims were not prosecuted. By digging much deeper, a small sample of cases was collected where First Nations children gave evidence in court. While it is impossible to conclude that these cases are representative of what occurred in courts during the twentieth century, the examination of these cases in Chapter 8 contributes to understanding if, and how, Indigenous children participated in the criminal justice process as witnesses. These child witnesses participated in the same process and were largely treated in the same way as the non-Indigenous children who appear throughout the book. Some were treated very well; others dreadfully. It is in the peripheral details of these few cases though, where we see how Indigenous cultural practices (or assumptions about such practices) were used against the witnesses, how the criminal justice system exploited these children and how, as the Women's Christian Temperance Union said in 1934, the law that served to protect Indigenous peoples "crushed them" (*Daily News* 1934, 5).

While this book uncovers a story about children that has been largely overlooked until now, it also illustrates the extent to which, as legal scholar Roscoe Pound observed in 1910, "changes in law [are] full of danger" (Pound 1921, 167). The findings of each chapter are remarkably similar. In describing child witness law, policy and procedure, they each demonstrate the child witness's journey did not change throughout the first three-quarters of the century. There was little (if any) reform during this period. And yet, each chapter also uncovers evidence of opposition to those long-held practices and procedures. Such opposition, while forward-thinking for its time, was uniformly ignored by judges and lawmakers until the mid-1970s onwards, when there was a period of substantial reform. But even the changes that occurred in the late twentieth century still demonstrate how the system remained largely the same as it ever was. Reforms aimed to make it easier for child witnesses to give evidence, but only to the extent that the system—the adversarial trial—remained unchanged. Barrister Andrew Boe made a similar observation of the legal system generally, saying "[t]his system has hardly changed over the century or so since Federation. Its edges have been tweaked by incremental reforms, but some aspects are due for a fundamental rethink" (Boe 2020, 2). In tracing over a century of reforms (and lack thereof) in child witness procedure and policy, this book raises the question of whether, given the long history of ignoring the need for reform, this is one aspect of the system that is due for such change.

Note

1. For details of the first and second inquests, the trial, Federal Court appeal and High Court appeal, see *Chamberlain v The Queen (No. 2)* (1984) 153 CLR 521. For the Royal Commission, see *Re Conviction of Chamberlain* (1988) 38 NTLR 82. Third inquest—13 December 1995, Mr Lowndes, Coroner Northern Territory, see https://justice.nt.gov.au/__data/assets/pdf_file/0005/209057/azaria-hamberlain-appendix-av-web.pdf. Fourth inquest: *Inquest into the death of Azaria Chantel Loren Chamberlain* [2012] NTMC 020 accessed 29 October 2020 at https://justice.nt.gov.au/__data/assets/pdf_file/0006/205377/azaria-chantel-chamberlain.pdf.

References

The Advertiser (Adelaide). 1923. "A Chief Justice and a Child Witness." February 22, 1923.

The Argus (Melbourne). 1924. "Carlton Murder." February 16, 1924.

The Argus (Melbourne). 1932. "To-Day's News." July 8, 1932.

Australian Human Rights Commission, *Bringing them home: National Inquiry into the Separation of Aboriginal and Torres Strait Islander Children From their Families* (Report, April 1997).

Australian Law Reform Commission and Human Rights and Equal Opportunity Commission, *Seen and Heard: Priority for Children in the Legal Process* (Report No. 84, 1997).

Backhouse, Constance. 2001. "The Doctrine of Corroboration in Sexual Assault Trials in Early Twentieth Century Canada and Australia." *Queen's Law Journal* 26 (2): 297–338.

Boe, Andrew. 2020. *The Truth Hurts*. Sydney: Hachette.

Cashmore, Judy, and Marion Horsky. 1987. *Child Sexual Assault – The Court Response*. Sydney: New South Wales Bureau of Crime Statistics and Research Attorney General's Department.

Ceci, Stephen J., and Maggie Bruck. 1993. "Suggestibility of the Child Witness: A Historical Review and Synthesis." *Psychological Bulletin* 113 (3): 403–439.

Chamberlain v. The Queen (No. 2) (1984) 153 CLR 521.

Cooper, Debbie. 2005. "Pigot Unfulfilled: Video-Recorded Cross-Examination Under Section 28 of the *Youth Justice and Criminal Evidence Act 1999.*" *Criminal Law Review* (June): 456–466.

Daily News (Perth). "Suggestions for Native Welfare Progress." April 6, 1934.

Evil Angels, directed by Fred Schepisi (1988; Australia, Cannon International).

Fogarty, John. 2008. "Some Aspects of the Early History of Child Protection in Australia." *Family Matters* 78: 52–59.

Goodman, Gail. 1982. "Children's Testimony in Historical Perspective." *Journal of Social Issues* 40 (2): 9–31.

Goodman, Gail. 1984. "The Child Witness: An Introduction." *Journal of Social Issues* 40 (2): 1–7.

Inquest into the Death of Azaria Chantel Loren Chamberlain [2012] NTMC 020.

Jordan, Jan. 2015. "Justice for Rape Victims? The Spirit May Sound Willing, But the Flesh Remains Weak." In *Crime, Victims and Policy: International Contexts, Local Experiences*, edited by Dean Wilson and Stuart Ross, 84–106. London: Palgrave Macmillan.

Lyon, Thomas D., and Raymond Lamagna. 2007. "The History of Children's Hearsay: From Old Bailey to Post-Davis." *Indiana Law Journal* 82 (4): 1029–1058.

McGough, Lucy S. 1994. *Child Witnesses: Fragile Voices in the American Legal System*. New Haven: Yale University Press.

New Zealand Law Commission, *The Justice Response to Victims of Sexual Violence* (Report No 136, 2015).

Pound, Roscoe. 1921. "The Spirit of the Common Law." College of Law, Faculty Publications. 1. https://digitalcommons.unl.edu/lawfacpub/1. Last accessed 29 October 2020.

Royal Commission into Institutional Responses to Child Sexual Abuse. 2017. "Final Report." https://www.childabuseroyalcommission.gov.au/final-report. Last accessed 9 March 2021.

R v Brasier (1779) 168 E.R 202.

Saywitz, Karen, and Rebecca Nathanson. 1993. "Children's Testimony and the Perceptions of Stress In and Out of the Courtroom." *Child Abuse and Neglect* 17 (5): 613–622.

Scott, Dorothy, and Shurlee Swain. 2002. *Confronting Cruelty: Historical Perspectives on Child Abuse*. Melbourne: Melbourne University Press.

Victorian Law Reform Commission, *Sexual Offences* (Final Report, August 2004).

Weekly Times (Melbourne). 1923. "Woman's Throat Cut." December 8, 1923.

Zajac, Rachel, Sarah O'Neill, and Harlene Hayne. 2012. "Disorder in the Courtroom? Child Witnesses Under Cross-Examination." *Developmental Review* 32 (3): 181–204.

2

Child Witnesses and the Common Law

Bailiff: Calling Bartholomew J. Simpson to the stand.
[Bart, covered in bandages, makes his way to witness stand in a wheelchair]
Mr Burns: Oh please.
Judge: Hello Bart. Now you know the difference between telling the truth and telling a lie don't you son?
Bart: Maybe.
Judge: Well, you wouldn't lie to the United States would you Bart?
[Homer Simpson and lawyer Lionel Hutz gesture towards Bart, "No, no!"]
Bart: No.
Judge: Good. Proceed, Mr Hutz.
Mr Hutz: Thank you, your Honour. Now Bart, I want you to tell the jury in your own words exactly what happened on the day of the accident.
Bart: Yes Sir. It was a beautiful Sunday afternoon. I was playing in my wholesome childlike way, little realising that I was about to be struck down by the luxury car of death [recounts accident]. Luckily, I was not killed that day although sometimes (sobbing) … I wish … I had been.

R. Blewer, *Child Witnesses in Twentieth Century Australian Courtrooms*, Palgrave Histories of Policing, Punishment and Justice, https://doi.org/10.1007/978-3-030-69791-4_2

[Jury and public gallery visibly moved and crying]
Mr Burns (stands): Oh, he's lying.
Mr Hutz: Now that's believable testimony. (*The Simpsons* 1991)

This image of the popular cartoon character, Bart Simpson, tugging at the heartstrings of the jury and holding the public gallery in the palm of his hand exemplifies the nature of the common law adversarial trial process. The scene bears the hallmarks of many of the questions considered in this book. Before embarking on this exploration of the child witness in Australian criminal courts, it is appropriate to consider the broader legal framework that underpins the following chapters. In his battle against Mr Burns, Bart Simpson's testimony just had to be believable—not necessarily truthful. This is the nature of the adversarial trial process, a process that has been described by legal historian John Langbein as the defining feature of criminal justice in England and other common law countries like Australia, New Zealand and Canada (Langbein 2005, 106).

In 1883, English judge James Fitzjames Stephen described the adversarial trial as "always more or less of a battle" where the

> object of the rules of evidence and procedure is to keep such warfare within reasonable bounds, and to prevent the combatants from inflicting upon each other, and upon third parties, injuries, the inflicting of which is not absolutely essential to the purposes of the combat. (Fitzjames Stephen 1883, 432)

With descriptors such as "warfare," "combatants," "injuries" and "combat,“ it is little wonder the capacity for this trial process to elicit accurate testimony from witnesses—adult and child alike—has been questioned (Muller 2001, 2; Steffen 1988, 799; Bowden et al. 2014, 539). It is, however, the process adopted in Australian criminal courts since the late eighteenth century. While early adaptations of the process were made in order to suit the needs of a penal colony, over time the criminal trial process came to mirror that of England.

Sources of Child Witness Law and Procedure in Australia

The law in Australia is essentially drawn from three sources: the rules and principles derived from decisions of judges in court; legislation made by parliament; and other sources such as state and federal constitutions, international law and instruments. The body of law made by judges is referred to as case law and, further still, as the common law. The phrase "common law" is also used to describe the broader system of law "inherited" from England, which can be used to describe case law and legislation collectively. Australia, for example, like England, Canada, New Zealand and, in parts, the United States, is described as a "common law" country.

The common law as a legal system has its origins in the early twelfth century and thus has a long history (van Caenegem 1988, 3–4). It can be contrasted with civil systems often found in European countries, where law is codified or written down as one cohesive source. The common law is not codified. It is written in the form of judgments but is not set down as a single source. This system of documenting and following earlier decisions of judges became known as the common law because the law and legal principles in these court decisions were said to be "common" to all of England. To maintain this sense of commonality, the reasoning process of judges of superior courts in similar kinds of cases had to be adopted by lower courts as a precedent for their own decisions. This so-called "doctrine of precedent" has always been inherently rigid to give the common law the requisite stability and consistency which, in turn, helps to ensure its legitimacy and longevity. Explaining this concept in the case of *Mabo No. 2*, which recognised native title and overturned the centuries-old doctrine of *terra nullius* (the notion that this land was uninhabited when the English arrived) in the process, Justice Brennan said:

> In discharging its duty to declare the common law of Australia, this Court is not free to adopt rules that accord with contemporary notions of justice and human rights if their adoption would fracture the skeleton of principle which gives the body of our law its shape and internal consistency.

> Australian law is not only the historical successor of, but is an organic development from, the law of England. (*Mabo v Queensland (No. 2)* (1993) 175 CLR 1, 29)

Thus, in a common law legal system, earlier cases decided by judges are difficult for subsequent courts, including the High Court, to overturn without carefully considering the impact of such a departure, and whether it would threaten the "skeleton of principle" Brennan J describes.

The phrase "common law" is not only used to describe a legal system. It is also used to refer to the case law comprised of decisions of judges, as opposed to legislation made by parliaments. When discussing rules and principles of law, judicial decisions will often be referred to as "common law" rules, principles or doctrines. Thus, because there are two primary sources of law, there can be two different sets of laws applying to a topic or issue at the same time. In Chapter 6 on corroboration, for example, the "common law" approach to corroboration of a child's testimony and the approach in statute are different and evolve separately. Similarly, in Chapter 4, the procedure for a child to demonstrate their competency to give evidence was historically found in common law (i.e. case law) but in the late nineteenth century, the procedure was supplemented by statute to allow unsworn evidence in certain cases. The doctrine of parliamentary sovereignty means that, as long as legislation is made within the powers of the legislature, if there is a conflict between the common law rules and statute, the law made by parliament is supreme (Sanson and Anthony 2019, 115).

While all Australian states and territories are common law jurisdictions and thus able to draw on case law, the federal composition of the Commonwealth of Australia impacts upon the administration of criminal justice. When designing the new federation and drafting its constitution in the late nineteenth century, the Australian colonies conceded to the federal government only those powers that would be necessary for, and in the interests of, the nation. Criminal justice was thought of primarily as a matter for the states. Thus, when the Commonwealth came into existence on 1 January 1901, each state retained the power to administer its own criminal justice system with a possible right of appeal from state courts to the High Court of Australia and, ultimately, to the Privy Council in England. It is for this reason Australia now has nine separate criminal justice systems—a federal system and systems for each of the six states, and one for each of the two territories. Within each jurisdiction, the reception of English law meant the reception of the common law and the combination of legislation and case law as the two primary sources of law.

Pre-twentieth-century Attitudes Towards Children and Child Witnesses

In addition to understanding the interplay between common law and legislation, and the different state and federal jurisdictions, in considering child witnesses, it is also important to consider the definition of "child." The child is a concept the law has constructed and reconstructed over centuries. There is not the scope in this book to provide a comprehensive account of this history, but the following brief overview provides the relevant background to the issue of defining who is, and is not, a child for the purpose of considering child witnesses in the twentieth century. The process of defining and redefining childhood could be viewed as a reflection of the common law's capacity to adapt to meet changing notions of childhood. It may also be understood, though, as an example of the artificial construct that is "childhood." In her book *By Birth or Consent: Children, Law and the Anglo-American Revolution in History*, historian Holly Brewer traces the law's shifting approach to the status of children. She writes:

> In sixteenth-century England, children over age seven were of "ripe age" to marry (under seven they could contract only "espousals," or betrothals). Four-year-olds could make wills to give away their goods and chattels. Children of any age could bind themselves into apprenticeships. Eight-year-olds could be hanged for arson or any other felony. Teenagers were routinely elected to Parliament. Children who owned sufficient property could vote. And custody as we know it did not exist. (Brewer 2005, 1)

To twenty-first-century sensibilities, the idea that a four-year-old could make a will seems inexplicable. But in the sixteenth century there was no such thing as "childhood." During the seventeenth and eighteenth centuries, there was a shift in the law's approach to the status of children. In this "age of reason," Brewer argues, those without the capacity for reason, including children, "became unable to make most legal decisions that affected themselves or others" (2005, 3). The impact of this new approach to authority and reason led prominent lawyers, legal scholars and judges from the eighteenth century such as Matthew Hale in 1736 (Backhouse 2000, 79), Henry Bathurst in 1761 (Lyon and LaMagna 2007, 1031) and William Blackstone in 1765 (Blackstone 1765–1769, IV Ch. 27), to consider the dilemma the child witness posed for the administration of justice. Each thought the testimony of children should be accepted on the basis that it may be the best evidence available, and preferable to accepting hearsay evidence. Each also questioned the extent to which the testimony of children should be relied upon to convict an accused, lest an innocent man be convicted. Blackstone articulated this concern in the eighteenth century, when he wrote it was "better that ten guilty persons escape than that one innocent suffer" (Blackstone 1765–1769, IV Ch. 27). "Blackstone's ratio," as the statement came to be known, has been "firmly rooted in fundamental moral and legal discourse" ever since (de Keijser et al. 2014, 43). Benjamin Franklin echoed Blackstone's sentiments, arguing it would be better for one hundred guilty persons to escape than one innocent person suffer (Franklin 1706–1790, 293). Jeremy Bentham, however, took exception to this principle, arguing in 1825 that Blackstone was effectively suggesting "nobody ought to be punished, lest an innocent man be punished" (Bentham 1825, in Halvorsen 2004, 3).

At the time these legal scholars were writing about children and the law, the concept of "childhood" was being redefined. A case documented by Holly Brewer provides an example of the law's struggle to arrive at an appropriate understanding of childhood for the time. In 1748, ten-year-old William was found guilty of murdering a five-year-old girl. The punishment for murder was execution. The boy was guilty of murder, and by law, should have been hung, yet William's punishment no longer seemed right, even though it once had. William's life lay in the balance.

For the next nine years, he was imprisoned while his fate was debated. William was imprisoned between the ages of ten and nineteen, when he was pardoned by the King on the condition that he join the navy. "His case," Brewer writes, "helped to define a transition in standards for authority and responsibility, standards that applied not simply to children but to all members of society" (2005, 5).

William's murder conviction occurred "at a crossroads in the history of justice" (Brewer 2005, 5). Despite his young age, William was capable of forming the requisite intent to murder his five-year-old co-worker, who had wet the bed they were sharing. The issue of criminal responsibility provides a fitting example of the law's complicated approach towards children changing over time. The "ancient" common law doctrine of *doli incapax* established the principle (still applicable today) that children under ten years of age are incapable of forming the intent to commit a crime. Between ten and fourteen years of age, their responsibility is conditional upon issues such as their capacity to understand that what they were doing was wrong (van Krieken 2020, 86). The *doli incapax* case law, which developed in the nineteenth and early twentieth centuries, clarified that just the doing of a criminal act was not enough to convict a child; they had to have the requisite knowledge the act was wrong also. This case law, as sociologist Robert van Krieken notes, created difficulties for the application of the doctrine in the second half of the twentieth century, as the concept of "childhood" changed again and children came before the courts in different circumstances than in the earlier centuries (van Krieken 2020, 89). "Real, live children and young people often fit poorly within the criminal law's usual approach to legal subjectivity…" (van Krieken 2020, 101).

After redefining the concept of childhood in the seventeenth and eighteenth centuries, children once again became a focus of law reform as a result of the child protection movement of the mid- to late nineteenth century. Newly established child protection organisations were concerned about the plight of child victims of abuse and neglect (Jackson 2000, 52). Law reforms focussed on the welfare of children and, for modern criminal justice systems in Australia and throughout the western world, this involved the establishment of reformatory schools and children's courts. The advocacy of child protection organisations and their particular concern about the sexual abuse of young girls was vital to the widespread increase in the age of consent for children. Providing further evidence of the challenge of defining childhood, chronological age limits for consent as defined in legislation differed across state jurisdictions. In 1891, Victoria raised the age of consent from 12 to 16 years, while Queensland raised it from 12 to 14, and in 1910, NSW raised their age of consent from 14 to 16, having raised it from 12 to 14 in 1883 (Smaal 2013, 715–716; Kaladelfos 2009, 14–15).

The child as a concept remained undefined into the twentieth century. Neither the 1924 nor 1959 versions of the *Declaration on the Rights of the Child* contain a definition of who is a child, even though children are clearly the focus of such instruments (Tobin and Oxford University Press 2019, 21–22). As many of the cases in this book demonstrate, the problem of obtaining evidence even of birth, let alone age, was a challenge for many children and courts, and the reason for use of such vague terms as "tender years" found in case law and legislation. In 1989, the United Nations Convention on the Rights of the Child settled on a chronological definition, stating:

> For the purposes of the present Convention, a child means every human being below the age of eighteen years unless under the law applicable to the child, majority is attained earlier. (UN Convention on the Rights of the Child 1989, Article 1)

Even then, this definition was acknowledged by the Convention Committee as being limited, in that it relied on the capacity for records to be available which, for many children, may be impossible to produce (Tobin and Oxford University Press 2019, 31). In his commentary on the Convention on the Rights of the Child, lawyer and academic John Tobin emphasises the importance of recognising the heterogeneity of childhood, regardless of what approach is taken to defining such a concept (Tobin and Oxford University Press 2019, 31).

The Impact of Psychology and Medicine on Child Witness Law and Procedure

The interest in children, delinquency and child protection in the nineteenth century extended to psychology as numerous child psychologists undertook studies to contribute to a more scientific understanding of children. The suspicion legal scholars, like Hale and Blackstone, had previously expressed about testimony of child witnesses was confirmed in a number of psychological studies of children's memory and suggestibility carried out in the mid-nineteenth century (Davis 1998, 186). Despite methodological problems with these studies, the results gave credence to the view that children were unreliable witnesses. Psychologists Alfred Binet and Julien Varendonck each published research questioning the suitability of children giving evidence (Binet 1900; Varendonck 1911, in Ceci and Bruck 1995, 52). In 1910, French psychologist Ernest Dupré claimed his research proved "practically all that [children] say is erroneous" and judges "should not, in any case, give any effective value to the testimony of a child" (Dupre 1910, in Meyer 1997, 36). In his 1911 study, German paediatrician Adolf Baginsky argued children were "the most dangerous of all witnesses" (Baginsky 1911, in Goodman 1984, 2). British psychologists T.H. Pear and Stanley Wyatt were a rare exception to the scepticism featured in so much psychological research during this period. They claimed a child's testimony was "worthy of the utmost consideration" (Pear and Wyatt 1914, 401).

After this apparent flurry of research in the early twentieth century, the next two decades reflect a waning interest in child witnesses, with no new research on child witnesses published in the 1920s or 1930s (Goodman 1984, 22–23). Psychologists Stephen J. Ceci and Maggie Bruck refer to the period 1915 to 1963 as "the dry middle years" of twentiethcentury research. During this period, they note only 16 studies on children's suggestibility and memory (Ceci and Bruck 1995, 58). This may have been a result of the tension between the psychological and legal professions during the first half, at least, of the twentieth century. Even though the law and psychology were essentially in agreement as to the competency of child witnesses, the law showed little interest in listening to psychologists (Ceci and Bruck 1993, 407–408).

In 1935, American judge and scholar John Henry Wigmore challenged the relevance of psychological research to the law. Psychological tests, he maintained, were based on group averages and thus of no use to a court whose sole concern was the evidence of the particular witness in the courtroom during the hearing. Law as a practice, Wigmore argued, was based on rules developed over time in reference to specific problems. Psychology, on the other hand, was a scientific discipline more concerned with describing, explaining and predicting human behaviour (Wigmore, in Ceci and Bruck 1995, 50).

Although the legal system was dismissive of psychological research throughout the first half of the twentieth century, like the psychology profession, legal scholars and lawyers were rarely concerned with child witnesses as a topic of academic study. When they did turn their attention to children, the observations made were often distrustful and pessimistic. A review of twentieth-century legal academic writing on child sexual abuse in the United States found very few articles were published between 1900 and 1975 (Myers et al. 1999, 201). Of those that were found, four common themes emerged: a fear of fabricated allegations; fear of "crazy women"; a preoccupation with consent; and the need for corroboration of the victim's testimony (Myers et al. 1999, 203).

Professionals working in courtrooms, however, may not have been as distrustful as legal scholars. Myers and colleagues analysed 463 appellate court decisions on child sex abuse cases delivered between 1900 and 1950 in the United States. Their research found the appellate judges did not exhibit the level of scepticism towards children's testimony they had predicted based on their findings on the academic articles published during the same period. This, they concluded, may be attributed to the seriousness with which judges approached their role and the "powerful" impact of the evidence of children on those in the courtroom, including judges. The authors speculated that "face-to-face confrontation with the harm of sexual abuse dampens skepticism" (Myers et al. 1999, 212). These conclusions suggested the practice of law, particularly dealing first-hand with the testimony of children, had the potential to challenge the deficit views of children's capacity to give evidence commonly held by contemporary psychologists and legal academics.

The child protection movement of the late nineteenth and early twentieth centuries was born largely out of humanitarian or philanthropic concerns. A century on, child welfare again became the focus of law reform. The renewed interest in child protection that emerged during the 1960s, however, occurred primarily as a result of medical research and scientific understanding of children, rather than humanitarian or philanthropic ideals, although child welfare was a significant part of the reason for such attention. Dr. Henry Kempe and colleagues' research into "battered child syndrome," along with Dr. Dora Bialestock's "failure to thrive" research and the research of Drs. John and Robert Birrell on the impact of child abuse are regularly cited as representing the origins of this second wave of child protection. Given the first wave of child protection a century beforehand, it is erroneous to credit these doctors with "discovering" child abuse, but their research nevertheless attracted significant attention which, in turn, increased public awareness of child protection issues (Scott and Swain 2002, 120–135).

The development of medical research on children and child welfare had a direct impact on psychological research on child witnesses. Between 1979 and 1992, over one hundred new psychological studies involving child witnesses were carried out in the United States alone (Ceci and Bruck 1993, 408). These studies frequently resulted in positive perceptions of children and their capacity for giving truthful testimony (Davies and Westcott 2006, 153–169). With the results of these new studies, the legal profession exhibited more interest in behavioural sciences data that focussed on how to elicit testimony from children more effectively (Ceci and Bruck 1993, 403). In 1984, American psychologist Gail Goodman edited a special issue of the *Journal of Social Issues* which, she claimed, represented "perhaps the first attempt to provide a comprehensive, book-length treatment of psychological research, laws, and legal practices concerning child witnesses" (Goodman 1984, 2).

In Australia, psychologists conducted three important studies in the late 1980s, starting with Mark Brennan and Roslin E. Brennan's research in 1988, which considered the language of the legal process and the capacity of child witnesses to interpret this language (Brennan and Brennan 1988). Their research highlighted the substantial difficulties faced by child witnesses while trying to communicate with a court. A year later, in 1989, Peter Mertin published a study in which he found, when questioned appropriately, child witnesses gave reliable testimony (Mertin 1989, 23–32). The following year Judy Cashmore examined the advantages and disadvantages of using closed-circuit television and video-taped recordings of children's evidence (Cashmore 1990, 228). Later in the 1990s, Christine Eastwood and colleagues studied the experiences of child victims of sexual abuse in the criminal justice system (Eastwood, Patton and Stacy 1998).

The growing body of psychological research into child witnesses that emerged in the 1980s and 1990s led to the development of new research questions. Although still concerned with the reliability and accuracy of children's memory and testimony, psychologists began considering the effect giving evidence in court had upon children. The particularly brutal nature of the adversarial trial raised concerns for researchers. They considered the impact the stress of giving evidence might have on a child's development, including the effects of having to confront the accused in court (Follmer et al. 2009, 36–56; Goodman et al. 1991, 1–142). Other studies demonstrated the extent to which the adversarial trial process disadvantaged child witnesses and how children would each cope differently with the experience (Eisen and Goodman 1998, 717–738, Goodman et al. 1992, 8). This research made a significant contribution to statutory reforms of the late twentieth century, which sought to protect children from the potentially damaging impact of trial procedure (Ghetti et al. 2002, 241).

Child Witnesses in the Media

The increase in research into child witnesses in the late twentieth century may be attributable to the extensive press reporting of high-profile criminal cases involving the testimony of children (Goodman 1982, 10; Meyer 1997, 9). Criminologist Adam Tomison has suggested, in the Australian context at least, the media attention at this time could be as important to the second wave of child protection reform as the psychological research (2001, 50). There has always been something about child victims as witnesses that makes them a topic of fascination for the press. Indeed, without the press, this book would likely have been a dry, doctrinal account of case law and legislation, instead of one infused with stories of children, often told in their own words and reported verbatim by journalists.

During the 1970s and 1980s, a number of sensational child sexual abuse cases attracted considerable attention in the United States, the United Kingdom and Australia. Ceci and Bruck provide an overview of a number of these cases in their 1995 book, *Jeopardy in the Courtroom – A Scientific Analysis of Children's Testimony*. In addition to noting the prominence of the Salem Witch Trials in American jurisprudence—and popular culture—they highlight a number of cases such as the Little Rascals Day Care case, the Wee Care Nursery School case, the Old Cutler Presbyterian case and the Country Walk Babysitting Service case, which all concern allegations against child-care workers or carers (Ceci and Bruck 1995, 9–16). Lucy McGough notes even more child-care cases that gained considerable attention in the United States in the 1980s, such as the 1983 McMartin Pre-School case in which "at least 350" children made accusations against the school's founder and six teachers (McGough 1994, 8). In a pre-trial hearing in the McMartin case, a child spent one day in court being examined by the prosecutor, and then a further seventeen days in court being cross-examined by the defence (McGough 1994, 9).

Australia has its own cases involving highly publicised allegations of child sexual abuse in the 1980s and 1990s. New South Wales' Royal Commission into the New South Wales Police Service (also known as the Wood Royal Commission) details the circumstances and investigations of two of these cases in *Volume IV – The Paedophile Inquiry* (Wood 1997, 561–896). The Seabeach Kindergarten and North Shore Kindergarten cases involved allegations of sexual abuse of children attending these two centres in Sydney in 1988. During the Seabeach investigation (also known as the "Mr Bubbles" case), police interviews with children had been undertaken by a probationary constable "who had no experience in child sexual assault cases and who had never interviewed a victim of such an assault" (Wood 1997, para 7.151). The committal hearing for the accused carers concluded with the magistrate deciding the evidence of the children had been contaminated to such an extent that no trial could go ahead. The North Shore investigation had a similar outcome. It was led by the head of the Child Mistreatment Unit, Detective Sergeant Pat Clear. Clear had no "specialist experience in child sexual abuse" before his appointment (Wood 1997, para 7.203). Following his investigation, Clear decided no further action could be taken due to a "lack of corroboration," as well as his own judgement as to the "capacity of the children to give evidence" and the possible contamination of the children's evidence because of the multiple interviews in which they had participated (Wood 1997, para 7.216–217).

The press attention on cases had various effects. On the one hand, it led to an increased focus on child witnesses and pressure on the justice system to effectively prosecute child sex abuse allegations. Reporting of these cases in the United States "depicted a modern legal system that was insensitive to the cries of abused children and revictimized them by its hostile trial procedure" (McGough 1994, 9). The Australian Press Council upheld a complaint made in relation to an article in the *Sydney Morning Herald* about the Seabeach case. The article "Mr Bubbles – Where the Witch Hunt Went Wrong" was found by the Council to have drawn "sweeping, far-reaching conclusions" and "sought totally to dismiss the allegations and the public concern caused by them" (*The Canberra Times* 1990, 4). On the other hand, press coverage could also serve to further reinforce stereotypical views of child witnesses. With the frequency of childcare cases, the media questioned a perceived increase in the number of "unsubstantiated, and sometimes bizarre" cases of child abuse (Zaragoza 1995, 195).

Conclusion

The objective of this chapter has been to provide an introduction to some of the concepts that are important to the remaining chapters. The contradictions and complexities of the adversarial process, the legal definition of who is a child, child witness research and the media's approach to children, have each impacted significantly on the development of child witness law, policy and procedure. This reality is reflected in the fictional "Bart Gets Hit by a Car" episode of *The Simpsons* that opened this chapter. After Bart gives evidence, the scene continues. Mr. Burns takes the stand:

> *Mr Burns' Lawyer*: Now Mr Burns, would you please relate in your own words exactly what *really* happened on the day of the accident?
> *Mr Burns*: Certainly. It was a beautiful day. The sun was shining. I was driving to the orphanage to pass out toys. Suddenly that incorrigible Simpson boy darted in front of me … [recounts accident] … That's what happened.
> [Jury and public gallery visibly unmoved, hostile]
> *Mr Burns* (to those in the room): What are you looking at me like that for? You believed *his* story.
> *Mr Lutz* (to Homer): It's looking good Mr Simpson. It's looking very, very good.

The testimony of the two witnesses is virtually identical. They both speak of the "beautiful day," the unexpected and sudden impact of the collision. They both inject drama "the luxury car of death" and "that incorrigible … boy darted in front of me" and yet the jury and public gallery clearly side with Bart. Mr. Burns acknowledges as much before he even leaves the witness box. The scene highlights the inexact nature of the adversarial process. On this occasion, everyone believes the boy. Irrespective of what the law is, what the research says, or what the media reports, at the end of the day, it still comes down to a question of who is believed … or not believed.

References

Backhouse, Constance. 2000. "Skewering the Credibility of Women: A Reappraisal of Corroboration in Australian Legal History." *University of Western Australia Law Review* 29 (1): 79–107.

Bentham, Jeremy. A Treatise on Judicial Evidence (London: I.W. Paget, 1825) cited in Vidar Halvorsen. 2004. "Is it Better that Ten Guilty Persons Go Free than that One Innocent Person be Convicted?" *Criminal Justice Ethics* 23 (2): 3–13.

Binet, Alfred. La Suggestibilité (Paris: Schleicher Frères, 1900) cited in Stephen J. Ceci and Maggie Bruck. 1995. *Jeopardy in the Courtroom: A Scientific Analysis of Children's Testimony*, 52. Washington, DC: American Psychological Association.

Blackstone, William. 1765–1769. "Of Trial and Conviction." In *Commentaries on the Laws of England*, Book IV, Chapter 27. https://avalon.law.yale.edu/18th_century/blackstone_bk4ch27.asp.

Bowden, Phoebe, Terese Henning, and David Plater. 2014. "Balancing Fairness to Victims, Society and Defendants in the Cross-examination of Vulnerable Witnesses: An Impossible Triangulation." *Melbourne University Law Review* 37 (3): 539–584.

Brennan, Mark, and Roslin E. Brennan. 1988. *Strange Language: Child Victims Under Cross Examination.* Wagga Wagga: Riverina-Murray Institute of Higher Education.

Brewer, Holly. 2005. *By Birth or Consent: Children, Law, and the Anglo-American Revolution in Authority.* Chapel Hill: University of North Carolina Press.

The Canberra Times (ACT: 1926–1995). (1990). "'Mr Bubbles' Article Greatly Overstated." July 9.

Cashmore, Judy. 1990. "The Use of Video Technology for Child Witnesses." *Monash University Law Review* 16 (2): 228–250.

Ceci, Stephen J., and Maggie Bruck. 1993. "Suggestibility of the Child Witness: A Historical Review and Synthesis." *Psychological Bulletin* 113 (3): 403–439.

Ceci, Stephen J., and Maggie Bruck. 1995. *Jeopardy in the Courtroom: A Scientific Analysis of Children's Testimony*. Washington, DC: American Psychological Association.

Davies, Graham, and Helen Westcott. 2006. "Investigative Interviewing with Children: Progress and Pitfalls." In *Witness Testimony: Psychological, Investigative and Evidential Perspectives*, edited by Anthony Heaton-Armstrong, Eric Shepherd, Gisli Gudjonsson and David Wolchover, 153–169. Oxford: Oxford University Press.

Davis, Suzanne, L. 1998. "Social and Scientific Influences on the Study of Children's Suggestibility: A Historical Perspective." *Child Maltreatment* 3 (2): 186–194.

de Keijser, Jan W., Evianne GM de Lange, and Johan A van Wilsem. 2014. "Wrongful Convictions and the Blackstone Ratio: An Empirical Analysis of Public Attitudes." *Punishment & Society* 16 (1): 32–49.

Eastwood, Christine Jane, W. Patton, H. Stacy, and Australian Institute of Criminology. 1998. *Child Sexual Abuse & the Criminal Justice System*, Vol. 99. Canberra, ACT: Australian Institute of Criminology. http://aic.gov.au/publications/current%20series/tandi/81-100/tandi099.html.

Eisen, Mitchell L., and Gail S. Goodman, 1998. "Trauma, Memory, and Suggestibility in Children." *Development and Psychopathology* 10 (4): 717–738.

Fitzjames, Stephen James. 1883. *A History of the Criminal law of England Volume I*. London: Macmillan.

Follmer, Andrea, Greenhoot, and Sarah L. Bunnell. 2009. "Trauma and Memory." In *Children as Victims, Witnesses and Offenders – Psychological Science and the Law*, edited by Bette L. Bottoms, Cynthia J. Jadowski, and Gail S. Goodman, 36–56, New York: The Guilford Press.

Franklin, Benjamin, 1706–1790 and Albert Henry Smyth 1863-1907. 1970. *The Writings of Benjamin Franklin*. New York: Haskell House.

Ghetti, Simona, Kristen Weede Alexander, and Gail S. Goodman. 2002. "Legal Involvement in Child Sexual Abuse Cases." *International Journal of Law and Psychiatry* 25 (3): 235–251.

Goodman, Gail. 1982. "Children's Testimony in Historical Perspective." *Journal of Social Issues* 40 (2): 9–31.

Goodman, Gail S., Murray Levine, Gary B. Melton, and David W. Ogden. 1991. "Child Witnesses and the Confrontation Clause: The American Psychological Association Brief in Maryland v. Craig." *Law and Human Behavior* 15 (1): 13–29.

Goodman, Gail, E.P. Taub, D.P.H. Jones, P. England, L.K. Port, L. Rudy, and L. Prado. 1992. "Testifying in Criminal Court - Emotional Effects on Child Sexual Assault Victims." *Monographs of the Society for Research in Child Development* 57 (5): 1–142.

Goodman, Gail. 1984. "The Child Witness: An Introduction." *Journal of Social Issues* 40 (2): 1–7.

Jackson, Louise A. 2000. *Child Sexual Abuse in Victorian England*. New York: Routledge.

Kaladelfos, A. 2009. "'Call all Male Offenders by their Right Name': Masculinity and the Age of Consent." *Melbourne Historical Journal* (Special issue 1): 1–19.

Langbein, John H. 2005. *The Origins of Adversary Criminal Trial.* Oxford: Oxford University Press.

Lyon, T.D., and R. LaMagna. 2007. "The History of Children's Hearsay: From Old Bailey to Post-Davis." *Indiana Law Journal* 82 (4): 1029–1058.

Mabo v Queensland (No. 2) (1993) 175 CLR 1, 29.
McGough, Lucy S. 1994. *Child Witnesses: Fragile Voices in the American Legal System*. New Haven: Yale University Press.
Mertin, Peter M. 1989. "The Memory of Young Children for Eyewitness Events." *Australian Journal of Social Issues* 24 (1): 23–32.
Meyer, Jon'a. 1997. *Inaccuracies in Children's Testimony: Memory, Suggestibility, or Obedience to Authority?* New York: Haworth Press.
Muller, Karen. 2001. "An Inquisitorial Approach to the Evidence of Children." *Crime Research in South Africa* 4 (4): 1–13.
Myers, John E.B., Susan Diedrich, Devon Lee, Kelly McClanahan Fincher, and Rachel Stern. 1999. "Professional Writing on Child Sexual Abuse from 1900 to 1975: Dominant Themes and Impact on Prosecution." *Child Maltreatment* 4 (3): 201–216.
Pear, T.H., and Stanley Wyatt. 1914. "The Testimony of Normal and Mentally Defective Children." *British Journal of Psychology* 6 (3): 387–419.
Sanson, Michelle, and Thalia Anthony. 2019. *Connecting with Law*, 4th ed. Docklands, VIC: Oxford University Press.
Scott, Dorothy, and Shurlee Swain. 2002. *Confronting Cruelty: Historical Perspectives on Child Abuse*. Melbourne: Melbourne University Press.
Smaal, Yorick. 2013. "Historical Perspectives on Child Sexual Abuse, Part 1: Historical Perspectives on Child Sexual Abuse." *History Compass* 11 (9): 702–713. https://doi.org/10.1111/hic3.12083.
Steffen, Thomas L. 1988. "Truth as Second Fiddle: Re-evaluating the Place of Truth in the Adversarial Trial Ensemble." *Utah Law Review* 4: 799–845.
The Simpsons, Season 2, Episode 10. "Bart Gets Hit By a Car." 1991. Directed by Mark Kirkland, written by John Swartzwelder.
Tobin, John, and Oxford University Press. 2019. *The UN Convention on the Rights of the Child: A Commentary*. Oxford: Oxford University Press.
Tomison, Adam. 2001. "A History of Child Protection: Back to the Future?" *Family Matters* 60: 46–57.
UN Convention on the Rights of the Child 1989. https://www.ohchr.org/en/professionalinterest/pages/crc.aspx.
van Caenegem, R.C. 1988. *The Birth of the English Common Law*. Cambridge, Eng: Cambridge University Press.
van Krieken, Robert. 2020. "Naughty or Bad: Children and Crime." *Sociological Studies of Children and Youth* 25: 85–105.
Varendonk, Julien. "Les témoignages d"enfants dans un process retentissant" *Archives de Psychologie* 11 (1911): 129–171, cited in Stephen J. Ceci and Maggie Bruck. 1995. *Jeopardy in the Courtroom: A Scientific Analysis*

of Children's Testimony, 55–56. Washington, DC: American Psychological Association.

Wood, J.R.T. 1997. *Royal Commission into the NSW Police Service: Final Report*. Sydney: NSW Government.

Zaragoza, Maria S. 1995. *Memory and Testimony in the Child Witness.* Thousand Oaks, CA: Sage.

3

"Those Troublesome Men in Blue": Police

The start of any child witness's journey through the criminal justice system invariably begins with the police. Widely regarded as the "gatekeepers to the criminal justice system," police have prosecuted crime since the early nineteenth century (Emsley 1996, 254).[1] They had—and continue to have—a fundamental role in investigating cases. They decide whether or not to press charges. Today, their recorded interviews with children will usually form the basis of a child's evidence-in-chief at a trial, which would have been led by the prosecutor in the past. The importance of the police to the criminal trial is thus undeniable and remains unchanged since the turn of the twentieth century. If anything, the significance of the part that police play in determining whether a child witness will be heard is greater than ever before.

For most of the twentieth century, police practices with respect to child witnesses were largely unregulated, with the prime policing focus being controlling crime and criminals. This preoccupation with crime control is evident in the various guides, circulars, manuals, commissioners' standing orders and gazettes advising police on the execution of their duties. These sources provided officers with comprehensive

R. Blewer, *Child Witnesses in Twentieth Century Australian Courtrooms*, Palgrave Histories of Policing, Punishment and Justice,
https://doi.org/10.1007/978-3-030-69791-4_3

instruction on procedures for the arrest and prosecution of offenders, but very little direction on how to interact with victims and witnesses, including children (Finnane 1994, 152–159). Police in the early decades of the twentieth century thus had significant discretionary powers when conducting criminal investigations, particularly with child witnesses, who were not mentioned in any legislation. The interests of child witnesses were a secondary concern, if considered at all, for investigating officers.

Policing was, and is, not just a collective task. It is also an individual task. Guides, circulars and codes may have provided police as a force with some direction on procedures, but otherwise police relied upon their own discretion to decide how to engage with children. Children were thus often at the mercy of individual personalities of officers in their interactions with police, each of whom could determine if children were listened to, supported emotionally or even believed. Until the 1980s, when greater regulation and organised practices for interviewing children were introduced, police engagement with child witnesses reflected each officer's personal assumptions and preconceptions about children—including how a child's memory functioned, children's propensities for lying or fantasising, and the ongoing effects of having been a victim or witness of crime.

The assumptions officers made about their *own* capacities, roles and responsibilities also impacted upon police engagement with child witnesses and the reform of police practices. The appointment of women officers in the early decades of the twentieth century, an undoubtedly political and controversial move at the time, evidences a perception amongst the police that male officers were ill suited to looking after matters involving women and child witnesses—"duties which it was extremely difficult for male police to handle with the requisite delicacy" (*The Capricornian* 1929, 10). It was expected that the "inherently maternal" qualities of women would make them better suited to "mothering-type" police work in a way that would complement the male police function, not supplant it (Sutton 1992, 67).

The introduction of women into police forces reflects an understanding that children might have particular needs when it came to police investigations. The later decades of the twentieth century saw the continued development of this awareness, along with a recognition of the necessity for consistent formal procedures to address children's unique requirements. These new procedures are attributable to the increased, or at least more visible, concern within police forces for abused children and the acceptance of scientific, evidence-based research on children as witnesses emerging from the late 1960s onwards. The resulting procedural reforms are characterised by greater engagement between the police and other services or disciplines such as medicine, social work and psychology. The adoption of modern audio-visual technologies further reformed police practices by providing new methods for interviewing children and identifying suspects.

The Relationship Between Police and Child Witnesses

While Australia has been policed in one way or another since the arrival of the First Fleet in 1788, centralised police forces were only established in the colonies from the middle of the nineteenth century (Finnane 1994, 9). Thus, by the turn of the twentieth century and the time of Federation in 1901, each state's forces were still relatively new. Established policies or procedures were rudimentary (Finnane 1989, 95), but demonstrate police had significant discretionary powers, particularly with child witnesses. Police manuals, standing orders, case law, depositions, press reports and archival material indicate police practices in the early twentieth century included taking children to confront the suspect directly before any charges were laid; having children participate in face-to-face identification parades; interviewing child witnesses and police themselves participating in committal and trial proceedings.

Further, police—as a force or presence—held considerable power over young people. Police power over suspects has been acknowledged, researched and written about elsewhere (Finnane 1994, 75–92; Fitzgerald 1989, 206). Far less has been documented, however, about police authority over victims and witnesses, over whom police would have wielded as much, if not more, power and influence than they had over criminals or suspects (Eijkman 1992, 266). Police power and importance in the minds of children are evidenced in a 1914 case from the Adelaide Police Court when an eleven-year-old girl gave evidence of an alleged misdemeanour she had witnessed:

> "You had a lot of trouble in finding a policeman, didn't you?" asked counsel for the defence.
> "Yes" replied the girl.
> "They're a great nuisance aren't they?"
> "Yes!" came the response with a sympathetic inflexion.
> "Never there when they're wanted?"
> "No!" came the monosyllabic reply, and the court laughed. (*Daily Herald* 1914, 4)

This girl provided the courtroom with some levity in what might otherwise have been a serious, sad place. But her testimony nonetheless tells us that she knew to report what she had seen to the police. The almost omnipresent power of police, at least in the minds of much younger children, was demonstrated in a case heard in the Melbourne Coroner's Court in 1929. This time, a boy of just four years old was called as a witness. The coroner was examining the boy to establish whether he could swear an oath. The coroner said:

> "There is someone who watches over us and knows everything we do. Do you know who that is?"
> "Yes", the boy replied.
> "Well who is it?" said the coroner.
> The boy answered, "The police." (*Cairns Post* 1929, 10)

Women Police Officers

Notwithstanding the almost mythical power police may have had over the minds of some children, the appointment of women officers provides evidence of an assumed deficiency with respect to how male officers engaged with children. As the *Darling Downs Gazette* reported, within policing "there is much also in which moral force and tactful supervision are of more value than muscle. In matters concerning women and children especially, the policewoman has powers sometimes denied to the man" (1917, 3). Women first served in the police force of New South Wales from July 1915, followed by South Australia five months later in December 1915 and Victoria, Western Australia and Tasmania throughout 1917. Queensland did not employ female officers until 1931 (Prenzler 2015, 3). Various views have been advanced as to why women officers were introduced into police forces. According to criminologist Tim Prenzler, reasons for the appointment of women include, for example, to supplement depleted forces during the First World War, or in response to social changes taking place during this same period, where the apparent frequency with which widowed women and girls turned to prostitution to support themselves during the war period became a cause for concern (Prenzler 1994, 79). It was hoped engaging women officers in "specialist" police roles might have a positive effect on the control of social problems such as neglected children and immoral females (Prenzler 1994, 79). The fact the protection and support of child witnesses was often cited as one of the tasks women officers undertook suggests male police forces were cognisant of a need, or at least potential opportunity, to improve existing practices to better address the needs of child witnesses (Jackson 1999, 17).[2] The Tasmanian Police, for example, reported in 1919 of the "satisfactory" work (Parliament of Tasmania 1919, 7, cited in Prenzler 2015, 37) of policewomen attending court: "her presence is often very useful in and about the courts when women and young girls are in attendance in varying roles, and especially in the case of female witnesses of tender years" (*Examiner—Launceston* 1919, 4).

The work women officers did with child witnesses was widely reported in the press. The general opinion conveyed in newspaper articles appeared to be positive, concluding that a "firm, so long as she is a tactful, woman can render the community excellent and yet unobtrusive service" (*Examiner—Launceston* 1919, 4). *The Brisbane Courier* published a letter to the editor in 1929 from a member of the Queensland branch of the National Council of Women, Ms. E. A. Mallalieu. Queensland was yet to appoint women to their force, but Ms. Mallalieu and her colleagues were agitating for change to bring their state into line with others. Advice Ms. Mallalieu had received from her South Australian colleagues said women officers in their state attended to all minors in court, in addition to taking statements from female victims. "This work," the colleague had told Ms. Mallalieu:

> should be done exclusively by women in every civilised community, for that women and girls have to tell their sordid stories to men is fair neither to the men nor to the women and girls. (*The Brisbane Courier* 1929, 8)

As Ms. Mallalieu was calling on the Queensland government for change, by 1929 South Australia already had over a decade of experience with female officers. The innovation had been received with considerable approval. In Myrtle Slape's high-profile child-neglect case in 1918, for example, Magistrate Mr. S. J. Mitchell congratulated Constable Kate Cocks and Miss Alice Kentish on the "praiseworthy manner" in which they had gathered evidence and prepared the case. The prosecutor, Mr. F.V. Smith, agreed, noting the "state was indebted" to the two women for the work they had done. "Seldom had cases been brought before the Police Court" he proclaimed, that had been "more skilfully prepared" (*Register* 1917, 4).

The press reported cases like Ms. Slape's extensively and the contribution made by the women officers involved was often celebrated. In other reports, however, the involvement of female officers was reported in very matter-of-fact terms, suggesting forces had quickly adapted to the presence of women officers, in the context of child witnesses at least, and could see the benefit of the addition of women to police forces. In 1921, seven-year-old Matthew, for example, was reported to have been talking so animatedly and happily to the two women officers sitting with him outside a courtroom that he had not noticed his father, who was on trial for murdering the child's mother, walk right by (*Mirror* 1937, 22).

In the context of this twentieth-century study, women police officers were a reasonably constant—though likely rare—presence, at least until the late decades of the century (Jackson 2003, 624; Prenzler 1994, 79; Finnane 1994, 106, 137). The work women officers are reported to have done in supporting child witnesses is significant to this research, even if few women were appointed across the nation. While women were a significant addition to Australian police forces in the twentieth century, it undoubtedly remained male officers who would have carried out majority police work involving child witnesses for most of the century.

Police Practices—Investigating Crime

Children generally could present quite a challenge for police officers. "Child witnesses are not usually the most reliable for a criminal investigator," wrote Harry Mann, a former Criminal Investigation Bureau Chief of Police, in Perth's *Mirror* in 1952. "Children," he continued, could nevertheless be "powerful witnesses." Mann noted "a child's simple words have put the noose around [a defendant's] neck" in circumstances where scientific evidence could not (*Mirror* 1952, 7).

Notwithstanding such acknowledgement, there was a distinct absence of formal, written instructions for police on how to deal with child witnesses for much of the twentieth century. During the early decades of the twentieth century, police had wide-ranging powers to discover who had committed a crime and, in order to make such a discovery, to question any person they thought might have useful information (Brampton in Vincent 1905, ix). Police gazettes, information manuals and guides often reminded officers of the need to act fairly towards suspects by complying with rules about what questions could be asked of suspects and the admissibility of their statements later on, in court. Once arrested or in custody, police were not permitted to force a suspect to answer questions. They were further instructed:

> [n]ever act unfairly to a prisoner by coaxing him by word or conduct to divulge anything. If you do, you will surely be severely handled at the trial, and it is not unlikely that your evidence will be disbelieved. (Brampton in Vincent 1905, ix)

These sources indicate officers were instructed on the criminal trial process and would be made aware of, for example, rules of evidence. Guides and manuals appear also to have only provided police with information on the legal limits of the testimony of children. They were advised on the law, for example, of the need for children to swear an oath and for their evidence to be corroborated (O'Callaghan et al. 1906, Rules 536 and 537; Paul and Victoria Police Force 1924, 172, par 6).[3] In Victoria, officers were referred to relevant legislation for advice as to when children could be witnesses and relevant case law on various types of offences.[4] Aside from these few directions, though, officers do not appear to have been advised of policies or practices that should—or should not—apply to their interactions with child witnesses. As the following case examples illustrate, police practices with respect to these limitations on the evidence of children played an important role in determining which cases would result in charges being laid against a suspect.

Despite a dearth of written direction as to how officers should deal with children, it has nevertheless been possible to glean some common investigative practices. It is unclear whether these procedures were mandatory or even applied consistently; indeed, they may have been applied *inconsistently.* They were, however, referred to frequently enough and reported on in such ways to suggest they were, at the very least, not out of the ordinary.

Confronting the Suspect

The investigative process often began with a police officer having the child witness directly confront the accused. On the morning of 24 October 1901, in Queanbeyan, just outside Canberra, three little girls were searching for baby magpies. At some point, Joseph Campbell, twenty-four, joined the search. He convinced the girls to venture further and further away from the town into the bush, where he violently assaulted the eldest of the three girls. Once the assault was over, Campbell accompanied the girls almost to their homes. The victim of the assault was so badly injured that it didn't take long for the offence to be detected and for police to begin the hunt for the perpetrator of what became known as the "Queanbeyan Outrage." Within hours, Campbell had been detained nine miles out of town. It was reported that "[t]he whole town turned out to see his arrival on foot." Police took Campbell to the girl's home, right into her bedroom. The officers asked her if she recognised the man who had assaulted her that morning. She pointed to Campbell, who claimed the girl was lying (*Evening News* 1901, 4). Campbell was also taken to the other girls who "identified him at once" (*The Australian Star* 1901, 5).

The practice of having children confront suspects formed the basis of an appeal to the High Court in 1910 (*R v Grills* (1910) 11 CLR 400). After reporting various offences that had been committed against him, a boy of nine was taken by Constable George Grove to the suspect to discuss the allegations. In front of the suspect, the officer said to the boy "Did this man pull you into the cart and pull your trousers down?" The boy answered, "Yes" (*R v Grills* (1910) 11 CLR 400, 402). Accusing the officer and boy of having concocted a story between them, the suspect demanded he be allowed to interrogate the boy directly. Constable Grove acquiesced. The interaction between the suspect and the child was subsequently recounted in the High Court's judgment. Grills said to the boy:

> "Do you say that I pulled your trousers down?"
> The boy did not answer.
> Accused again said, "Do you say that I pulled your trousers down?"
> The boy replied, "No; a button came off and they fell down." (*R v Grills* (1910) 11 CLR 400, 402)

At this point in the confrontation, Constable Grove interjected, saying "[t]he boy is frightened. Harold is it true what you told your mother and what you told me last night? Do not be frightened. Tell the truth." Harold confirmed that what he had told Constable Grove and his mother the night before was true and what he had just said in reply to Grills was not (*R v Grills* (1910) 11 CLR 400, 402). Grills, was convicted and sentenced to seven years' imprisonment (*R v Grills* (1910) 11 CLR 400, 401). On appeal, the New South Wales Supreme Court considered the testimony of Constable Grove and how, through his evidence, unsworn statements of the accused and the boy had effectively been put before the Court. The Court found the officer's testimony was admissible, but the jury should have been warned about how to treat such unsworn evidence

(*R v Grills* (1910) 10 SR (NSW) 309, 309). Grills' conviction was quashed. The Crown appealed to the High Court which decided three to one (with Justice Isaacs dissenting) that Constable Groves' evidence had been properly admitted. Grills' conviction and sentence were thus reinstated (*R v Grills* (1910) 11 CLR 400, 432).

Identifying Suspects

The practice of bringing children into close contact with suspects continued in cases where identification was required. In the *Grills* case, Harold, the child, was the accused's stepson. Like the majority of children making allegations of sexual abuse, he knew the accused. In cases where the child did not know the suspect, however, the identification of suspects was an important issue for police investigators. For at least the first half of the twentieth century, child witnesses might be asked to participate in an identification parade, or "line-up," as they are also known, just like adult witnesses. Parades had been a part of regular police procedures since the mid-nineteenth century (Davies and Griffiths 2008, 435). Children are reported to have participated in such line-ups from at least 1900. In *R v Carroll* in 1906, for instance, the child witness picked Carroll out of a line-up of men who stood right in front of her (*The Dubbo Liberal and Macquarie Advocate* 1906, 3). In another case in March 1941, an eleven-year-old girl gave evidence of going to the police station where she "saw a lot of men in a line…I went and touched that man there…He was the man I had seen at the station" (*Eltham and Whittlesea Shires Advertiser* 1941, 4). And in 1928 in New South Wales, a sixteen-year-old girl attended a line-up where she identified three of the four men who she alleged had raped her the night before by walking up to them and touching them (*Western Champion* 1928, 5). Carrying out identification parades like these was generally governed by commissioners' standing orders and case law (Australian Law Reform Commission 1975, 52). The law dictated that parades had to be carried out in a way that was fair to the accused. Line-ups gave the suspect the opportunity to participate in the process and immediately respond to any perceived unfairness. Should they be conducted *un*fairly, a court could use its discretion to refuse any evidence that had been so obtained. Fairness involved conducting parades as soon as possible after the initial allegation to ensure the witness's memory was fresh (Australian Law Reform Commission 1975, 52).

The extent to which this objective was prioritised is evident in the investigation of the "Ramsay's Bush Outrage" in 1901. On the morning of 2 October, nine-year-old Stella was found with her younger brother, sitting in a gutter in inner-city Sydney. The day before, a man had lured the two of them away from a confectionary shop with the promise of a gold watch. They had wandered around with the man all day, into the night. Overnight Stella was violently raped by the man. Her screams for help went unanswered as the man covered her mouth with his hand and some of her clothes until "she became terrorised into silence" (*Australian Star* 1901, 5). In the morning, the man took the children to the tram and gave them money to get home. He also gave Stella a package with some of her clothing. When the two children got off the tram, Stella was unable to walk. The two children sat in the gutter until their uncle (who was part of a sizable search party who had been out all night looking for the children) found them (*The Australian Star* 1901, 5). Stella was hospitalised. The police brought numerous men to her hospital bedside, but Stella failed to identify any of them as the alleged the perpetrator.

Some weeks later, Joseph Campbell, who had been arrested and charged with the previously mentioned "Queanbeyan Outrage," was brought from Queanbeyan to Stella's hospital bedside in Sydney, where he appeared along with five other men for another bedside identification parade. Campbell protested:

> "There's not a man there anything like me."
> Detective Keatinge replied: "You couldn't get five men in Sydney to come closer to it."
> "They're not a bit like me," said the accused man.
> "It's not fair; there are not enough of them, either." (*The Burrangong Argus* 1901, 4)

When the little girl was asked if she could see the man who assaulted her, she turned her face to the wall for some time. Her response was barely audible. The man was there, she confirmed, but she would not point him out. The men were asked to walk closer towards the girl's bed and hold up their hands. As Campbell, going last, moved towards the bed, the girl turned to her father and said, "That's him" before turning away again. Once Campbell left the room, Stella told her father and those present that she had known it was him as soon as he had walked in. It was reported that "the father of the child was much agitated, as was only natural, when the identification was over, and only controlled his feelings by a great effort." The following day, Stella's doctor informed the court that the "ordeal of identifying her alleged assailant had not prejudicially affected her" (*The Burrangong Argus* 1901, 4).

Extensive judicial commentary on identification evidence explains the legal principles behind procedures like these (*Alexander v the Queen* (1981) 145 CLR 395). There is very little in this case law dealing with the identification of suspects by children specifically. One exception is the case of *Croft* (*Croft v The King* (1917) 7 WALR 263). John Croft was charged in 1916 with indecently assaulting a young girl. The girl and her younger brother had attended a line-up together. The girl identified the accused immediately. Her brother, however, reportedly "cried and was afraid," before eventually identifying the same man his sister had identified just moments earlier. In summing up the case to the jury, Judge Burnside noted because of "so much haste on the part of the police" to have both children attend the line-up together, the brother and sister could not be thought of as independent witnesses (*Truth* 1916, 3). The brother had seen what his older sister had done. There was a risk that in identifying the accused, he was simply copying her. The jury did not share the judge's reservations about Croft's identity. They found him guilty (*The Daily News* 1916, 8).[5]

Misidentification of a suspect has been recognised as a common cause of wrongful conviction since the 1970s (Davies and Griffiths 2008, 436; Hall and Ostrom 2013, 66). Concerns about the practice were first raised in the United States in the 1960s, after two high-profile cases of wrongful conviction (neither involved child witnesses) (Davies and Griffiths 2008, 437). The Australian Law Reform Commission (ALRC) raised questions about the practice in one of its earliest reports. On the basis existing process was governed largely by common law (case law), it recommended the introduction of legislation to govern such procedures, and that photographs, preferably videos, be used rather than live parades (Australian Law Reform Commission 1975, 52). Shortly thereafter, in England, Lord Devlin conducted a review of identification procedures (Devlin and Great Britain 1976). Despite concerns about the practice, identification parades remained the preferred means of identifying a suspect for the duration of the century. In 1981, Chief Justice Gibbs of the High Court said identification parades represented "[t]he safest and most satisfactory way" of ensuring accurate identification of witnesses (*Alexander v the Queen* (1981) 145 CLR 395, 399–400). In 1988, the New South Wales Law Reform Commission recommended the introduction of legislation to regulate police investigations and identification procedures (New South Wales Law Reform Commission 1988, par 2.39). The capacity of children to identify suspects was studied by several researchers during the late 1980s and 1990s (Lindsay et al. 1997; Mapes 1995). This research indicated children were more likely than adults to incorrectly identify suspects (Fraser Parker and Ryan 1993, 17). The findings of such studies led, in turn, to new methods of child witnesses participating in identification parades in the twenty-first century (Brewer and Day 2005, 120; Pozzulo and Lindsay 1999; Rush et al. 2014).

Interviewing Children

The identification of a suspect is a vital issue for criminal investigations, but the "cornerstone of investigation" is generally agreed to be the police interview where an interviewer's skill in enhancing a witness's reliable recall and ability to communicate is of "paramount importance" to the investigative process (Milne and Bull 1999, 1–2; Powell et al. 2016). Again, there is little evidence of formal instructions or guidance for investigative officers with respect to child interview techniques or procedures prior to the twentieth century. Various editions of the *Criminal Investigation Practical Textbook for Magistrates, Police Officers and Lawyers*, first published in 1893 by Austrian lawyer Hans Gross and subsequently translated into English, were used by Victorian police (Adam et al. 1934, 1949, 1962). The text advises interviewers to be cautious when interviewing children. At the same time, the authors note that a child's evidence could be "of great value" (Adam et al. 1934, 1949, 1962, 62).[6] In stark contrast to the studies undertaken in the latter decades of the twentieth century, the guidance given to officers in this text appears to be unproven and based on assumption rather than empirical evidence. This is particularly so regarding issues of gender. The authors claim "... just as sex differentiates in external appearance the [male] youth from the girl, so are they differentiated in their methods of perception ... An intelligent boy," they continue, "is as a rule the best witness in the world." Young girls, however, could be "very dangerous" witnesses, whose potential harm could continue into adulthood and was particularly apparent "before and during each period of menstruation" (Adam et al. 1934, 1949, 1962, 62). "In short," they concluded, "too great care cannot be observed in interrogating a young girl, to whatever class of society she belongs" (Adam et al. 1934, 1949, 1962, 46).

This view would likely have influenced police officers conducting interviews with child witnesses. Given the small of Australian cases available featuring child witnesses, and the high proportion of females within these cases, it was not possible for this research to determine if police conducted interviews differently for male and female children. The suggestions made to officers that female witnesses were less reliable may still have resulted in interviewers treating girls differently to boys. A number of children had some difficulty with the police interview process. In a 1954 case in Western Australia, the fourteen-year-old witness testified in court she had lied to the women police officers who interviewed her because she had "wanted to get away from the Women Police Office and go home." She had not read her statement before she signed it "because she was crying" (*Mirror* 1954, 5). In 1912, an eleven-year-old girl recanted her police statement in court (*The Sydney Morning Herald* 1912, 5), as did another in 1913 (*Independent* 1913, 1).

Police interview practices caused problems for all concerned in the trial of Mary Ryan in Queensland in 1900. Mary was abandoned by her husband and left to raise their five children. Her husband would return periodically for short intervals. The police played a particularly crucial, and at times controversial, role in Mary's prosecution for the murder of her sixth child, a newborn boy. Mary's ten-year-old daughter, Margaret, gave evidence that one of the investigating officers, Constable Wilkinson, had lived temporarily with them in their family home following her mother's arrest (Queensland State Archives, ID95466, 61 [Margaret]).

Along with Constable Wilkinson, Acting Sergeant Alexander Leslie also investigated the case and attended the Ryan residence, talking to Mary and her three eldest children—Bridget, Margaret and Mary Jnr (Queensland State Archives, ID95466, 17 [Leslie]). The girls each initially told the officer they had not seen or heard a baby on the day in question. Leslie was not convinced. By the end of his interviews with the girls, all three had told him they *had* seen and heard a baby crying (Queensland State Archives, ID95466 [Leslie]).

During Mary Snr's committal hearing, Margaret was examined at length. She testified that Leslie had interviewed her a number of times, asking each time if she had heard the baby cry and each time, she had told him that she had not heard a baby cry. Margaret testified that Leslie eventually told her if she did not say she had heard the baby cry, she would be put in gaol (Queensland State Archives, ID95466, 89 [Margaret]). It was only after this threat that she told Leslie she *had* heard the baby cry. On cross-examination by her mother's barrister, Mr. O'Shea, Margaret admitted she had been afraid when Leslie had threatened her with gaol (Queensland State Archives, ID95466, 90 [Margaret]). Despite having changed her story numerous times, Margaret's final interview gave Sergeant Leslie what he had been looking for. The police were only able to charge the girls' mother with murder once they had evidence the baby had been born alive.

Problematic police interview techniques, like those in Mary Ryan's case, were raised in several government reports and courtrooms over the course of the twentieth century. In 1940, a Victorian police magistrate, referring to a case over which he had presided where the police had been unable to obtain coherent statements from two children, suggested officers wear plain clothes to appear less intimidating. Detectives rejected this call. Wanting to teach children to recognise police officers as their friends, the officers argued it was preferable for them to be in uniform when interviewing children (*The Argus* 1940, 8).[7] In a case in Western Australia in 1954, the investigating officers admitted to having deliberately decided not to interview a child witness in a public drunkenness case. This case had begun as an indecent interference matter. A group of small children had left their homes to go to a nearby shop together. A six-year-old girl, pushing her doll's pram, had fallen behind the group. The defendant, Dwyer, grabbed the girl, but a woman passing by heard her cries and approached the pair. The police charged Dwyer with drunkenness. This was later changed to a charge of indecent interference but, at trial, the child, standing on a seat in the witness box, wept as she was asked by the magistrate whether she knew the difference between truth and "fibs." The magistrate queried whether the girl even knew why she was in court that day. Sergeant Williams advised that the Police had "purposely not talked about the incident to the child" (*Border Watch* 1954, 13). Without any evidence from the girl, there was little point in the Crown proceeding with the matter. As the magistrate dismissed the complaint, he commended the police for choosing not to interview the child. Alluding to broader concerns about police practices, he said while the decision to not interview the child may have "increased their difficulty," it nevertheless "increased respect for the integrity of police" (*Border Watch* 1954, 13).

Despite coming from just one magistrate in a remote part of Western Australia, this comment raises important concerns regarding the prosecution of offences against children in the mid-twentieth century. What was the integrity problem police were encountering with respect to investigating these allegations? Does the positive feedback the police received from the magistrate in this case point to a broader desire for children to not be questioned at all about such offences? Does it point to a general belief that police practices in investigating such allegations may have been harmful? Is there a suggestion the preferable approach at that time was to simply avoid the pursuit of justice? Contemporary research confirms the tendency of children to suggestibility or to acquiescence to authority, as Mary Ryan's daughters did. It also confirms the potentially stressful interview environment; problems of using leading questions; the cognitive and linguistic capacities of the child; the child having to recount, sometimes repeatedly, a traumatic event; and how to accurately record the child's evidence (Bull and Corran 2002, 316). But research also shows children can, and do, make effective witnesses when asked developmentally appropriate questions by investigating officers (Ceci and

Bruck 1993, 434; Jackson 1999, 95). The recommended approach today would not be to avoid interviewing a child, as the Mount Gambier police did in 1954, but rather to ensure the interviews techniques used were appropriate for the child.

Police and the Trial Process

Police involvement with child witness cases did not end with the interview or even the pressing of charges. It often extended to the trial itself. During Mary Ryan's committal hearing, for example, Margaret and her sisters gave evidence they had seen their mother carrying a baby and had heard it crying. On the strength of this evidence, which Sergeant Leslie had appeared so determined to extract from the girls during their interviews, Mary was committed to stand trial. At the trial, however, some five months later, Margaret and her older sister, Bridget, both gave evidence that since the committal they had been taken back to their house by police officers and "shown" they could not have observed their mother carrying a baby. Margaret and Bridget both subsequently changed their evidence from that they had given at the committal, and instead testified that they had not seen or heard a baby crying (Queensland State Archives, ID95466). Nothing appears to have been made of the police "showing" the girls they could not have seen their mother from where they had said they were standing. Instead, defence counsel and the judge remarked that this change in the girls' testimony only confirmed just how unreliable child witnesses were (*The Week* 1900, 26). The outcome of Mary's trial, and how her daughters gave evidence, is considered further in Chapters 5 and 6.

Another case in which the investigating officer occupied a vital role in the defendant's trial was *R v Sparkman,* heard in 1930 in Sydney. The defendant had been charged with one count of assault and one act of indecency (*R v Sparkman* (1930) 31 SR (NSW) 80, 80). The complainant was a twelve-year-old girl, who, like many child witnesses, was unable to give evidence because the trial judge had declared she was not "sufficiently mentally alert" to do so (*The Sydney Morning Herald* 1930, 8; *R v Sparkman* (1930) 31 SR (NSW) 80). Securing a conviction without the evidence of the child complainant would be a near-impossible task. In this case, however, the police officer gave evidence during which the jury heard—twice—that the girl had identified the defendant as her assailant. The defendant was found guilty and sentenced to three years' imprisonment (*The Sydney Morning Herald* 1930, 8). Sparkman's conviction was subsequently quashed on appeal. Chief Justice Street found the police officer's testimony would "have had enormous weight with the jury in determining what their verdict should be" (*R v Sparkman* (1930) 31 SR (NSW) 80, 81). He noted if this had been the only issue with the trial, he would have quashed the conviction and ordered a re-trial. Instead, the conviction was quashed outright due to other issues relevant to the apparent lack of physical evidence of an assault. This case exemplifies the highly technical aspects of rules of evidence and, in turn, the adversarial process. The unsworn statements of the girl identifying the defendant via the officer's testimony were detrimental to the prosecution. The lack of physical evidence, fatal. The Chief Justice emphasised he was not suggesting the constable had acted improperly or had intended to be unfair to the accused in giving his testimony (*R v Sparkman* (1930) 31 SR (NSW) 80, 81).

New Approaches to Child Witness Practices

The second half of the twentieth century heralded considerable reform of police practices with respect to child witnesses. A new collaborative approach to dealing with children saw police engage with other disciplines like social work, medicine and psychology. New audio-visual recording technologies were also utilised to improve the quality of evidence police and interviewers were able to obtain from children. The objective was to elicit the best evidence from child witnesses while minimising the risks of harm associated with the adversarial process.

Interview Practices

In 1969, Harold Snelling, the then New South Wales Solicitor-General, gave a paper at a criminology symposium held in Sydney. Speaking to the attendees, he said there was a need for improved communication strategies for child witnesses. He recommended New South Wales adopt the Israeli practice of using so-called "youth examiners" who with "[s]pecial skills would be likely to get more information from the child than could the police, and also to be more capable of assessing the veracity of the child" (Snelling 1969, 61).

Snelling's recommendation was not taken up but concerns about police interviewing techniques gained increased attention both in Australia and internationally in the following years. During the late 1970s and early 1980s, new psychological research considered how improved interview techniques could enhance the reliability of information children reported (Lamb 2008, 19; Ceci et al. 1987, 39–40; Westcott and Davies 1996, 452–454). This research coincided with increased attention being paid to the prosecution of offences involving child victims (Bull and Corran 2002, 315). The considerable scepticism with which child testimony had previously been viewed was replaced (or at least reduced) by concern as to how best to communicate with children to ensure they were able to clearly express what they remembered (Bull and Corran 2002, 315). The importance of training and the need for interviewers to consistently apply appropriate interview techniques was highlighted as necessary for overcoming problems with child witness interviews (Lamb 2008, 13). The Law Reform Commissioner of Tasmania recommended reforms in a 1990 report. Echoing the Victorian police magistrate's suggestions from half a century earlier, the Commissioner recommended police conduct interviews in plain clothes rather than in uniform (Law Reform Commissioner of Tasmania 1990. 5).

In response to issues with police interviews, states started to establish specialist police investigation teams (Humphreys 1996, 338). Queensland, for example, introduced Suspected Child Abuse and Neglect teams (SCAN) as early as 1980 (Queensland Police Force 1985, 2), comprised of medical practitioners, childcare officers from the Department of Children's Services and police officers (Queensland Police Force 1985, 3).

A Queensland Juvenile Aid Bureau report from 1985 confirms over one hundred offences against children were investigated during that year. The report mentioned the challenges of investigating offences against children, saying it was "tedious and mostly unrewarding" work due to the child's "natural reticence and lack of cooperation" as well as the "laws and court procedures which hinder rather than help the course of justice." The bureau did note, though, that in their experience, children were "usually truthful … and with a considerate, skilful approach provide valuable evidence" (Queensland Police Force 1985, 4). In Victoria, Sexual Offences and Child Abuse Investigation Teams were introduced in Victoria in 1991. A "dual track system" of investigating child abuse cases was developed whereby police and child welfare agencies shared investigative responsibilities. Under this system, social workers and healthcare professionals, as well as police, conducted investigative interviews (Scott and Swain 2002, 177).

In the United Kingdom, the "Cleveland Affair" in 1988 drew considerable attention to the many interviews in which child witnesses were often required to participate as they moved through the criminal justice system (Morgan and Zedner 1992, 77). This "affair" involved widespread allegations of incest and child sexual abuse in Cleveland (United Kingdom) families. Several children were removed from their homes based on the erroneous medical assessments of two doctors at the local hospital (Soothill and Francis 2002, 2). Following this scandal, the United Kingdom government published the "Report of the Advisory Group on Video Evidence" in 1989. This report made specific reference to police investigations of child sexual abuse in the context of "growing public concern" over such offences (Pigot 1989).

The impact of the "Cleveland Affair" reached Australia where, in addition to the outcome of the previously mentioned Seabeach and North Shore childcare cases, the issue of multiple interviews featured in proposed reforms. In 1990, Queensland SCAN officers highlighted the multiplicity of interviews child witnesses often had to undergo because of the increased number of agencies involved in the investigation process. The officers were concerned that each retelling by a child resulted in a loss of spontaneity and immediacy, which could impact on the effectiveness of the child as a witness in court. The number of interviews could result in some children relating their experience "without any emotional affect, with the result that their statements about abuse may appear to have a slick, rehearsed, or matter of fact quality to them" (Jefferies 1990, 2).

The potential problem of multiple investigative interviews with children was also acknowledged by the Australian Law Reform Commission (ALRC) in 1997 (Australian Law Reform Commission 1997, 14.27). The Commission recommended the creation and implementation of national interview standards, including ensuring appropriately qualified personnel conducted all interviews, that interviews be kept short and simple and that children be offered the opportunity to have an independent support person present during any interview. The ALRC further recommended the establishment of specialist interview teams like those in Queensland and Victoria, who could provide a coordinated response for these children. The desire to give additional support to children during the interview process was a significant departure from the days when there was little concern about children needing support during interactions and interviews with police, even while being taken to confront a suspect. Now, at the end of the twentieth century, measures of support included requiring any child who had made allegations about being abused by a family member being interviewed in an environment in which they could be open and frank (Australian Law Reform Commission 1997, 14.29). Other practices involved the use of anatomically correct dolls to help children explain what had allegedly happened (Goodman and Aman 1990).

New Technologies

The adoption of modern technologies towards the end of the twentieth century contributed significantly to changing police practices. Audio and visual recording technologies transformed the conduct of police interviews, identification parades and courtroom procedures. The use of video technology in this context was widely, but not universally, welcomed. Recorded interviews not only gave an accurate record of what had been said, they could also serve to reduce the number of times a child might have to tell and re-tell their story. The advent of video and recording technologies undoubtedly assisted researchers and officers alike in developing new ways to conduct child witness interviews to reduce the "rigours of curial proceedings" (*R v N.R.C* [1999] 3 VR 537, 540). Some, however, feared the only party likely to benefit from such recordings would be the defendant, who could use video to exploit inconsistencies in the child's subsequent testimony, thus making such evidence "potentially another weapon to be used against the child" (Wood 1997, 1074).

Notwithstanding reservations about using technologies in this way, the 1980s and early 1990s saw police forces across the country establish programs to record interviews with child witnesses. Queensland set up its "Interviewing Children and Recording Evidence" program (ICARE) in 1981. New South Wales followed with their own scheme ten years later, in 1991. The Wood Royal Commission into the Police Service (1995–1997) noted, however, the failure of the NSW scheme due to "the poor quality of police video interview skills," which resulted in *more*, not fewer, interviews (Wood 1997, 1073). The Tasmanian Law Reform Commissioner recommended in 1990 that interviews be recorded electronically and the videotape (edited to remove parts offending laws of evidence, like hearsay, for example) made admissible at trial (Law Reform Commissioner of Tasmania 1990, 11).

By the end of the 1990s, the perceived benefits of this technology resulted in police recorded interviews being used in court as a child witness's evidence-in-chief at trial (Aldridge and Wood 2000). Traditionally, the prosecutor would examine the child witness in the courtroom, often referring to the police interview. Now, with the advent of this technology, and to reduce the number of times a child would have to recount the events, the police interview would form the evidence judges and juries would hear. The Victorian case of *R v NRC* was one of the first Victorian cases in which this practice of using a recorded police interview as the child's evidence-in-chief was permitted. The defendant, NRC, was convicted of various offences including sexual offences and a threat to kill his five-year-old daughter, who was the complainant. NRC appealed against his conviction on the ground that the verdicts were unsafe and unsatisfactory. The interview played to the jury at trial had been conducted by a senior constable ten months after the alleged offence took place. The court noted the "laudable objectives" of allowing evidence to be received in this way, acknowledging as the reforms represented a "significant departure" from previous practice, trial judges needed to be cautious. They recognised their "overriding obligation…to ensure that…the accused is not exposed to the risk of an unfair trial" (*R v N.R.C* [1999] 3 VR 537, 540). This practice of having a child witness's evidence-in-chief put before the court through their police interview is now used across all Australian states, making police interview techniques and practices more important than ever.

Conclusion

While there were undoubtedly improvements over the century in how police engaged with child witnesses, for much of the twentieth century, it was a very unpleasant experience for most children. Existing policing practices at the start of the century meant that by the time a child witness was finished with a police investigation, they may have been taken back to the scene of the crime; been forced to confront the accused directly; been taken before a police line-up and asked to touch the suspect; participated in multiple interviews with police and, towards the end of the century, participated in interviews with the numerous other parties involved in the investigation. The century had begun with largely unregulated, informal interactions between children and police, but ended with highly regulated, strictly controlled procedures. These changes were informed by new research into the psychology of children and the adoption of new technologies that provided opportunities for police to reform interview techniques. The resulting improvements promoted a level of consistency and predictability in police practices that had not existed previously. Engagement with police officers was only the beginning, though, of the child witness's journey through the criminal justice system. A decision to press charges would set in motion the prosecution process and provide many more hurdles for a child witness to overcome in order to be heard.

Notes

1. See also: Australian Law Reform Commission, *Family Violence – A National Legal Response* (Report No 114—2010), par 26.8; New Zealand Law Commission, *The Justice Response to Victims of Sexual Violence* (Report No 136—2015); Victorian Law Reform Commission, *Sexual Offences (*Report—2004), 103; Cooper, Debbie. 2005. "Pigot Unfulfilled: Video-Recorded Cross-Examination Under Section 28 of the *Youth Justice and Criminal Evidence Act 1999*." *Criminal Law Review* (June): 456–466, 461.
2. The view that female officers were preferable to males in some circumstances mirrored that in the United Kingdom. See Logan, Anne. 2008. *Feminism and Criminal Justice: A Historical Perspective*. Great Britain: Springer Nature. https://doi.org/10.1057/9780230584136. In referring to "women police," it is acknowledged women officers were not introduced into the relevant state forces as equals of their male colleagues: Prenzler, Tim. 1995. "Equal Employment Opportunity and Policewomen in Australia." *Australian & New Zealand Journal of Criminology* 28 (3): 258–277. See also Allen, Judith. 1994. *Rose Scott – Vision and Revision in Feminism*. Melbourne: Oxford University Press, 160, on the inadequate representation and protection of women and children in criminal and divorce courts by men.
3. See, for example, Paul, William. 1924. *Victorian Police Manual*, 172, par 6. This manual contains extensive instructions on the process of examination, cross-examination and re-examination of witnesses (178–179) and for running a police prosecution (413–416). See also O'Callaghan, Thomas. 1906. *The Victorian Police Code, 1906*, Rules 536 and 537.
4. O'Callaghan, Thomas. 1906. *The Victorian Police Code, 1906*, Rule 2292 refers to the *Evidence Act 1890* (Vic) s 50 and the *Crimes Act 1891* (Vic) s 33. Case law cited includes *R v Bates & Brown* 8 VLR (L) 310 and *R v Macnamara* (1897) 22 VLR 668, in relation to evidence of complaints of rape. See also Vincent, Howard. 1905. "The Queensland Police Code and Justices." *Manual of the Criminal Law*. Sydney: The Law Book Co of Australasia Ltd. for similar instructions with reference to Queensland's *Criminal Code*.
5. See also: *The Prosecution Project Database*, https://prosecutionproject.griffith.edu.au/prosecutions, Trial ID #12096, Western Australian Supreme Court [WASC], John Joseph Croft, 1916.
6. The text is adapted from the *System der Kriminalistik* of Dr. Hans Gross, Professor of Criminology at the University of Prague. Copies of each of

these editions were located in the Victorian police archive material in the Victorian Supreme Court library call numbers: S 363.25 GRO.3/4/5. Additional versions are located in the Queensland Police Service Library, at Bond University and Murdoch University law libraries.

7. For further evidence of campaigns to foster better relationships between police and children generally, see *Newcastle Morning Herald and Miners' Advocate (NSW: 1876–1954).* "Making Friends." February 10, 1934, 8; *The Sun (Sydney, NSW: 1910–1954).* "Police as Friends." June 12, 1935, 7; *Advocate (Burnie, Tas: 1890–1954).* "Children Should Regard Police as Friends." March 24, 1941, 8.

References

Adam, John, J. Collyer, Norman Kendal, and Hans Gross. 1934, 1949, 1962. *System der Kriminalistik, Criminal Investigation Practical Textbook for Magistrates, Police Officers and Lawyers.* London: Sweet & Maxwell.

Advocate (Burnie, Tas: 1890–1954). "Children Should Regard Police as Friends." March 24, 1941.

Aldridge, Michelle, and Joanne Wood. 2000. "Interviewing Child Witnesses within Memorandum Guidelines – A Survey of Police Officers in England and Wales." *Children & Society* 14: 168–181.

Alexander v the Queen (1981) 145 CLR 395.

The Argus (Melbourne). "Children and Police." February 28, 1940.

Australian Law Reform Commission. 1975. *Criminal Investigation*, Report no. 2 – An Interim Report.

Australian Law Reform Commission and Australian Human Rights and Equal Opportunity Commission. 1997. *Seen and Heard: Priority for Children in the Legal Process*, Vol. 84. https://www.alrc.gov.au/publications/report-84.

Border Watch. "In the Mount Gambier Law Courts: Mount Gambier Police." November 11, 1954.

Brampton, Sir Henry Hawkins. 1905. "Address to the Police on Their Duties", quoted in Col. Sir Howard Vincent, 'The Queensland Police Code and Justices' *Manual of the Criminal Law.* Sydney: The Law Book Co of Australasia Ltd.

Brewer, Neil, and Katherine Day. 2005. "The Confidence-Accuracy and Decision Latency-Accuracy Relationships in Children's Eyewitness Identification." *Psychiatry, Psychology and Law* 12 (1): 119–128.
Bull, Ray, and Eleanor Corran. 2002. "Interviewing Child Witnesses: Past and Future." *International Journal of Police Science and Management* 4 (4): 315–322.
Cairns Post. "A Child Witness." October 11, 1929.
Ceci, Stephen J., and Maggie Bruck. 1993. "Suggestibility of the Child Witness: A Historical Review and Synthesis." *Psychological Bulletin* 113 (3): 403–439.
Ceci, Stephen J., David F. Ross, and Michael P. Toglia. 1987. "Suggestibility of Children's Memory: Psycholegal Implications." *Journal of Experimental Psychology: General* 116 (1): 38–49.
Croft v The King (1917) 7 WALR 263.
Daily Herald (Adelaide). "Those Troublesome Men in Blue." January 16, 1914.
Darling Downs Gazette. "Women Police." December 7, 1917.
Davies, Graham, and Laurence Griffiths. 2008. "Eyewitness Identification and the English Courts: A Century of Trial and Error." *Psychiatry, Psychology and Law* 15 (3): 435–449.
Devlin, Patrick, and Great Britain. 1976. *Report to the Secretary of State for the Home Department of the Departmental Committee on Evidence of Identification in Criminal Cases*. London: H.M. Stationery Office.
Eijkman, Henk. 1992. "Police, Victims and Democracy: Rewriting the Priorities." In *Policing Australia: Old Issues, New Perspectives*, edited by Henk Eijkman and Peter Moir, 266–298. Crow's Nest, NSW: Macmillan.
Eltham and Whittlesea Shires Advertiser (Vic: 1940–1942). "Whittlesea Court Man on Five Charges." March 14, 1941.
Emsley, Clive. 1996. *The English Police – A Political and Social History*, 2nd ed. Edinburgh Gate: Addison Wesley Longman.
Evening News (Sydney, NSW: 1869–1931). "The Queanbeyan Horror." November 21, 1901.
Examiner (Launceston, Tas: 1900–1954). "Women Police." November 4, 1919.
Finnane, Mark. 1989. "Police Rules and the Organisation of Policing in Queensland: 1905-1916." *Australian and New Zealand Journal of Criminology* 22 (June): 95–108.
Finnane, Mark. 1994. *Police and Government: Histories of Policing in Australia*. Melbourne: Oxford University Press.
Fitzgerald, Tony, and Queensland Commission of Inquiry into Possible Illegal Activities and Associated Police Misconduct. 1989. *Report of a Commission of*

Inquiry Pursuant to Orders in Council, dated 26 May 1987, 24 June 1987, 25 August 1988, 29 June 1989. Brisbane: Commission of Inquiry into Possible Illegal Activities and Associated Police Misconduct.

Fraser Parker, Janat, and Virginia Ryan. 1993. "An Attempt to Reduce Guessing Behavior in Children's and Adults' Eyewitness Identifications." *Law and Human Behavior* 17 (1): 11–26.

Goodman, Gail S., and Christine Aman. 1990. "Children's Use of Anatomically Detailed Dolls to Recount an Event." *Child Development* 61 (6): 1859–1871.

Hall, D. F., and T. M. Ostrom. 2013. "Accuracy of Eyewitness Identification After Biasing or Unbiased Instructions. Paper presented at the meeting of the American Psychological Association, Chicago, IL," cited by Nancy K. Stable, "Lineup Instructions." In *Reform of Eyewitness Identification Procedures*, edited by Brian L. Cutler, 66. Washington, DC: American Psychological Association.

Humphreys, Catherine. 1996. "Exploring New Territory: Police Organizational Responses to Child Sexual Abuse." *Child Abuse & Neglect* 20 (4):337–344.

Independent (Footscray). "Alleged Indecent Offence." August 23, 1913.

Jackson, Louise, A. 1999. *Child Sexual Abuse in Victorian England*. New York: Routledge.

Jackson, Louise A. 2003. "Care or Control? The Metropolitan Women Police and Child Welfare, 1919-1969." *The Historical Journal* 46 (3): 623–648.

Jefferies, David R. "Videotaping of Children's Evidence." Paper presented at Children and the Law Seminar, Brisbane, 10 July, 1990.

Lamb, Michael E. 2008. *Tell Me What Happened: Structured Investigative Interviews of Child Victims and Witnesses*, 2nd ed. Hoboken, NJ: Wiley-Blackwell.

Law Reform Commissioner of Tasmania, *Child Witnesses* (Report No 62—1990).

Lindsay, R.C.L., Joanna D. Pozzulo, Wendy Craig, Kang Lee, and Samantha Corber. 1997. "Simultaneous Lineups, Sequential Lineups, and Showups: Eyewitness Identification Decisions of Adults and Children." *Law and Human Behavior* 21 (4): 391–404.

Mapes, Bruce E. 1995. *Child Eyewitness Testimony in Sexual Abuse Investigations.* Brandon: Clinical Psychology Publishing Company.

Milne, Rebecca, and Ray Bull. 1999. *Investigative Interviewing: Psychology and Practice.* New York: Wiley.

Mirror (Perth, WA: 1921–1956). "Yes, That's My Daddy." December 11, 1937.

Mirror (Perth, WA: 1921–1956). "Girl Denies She Told Police of Alleged Offence." February 6, 1954.

Mirror (Perth, WA: 1921–1956). "Out of the Mouths of Babes." September 20, 1952.
Morgan, Jane, and Lucia Zedner. 1992. *Child Victims: Crime, Impact, and Criminal Justice*. Oxford: Clarendon Press.
New South Wales Law Reform Commission, *Evidence* (Report 56 1988).
Newcastle Morning Herald and Miners' Advocate (NSW: 1876–1954). "Making Friends." February 10, 1934.
O'Callaghan, Thomas, C. B. Finlayson, and Victoria Police Force. 1906. *Victorian Police Code*. Melbourne.
Paul, William, and Victoria Police Department. 1924. *Victorian Police Manual: For the Use of Officers and Members of the Victorian Police Force*. Melbourne: Albert J. Mullett, Government Printer.
Pigot, Thomas, Great Britain Home Office, and Great Britain Advisory Group on Video-Recorded Evidence. 1989. *Report of the Advisory Group on Video-Recorded Evidence*. London: Home Office, UK.
Powell, Martine, Nina Westera, Jane Goodman-Delahunty, and Anne Pichler. 2016. "Royal Commission into Institutional Responses to Child Sexual Abuse, *An Evaluation of How Evidence is Elicited from Complainants of Child Sexual Abuse*." Sydney: Royal Commission into Institutional Responses to Child Sexual Abuse.
Pozzulo, Joanna D., and R. C. L. Lindsay. 1999. "Elimination Lineups: An Improved Identification Procedure for Child Eyewitnesses." *Journal of Applied Psychology* 84 (2): 167–176.
Prenzler, Tim. 1994. "Women in Australian Policing: An Historical Overview." *Journal of Australian Studies* 18 (42): 78–88.
Prenzler, Tim. 2015. *100 Years of Women Police in Australia*. Samford Valley, Qld: Australian Academic Press.
Queensland Police Force. 1985. *Report - Juvenile Aid Bureau 1985*. Brisbane: Juvenile Aid Bureau (Queensland Police Museum).
Queensland State Archives, Queensland State Archives Item ID95466, Depositions and Indictments.
R v Grills (1910) 10 SR (NSW) 309.
R v Grills (1910) 11 CLR 400.
R v N.R.C [1999] 3 VR 537.
R v Sparkman (1930) 31 SR (NSW) 80.
Register (Adelaide). "Good Work by Policewomen." August 10, 1917.
Rush, Elizabeth B., Jodi A. Quas, Ilona S. Yim, Mariya Nikolayev, Steven E. Clark, and Rakel P. Larson. 2014. "Stress, Interviewer Support, and

Children's Eyewitness Identification Accuracy." *Child Development* 85 (3): 1292–1305.
Scott, Dorothy, and Shurlee Swain. 2002. *Confronting Cruelty: Historical Perspectives on Child Abuse.* Melbourne: Melbourne University Press.
Snelling, H.A.R. 1969. "Sexual Offences Involving Female Children." Paper presented at the University of Sydney Institute of Criminology Seminar on Sexual Offences Against Females, Sydney, 61–70. https://ses.library.usyd.edu.au/bitstream/handle/2123/14950/POIOC_06_1969.pdf.pdf?sequence=4&isAllowed=y.
Soothill, Keith, and Brian Francis. 2002. "Moral Panics and the Aftermath: A Study of Incest." *Journal of Social Welfare and Family Law* 24 (1):1–17.
Sutton, Jeanna. 1992. "Women in the Job." In *Policing Australia: Old Issues, New Perspectives*, edited by Henk Eijkman and Peter Moir, 67–101. Crow's Nest, NSW: Macmillan.
The Australian Star (Sydney, NSW: 1887–1909). "Queanbeyan Outrage." October 25, 1901a.
The Australian Star (Sydney, NSW: 1887–1909). "Revolting Outrage on a Little Girl." October 3, 1901b.
The Brisbane Courier (Qld: 1864–1933). "Women Police." April 11, 1929.
The Burrangong Argus (NSW: 1865–1913). "The Ramsay's Bush Outrage." November 16, 1901.
The Capricornian. "Women Police." June 27, 1929.
The Daily News (Perth, WA: 1882–1950). "A Serious Charge." September 6, 1916.
The Dubbo Liberal and Macquarie Advocate (NSW: 1894–1954). "Monday, April 9th – Alleged Indecent Assault." April 11, 1906.
The Prosecution Project Database [PP]. https://prosecutionproject.griffith.edu.au/prosecutions (version 1, 17 July 2016), Trial ID # 202466, New South Wales Quarter Sessions [NSWQS], Henry Grills, 1910.
The Prosecution Project Database [PP]. https://prosecutionproject.griffith.edu.au/prosecutions (version 1, 17 July 2016), Trial ID #12096, Western Australian Supreme Court [WASC], John Joseph Croft, 1916.
The Sun (Sydney, NSW: 1910–1954). "Police as Friends." June 12, 1935.
The Sydney Morning Herald (NSW: 1842–1954). "A Child Witness." May 9, 1912.
The Sydney Morning Herald (NSW:1842–1954). "Quarter Sessions." October 11, 1930.
The Week (Brisbane, Qld: 1876–1934). "Supreme Court Criminal Sittings." June 8, 1900.

Truth (Perth, WA: 1903–1931). "A Uniformed Ruffian." September 9, 1916.
Vincent, Howard. 1905. "The Queensland Police Code and Justices." *Manual of the Criminal Law.* Sydney: The Law Book Co of Australasia Ltd.
Westcott, Helen, and Graham Davies. 1996. "Sexually Abused Children's and Young People's Perspectives on Investigative Interviews." *The British Journal of Social Work* 26 (4): 451–474.
Western Champion (Parkes, NSW: 1898–1934). "Woodward Park Case: Hearing Lasts All Day." October 18, 1928.
Wood, J.R.T. 1997. *Royal Commission into the NSW Police Service: Final Report.* Sydney: NSW Government.

4

"If the Law Doesn't Get You, the Lord Will": Competency and Capacity

If you tell a lie, what will happen to you when you die? This is perhaps a tricky question for any adult to answer, but it was routinely asked of children in court to prove themselves to be competent witnesses. The decisions of police to press charges, and prosecutors to proceed to trial, were only the start of a child witness's struggle to be heard. For most of the twentieth century, until the 1990s, the law presumed children were incompetent to give evidence. Until any child witness was able to prove their competence, therefore, their evidence would not be received. To overcome this presumption of incompetency required children to demonstrate their understanding of the nature of the oath by demonstrating they understood they would go to hell if they lied. If they failed this test, and the case was one where unsworn testimony was potentially acceptable, child witnesses then had to demonstrate they were "sufficiently intelligent" to understand the need to tell the truth. Dating back to the seventeenth century, the expectation that children must leap these competency hurdles before a word of their evidence was received has its origins in the common law's need for witnesses to swear an oath to tell the truth. Having adopted the adversarial trial as its preferred mode of

R. Blewer, *Child Witnesses in Twentieth Century Australian Courtrooms*, Palgrave Histories of Policing, Punishment and Justice,
https://doi.org/10.1007/978-3-030-69791-4_4

prosecution, England and its common law empire were faced with the question of how to ensure witnesses would tell the truth (Finkelstein 2011, 135). For most adult witnesses, swearing an oath was a matter of taking the Bible in hand and promising to tell the whole truth and nothing but the truth. Realistically, though, all an oath could ever do was *symbolise* the ascertainment of truth (Green 1992, 699). It could not guarantee it.

The history of the common law is arguably one of pragmatism. Where an adult witness was not Christian or Anglo-Saxon, had another religious background or no religious beliefs, legislation provided alternative arrangements to swearing an oath, such as giving an affirmation. Even if witnesses could swear an oath, the common law presumed some classes of witnesses would be less inclined to tell the truth than Anglo-Saxon Christian, adult males. Indeed, the law presumed certain witness categories were inherently untrustworthy. Indigenous people, non-Christians and women, for example, were all subject to the same unease about competency as child witnesses (Robb and Kordyban 1989, 329). These witnesses were often forced to undergo far more intense testing of their capacity to swear an oath. Even if an adult swore an oath without holding Christian beliefs, their testimony would not necessarily be invalid (*Oaths Act 1889* (Tas) s 5). The law seems to have always understood the limits of this oath requirement. Developing ways to circumvent the competency test prevented courts from losing what could be vital testimony, reducing the risk that justice would not be served simply because a witness could not, or would not, swear an oath (*Cheers v Porter* (1931) 46 CLR 521). The law was quite flexible and fluid when it came to adults swearing oaths. This pragmatism and flexibility, however, was not applied to children in the same situation.

There is evidence from as early as the seventeenth century that juries tended to assess the evidence of children based on whether it was sworn or unsworn, regardless of whether they believed the child was telling the truth. Historian John Langbein cites the 1678 case of *Arrowsmith* as a striking example of the preference for sworn testimony—and the common law's pragmatism. A jury found Arrowsmith not guilty of raping a young girl. The court refused to accept this verdict, however, "not conceiving it to be according to their Evidence" (Langbein 1978,

293). Some jurors admitted to doubting the unsworn testimony of the two girls who had given evidence. The girls were recalled and re-examined on "whether they understood the nature of an Oath, and the danger of Perjury, which they gave a Rational account of" (Langbein 1978, 293). Assuring the jurors they did understand the nature of an oath, the verdict was taken again. Arrowsmith was convicted and executed the following day (Langbein 1978, 293). Having the child witnesses swear an oath seems to have made all the difference in this case.

A century on from *Arrowsmith*, the significance of sworn testimony was again confirmed in the 1776 English case of *R v Brasier*. Brasier was convicted of assaulting five-year-old Mary Harris (*R v Brasier* (1779) 168 E.R 202). Mary didn't give evidence at the trial. Instead, her mother and a lodger each gave evidence of what Mary had told them about the offence, including giving them an accurate description of the interior of the defendant's lodgings. In addition, Mary had identified the defendant in a line-up and a surgeon testified that the child had "received some hurt." Brasier was convicted. On appeal, though, the Court unanimously agreed the verdict was unsafe because of the hearsay evidence of Mary's mother and the lodger, and Brasier was pardoned. In their decision, the Court confirmed that children of any age could give evidence but "their admissibility depends upon the sense and reason they entertain of the danger and impiety of falsehood, which is to be collected from their answers to questions propounded to them by the Court" (*R v Brasier* (1779) 168 E.R 202, 203). Thus, while recognising the testimony of children of any age could be vital to the administration of justice and should, therefore, be received, the court limited the class of children who could testify to those who could swear an oath.

The difficulties associated with children passing this oath test from *Brasier* eventually led most Australian colonies to introduce statutory provisions allowing unsworn testimony of children in certain cases. South Australia was the first colony to introduce specific legislative provisions allowing for this. This reform in 1876 pre-dated similar English reforms and applied in cases of felonies or misdemeanours. It provided that unsworn testimony could be received from children under ten years of age without oath or formality (*Criminal Law Consolidation Act 1876*

(SA) pt IX s 377). Instead, judicial officers were required to explain to the child that he or she had to tell the truth. The child's testimony was then assessed according to the weight and credibility, which, in the opinion of the judicial officer or the jury, ought to be attached to evidence given "without the sanction of an oath" (*Criminal Law Consolidation Act 1876* (SA) pt IX ss 377–378).

The other Australian states did not follow South Australia's lead. They did, however, follow the English *Criminal Law Amendment Act 1885* (UK), which was introduced following the publication of a series of articles in London's *Pall Mall Gazette.* Known as "The Maiden Tribute to Modern Babylon" series (Stead 1885), the articles drew public attention to young English girls working as prostitutes in London:

> It is a veritable slave trade which is going on around us, but as it takes place in the heart of London, it is a scandal, an outrage on public morality, even to allude to it. We have kept silence far too long. The House, the school, the Church, the Press are silent. Law is actually an accessory to crime. (Stead 1885, July 6)

The *Criminal Law Amendment Act 1885* (UK) was concerned with prosecuting sexual offences. It increased the age of consent from thirteen to sixteen. It introduced new offences—including the notorious "Labouchere Amendment" (s 11), which re-introduced an offence of gross indecency between males (Smith 1976, 165–173). In what is arguably an overlooked part of the Act, a provision allowing for the receipt of unsworn testimony of children in certain cases was also introduced. The old common law rule in *R v Brasier* that children could only give evidence if they could swear an oath was implicated. As politician Samuel Smith argued:

> There were many charges of gross outrage on children which fell through owing to the ridiculous law which required the evidence of the child to be given on oath … A child might give the clearest possible testimony … leaving no reasonable doubt in any sound mind that she was telling the truth; but at the trial, perhaps two months afterwards, she was required to take the oath, and then it was discovered … that she did not know the nature of an oath. (United Kingdom *Hansard*, 31 July 1885 col 754)

Section 4 of the *Criminal Law Amendment Act 1885* (UK) allowed children to give unsworn testimony in relation to charges of defiling a girl under thirteen years of age on the following terms:

> Where, upon the hearing of a charge under this section, the girl in respect of whom the offence is charged to have been committed, or any other child of tender years who is tendered as a witness, does not in the opinion of the court or justices, understand the nature of an oath, the evidence of such girl or other child of tender years may be received, though not given up on oath, if, in the opinion of the court or justices, as the case may be such girl or other child of tender years is possessed of sufficient intelligence to justify the reception of the evidence, and understands the duty of speaking the truth: Provided that no person shall be liable to be convicted of the offence unless the testimony admitted by virtue of this section and given on behalf of the prosecution shall be corroborated by some other material evidence in support thereof implicating the accused: Provided also, that any witness whose evidence has been admitted under this section shall be liable to indictment and punishment for perjury in all respects as if he or she had been sworn. (*Criminal Law Amendment Act 1885* (UK) s 4)

This provision was a controversial one. It was initially defeated 123 votes to 120 (*Hansard*, 31 July 1885 col 763). To pass the provision, the parliament required two things: first, that unsworn evidence be corroborated, and second, that children who gave evidence pursuant to this provision could be charged with perjury if found to have lied in court.[1] The corroboration reforms arising out of this Act are considered further in Chapter 7.

News of the "Maiden Tribute" series reached Australia quickly. For some local publications, the series was re-printed verbatim, with the only comment being that it reflected "certain phases of 'London life'" (*Evening News* 1885, 3). The *Weekly Times*, however, included a lengthy editorial on the articles. Suggesting the commercial success of the *Pall Mall Gazette* was due to its sensational reporting style incorporating the "best and the worst features of journalism," the editor surmised, in this instance, the "Maiden Tribute" series, while very profitable for the

Gazette, had been published to "do a public service," also relevant in the Australian context:

> That it has been for the public good goes without saying. The "Pall Mall Gazette" has told nothing that is not well within the memory of all men of the world. It has told nothing that cannot be matched and paralleled in the cities of Australia. Its fearful record of lust and destruction is not new, although, alas ! true to the letter... We believe that not one word is exaggerated – that, on the contrary, the truth is only half told; and we are well aware that every line applies as well to Melbourne as to the Great Babylon, London. Girls are seduced, and children are sold into prostitution and debauchery, in Victoria as in England; people of note here are customers at the brothels, and the social evil flourishes just as vigorously as in the world's metropolis...we would ask whether it is not possible by legislative means to destroy or limit the evil. (Weekly Times 1885, 8)

It would take six years before Australian jurisdictions attempted to "destroy or limit the evil" by legislative means in the same way England had. New South Wales and Victoria passed legislation in similar terms to the *Criminal Law Amendment Act 1885* (UK) in December 1891 (*Criminal Law and Evidence Amendment Act 1891* (NSW) s 7; *Crimes Act 1891* (Vic) s 33).

Queensland did not introduce similar provisions to the other colonies at this time. In passing the *Child Protection Act 1896* (Qld), the colony provided for the receipt of unsworn testimony of children, but only in relation to offences under that Act specifically—namely ill treatment and neglect of a child (*Child Protection Act 1896* (Qld) s 7). Otherwise, Queensland retained its existing oaths legislation (*Oaths Act 1867* (Qld)), which had been amended in 1884 to allow a judge to receive evidence from any person who:

> objected to take an oath, or by reason of any defect of religious knowledge or belief, or other cause, appears incapable of comprehending the nature of an oath...if satisfied that the taking of an oath would have no binding effect on the conscience of such person and that he understands that

he will be liable to punishment if his evidence is untruthful. (*Oaths Act Amendment Act 1884* (Qld) s 2)

This provision appears to suggest a judge could take the evidence of any person, including a child, and declare in what manner the evidence was to be taken, and then treat that evidence as if an oath had been administered. Similar drafting in NSW formed the basis of a High Court challenge to a child's testimony in the case of *Cheers v Porter*, discussed below. Table 4.1 summarises the relevant legislation in each state providing for the receipt of unsworn testimony of children at the turn of the twentieth century.

In summary, at the turn of the twentieth century, under common law, all children were presumed incompetent to give sworn testimony, so had to undergo a convoluted process to give evidence. Anyone "of tender years" would be tested on their understanding of the nature of the oath. If the child passed this common law test, they were permitted to swear an oath, irrespective of the nature of the relevant offence. Children who failed the oath test could subsequently be tested according to the statutory requirements for unsworn testimony only if the offence was applicable in the relevant legislation and the child concerned was of the requisite age.

Questions of competency could be asked at any stage of a trial, even if a child had already been sworn and begun to give evidence, as in the case in *R v Whitehead* ((1897) 3 ALR 140 ("*Whitehead*")). James Whitehead was tried twice for indecently assaulting an eight-year-old girl in the Edinburgh Gardens, Fitzroy. At the trial, the girl, Myrtle, had been sworn and begun to give her evidence. It's not clear from the Argus Law Reports why, but it appears that part way through her evidence, questions were raised as to "whether she understood the nature of an oath" (*Whitehead*). There followed some debate as to whether this was a proper application of the oath test. The prosecutor, Mr. Finlayson, argued it was not. He submitted "once the child was sworn that she was a competent witness, and that it was too late to enquire into the matter." Counsel for Mr. Whitehead argued it was open to the court to "satisfy itself as to the competency of a witness at any stage of the proceedings" (*Whitehead*). Mr. Finlayson, after consulting the most recent edition of "*Russell*

Table 4.1 Pre-twentieth-century legislation permitting receipt of unsworn testimony of child witnesses

	SA	NSW	Tas	Vic	WA	Qld
Act/s	*Criminal Law Consolidation Act 1876* ss 377–378	*Criminal Law and Evidence Amendment Act 1891* s 7	*An Act to Amend the Law as to Oaths 1889* s 8	*Evidence Act 1890* s 50 and *Crimes Act 1890* s 33(1)	*Criminal Law Amendment Act 1892* s 4	*Child Protection Act 1896* s 7
Offences	felony or misdemeanor	amended *Criminal Law Amendment Act 1883* to allow unsworn testimony for offences under ss 41–44, 59–60—sexual offences committed against girls u14 and boys	general	s 50—general s 33(1)—rape, unlawful, carnal knowledge (and attempt) against girls	defilement of girls u12 (and attempt); girls 12–14 years	in respect of that Act only—ill-treatment and neglect
Age	under 10 years	tender years	under 7 years	s 50: under 7 years s 33(1)—tender years	tender years	tender years

	SA	NSW	Tas	Vic	WA	Qld
Required	judicial officer to explain to child need to tell truth—weight attached as per evidence given without sanction of oath	sufficient intelligence and understand duty to speak truth	sufficient intelligence and understand duty to speak truth	given upon affirmation or declaration to tell the truth, the whole truth and nothing but the truth—caution re. punish testimony	sufficient intelligence and understand duty to speak truth	sufficient intelligence and understand duty to speak truth

on Crimes 6th ed vol 3 at p671," acquiesced and agreed the judge could examine the child again as to her competency. Chief Justice Madden made the requisite further enquiries, "eventually determining that she was competent to give evidenced on oath" (*Whitehead*). The argument appears to be for naught, as the jury were unable to agree on a verdict (*The Age* 1897, 10).

Whitehead was again tried before Justice A'Beckett in the Criminal Court, Melbourne. This time he was found guilty. In sentencing Whitehead, Justice A'Beckett saw fit to make a comment on "the prevalence of assaults on young girls" (*The Argus* 1897, 10). His comments to the jury are worth noting. A'Beckett was recommending to the jury punishment by the lash, a punishment he "seldom directed." (*The Argus* 1897, 10) Prior to reviewing the evidence, his Honour told the jury that if any of them

> Thought that offences of the class under notice were simply to be regarded as a form of innocence [sic] amusement, and therefore not punishable, it was useless for him to address them. If they had made up their minds to acquit the prisoner apart altogether from the merits of the case, it would be useless for him to go into the evidence. But assuming that they were in a proper frame of mind he proposed to do so. A similar case had been tried before him in that court on the previous day; but although each of the two young ruffians who were accused stated in the course of their evidence for the defence that the other had behaved indecently towards the girl, the jury, evidently thinking it was to be regarded as a joke, brought in a verdict of not guilty. Mr. Justice A'Beckett then dealt with the evidence before the court, and the jury after a short retirement brought in a verdict of guilty. (*The Age* 1897, 10)

Whitehead was sentenced to twelve months' imprisonment with hard labour, periods of solitary confinement and to one whipping of fifteen strokes with the cat-o-nine-tails. It is not clear what was really going on in Justice A'Beckett's court or in Whitehead's first trial under Chief Justice Madden. But, for whatever reason, the capacity for Myrtle to give sworn testimony was at issue.

The Common Law Oath Test

The common law oath test set down in 1779 in the case of *Brasier*, to which Myrtle would have been subjected, required the resolution of two separate questions. First, was the witness a child of "tender years"? Second, if so, did they understand the nature of the oath? There were no specific rules on either aspect of the test in case law. Rather, each involved an exercise of the considerable discretionary powers of the presiding judicial officer. What was deemed a satisfactory demonstration of an understanding of the oath and the interpretation of the phrase "tender years" were subjects of frequent debate in courts and in parliaments throughout the twentieth century.

"Tender Years"

The rule in *Brasier* stipulated that only children "of tender years" needed to be tested on their understanding of the oath (*Brunsgard v Jennings* [1974] WAR 36). The first question for courts, then, was which children were "of tender years"? This phrase had been used to describe children from the early seventeenth century, if not earlier. John Langbein cites a pamphlet written by Mathew Hale in 1613 that used the phrase (Langbein 1978, 294). Its use may reflect the likelihood children would not have had evidence of their date of birth other than the hearsay evidence of what they had been told. This, in turn, may have been the reason it was subsequently included in various statutes across Australia in their unsworn testimony legislation in the nineteenth century (*Criminal Law and Evidence Amendment Act 1891* (NSW) s 7; *Crimes Act 1890* (Vic) s 33(1); *Criminal Law Amendment Act 1892* (WA) s 4). If so, this is another example of the law's concern that children still be able to give evidence and that courts would not lose important testimony purely because a child did not have access to a birth certificate to prove their exact age. But even if this was the case, it is strange that the phrase "tender years" remained undefined in case law or legislation for as long as it was in use. Its limitations were frequently discussed at length in court and in reported decisions. Children as young as four and adolescents as old as fourteen and fifteen were given the oath test, indicating the judges in these cases thought they were children "of tender years" (*The Dubbo Liberal and Macquarie Advocate* 1943, 2). In 1913, for instance, a judge refused to swear a five-year-old girl but changed his mind after counsel referred him to a Supreme Court case in which a child of that age had been sworn (*Independent* 1913, 1).

The vagueness of "tender years" was still being debated in 1974, some two hundred years after the English decision in *R v Brasier*. In the Western Australian case of *Brunsgard v Jennings,* Brunsgard was charged with exposing himself in the presence of two girls, eleven and twelve years of age (*Brunsgard v Jennings* [1974] WAR 36). The magistrate allowed the girls to give sworn evidence without first questioning them on their understanding of the oath, nor was there any objection from counsel to the girls being sworn in this way. Brunsgard was found guilty. He appealed against his conviction on the ground that the girls' sworn testimony was wrongly admitted. Brunsgard argued the girls were "of tender years" and should have been tested on their understanding of the oath before being sworn. The Supreme Court of Western Australia disagreed and found the evidence of the girls had been properly admitted. Chief Justice Jackson thought the phrase "tender years" referred to children "up to about ten years." Because the girls in this case were eleven and twelve, Jackson CJ said it was entirely a matter for the magistrate, and thus reasonable for the two to have been sworn without the need to be examined as to their competency. He cited the English decision of Lord Goddard CJ in *R v Campbell*, who said:

> [w]hether a child is of tender years is a matter for the good sense of the court, and though it may be difficult to decide whether a child understands the obligation of an oath, a court probably would have no difficulty in deciding whether he or she was of tender years. (*R v Campbell* [1956] 2 QB 432)

In his written judgment, Jackson CJ discussed the recent reduction in the age of majority from twenty-one years to eighteen years of age (*Brunsgard v Jennings* [1974] WAR 36, 38; *Minors (Property and Contracts) Act 1970* (NSW); *Age of Majority (Reduction) Act* 1971 (SA); *Age of Majority Act*

1972 (WA); *Age of Majority Act* 1973 (Tas)). He queried whether, in 1974, anyone over fourteen years would be considered a child. "Doubtless a young child up to about ten years of age should be qualified by questioning," he wrote, but otherwise he thought it should be a matter for the court's discretion as to whether they could be sworn without questioning. If the children gave evidence "in a competent manner," as the girls in this case had, there was no ground to appeal on the basis that such evidence had been improperly received (*Brunsgard v Jennings* [1974] WAR 36, 39). Despite Jackson CJ's opinion that judicial officers should be able to identify a child of tender years easily, the Western Australian Parliament amended the relevant section two years later, in 1976, replacing the general phrase "tender years" with the more specific qualification of children under twelve years (*Evidence Act Amendment Act (No. 2) 1976* (WA) s 5).

The relevant principles were applied inconsistently until the 1970s and 1980s, when legislative amendments clarified the process by replacing the phrase "tender years" with chronological age limits. Why the phrase remained undefined for so long is not clear. It may be that the judiciary were content with the discretion and flexibility it afforded them to determine for themselves which children were competent to give evidence. Twenty years after *Brunsgard v Jennings*, in 1993, the Tasmanian Supreme Court considered the meaning of the phrase in the case of *Mansell* (*Attorney-General's Reference No. 2 of 1993: Re R v Mansell* (1994) 4 TAS R 26). Here, Justice Cox thought the lack of authority or clarification was understandable. "It seems to me," he said:

> that what is meant by 'tender years' may very well differ according to the type of child who is about to give evidence but, as a general working rule, it is the experience of all three members of this court that for a proffered witness who is under the age of 14 the precaution which has been well established becomes necessary. (*Mansell*, 9)

Analysing the *Mansell* decision, legal scholar Terese Henning suggested the phrase reflected an intention for children to be assessed according to maturity, "not according to a pre-determined, arbitrarily prescribed age" (Henning 1995, 102). Despite Justice Cox's opinion in *Mansell* that the phrase "tender years" was reasonable, states began replacing it with chronological age limits at the end of the twentieth century, 400 years after it was first introduced into the common law as a way of defining who was and was not a young child.

Religious Belief

If a child was deemed to be "of tender years," they were then tested on their understanding of the oath. This often began with a very general enquiry to ascertain whether they understood what would happen to them if they lied. Such a question gave children no guidance as to what the desired answer might be. "Me mother will give me a hiding" was the response of one young boy when asked what would happen if he lied (*Barrier Miner* 1904, 3). A very astute boy (although described in the press as "precocious") was called to give evidence at Bungaree Court in Victoria in February 1905. He was asked if he knew what would happen if he did not tell the truth. The boy replied if he did not tell the truth, that meant he "would be telling a lie." The consequence of telling a lie, he continued, was he would "go to gaol for committing perjury" (*The Register* 1905, 6). A fourteen-year-old girl in Hobart in 1946 said swearing an oath meant "if the law doesn't get you, the Lord will" (*Examiner* 1946, 1). A thirteen-year-old said kissing the Bible meant she was "kissing God" (*Goulburn Evening Penny Post* 1905, 4), and another child, described in the press as "a bright young boarding school girl," said if she did not tell the truth her "expenses will be disallowed" (*Maryborough Chronicle, Wide Bay and Burnett Advertiser* 1937, 4).

Of course, what courts were looking for in these cases was the child's understanding that they would go to Hell if they lied. These responses show, however, the very literal way in which many children think. Where children did not immediately provide the desired answer, magistrates or judges often asked further questions, attempting to elicit from the child the extent of their knowledge of the Christian faith. In some cases, these additional questions were not much clearer than the initial question about what would happen to them if they lied. In Chapter 3, the boy who told the coroner it was the police who looked over us and knew everything we did was responding to precisely this style of questioning. His failure to pick up on this subtlety meant that he was not permitted to give sworn testimony (*Cairns Post* 1929, 10). Some judicial officers were very direct with their questions, like the magistrate who, after a failing to get the desired result after several preliminary questions, asked the boy outright "where would you *go* when you *died*?" "Oh, when I died, I would go to Hell," the boy replied (*The Register* 1905, 6). The child was sworn.

As was the case with the application of the term "tender years," the range of judicial approaches to the religious part of the oath test and its ill-defined, ambiguous nature resulted in widespread inconsistencies in application. Children were completely at the mercy of individual judges or magistrates presiding over the cases. In 1908, in the Queensland Supreme Court at Rockhampton, for example, Power J examined ten-year-old Mabel:

> *His Honour Mr. Justice Power*: How old are you Mabel?
> *Mabel*: Ten.
> *HH*: What happens to you if you do not tell the truth?
> *Mabel*: I will go to Hell. (*Morning Bulletin* 1908, 4)

Mabel's answer here should have been sufficient to satisfy the oath test. She had given the requisite answer to the oath question. Justice Power, however, was not satisfied. Along with defence barrister Mr. Douglas, who, incidentally, was the one calling Mabel as a witness, his Honour continued to examine the child:

> *HH*: That may be a long way off. Will anything happen to you now – in this life?
> [No answer]
> *HH*: Have you ever been told about gaol?
> *Mabel*: No.
> *Mr Douglas*: You said just now that you would go to Hell if you did not tell truth. Have you ever heard about Heaven?
> [No answer]
> *Mr Douglas*: Have you ever been at Sunday School?
> *Mabel*: No.
> *HH*: Have you ever been at a day school?

Mabel: Yes. The Sapphire Provisional School.
HH: They do not teach you anything about Heaven or Hell or anything else there, do they?
Mabel: No.
Mr Douglas: Have you ever heard anything about Heaven or Hell?
[No answer]
Mr Douglas: Has your mother ever told you anything about Heaven?
Mabel: No.
Mr Douglas: or about Hell?
Mabel: No.
Mr Douglas: You know you will be punished if you do not tell the truth?
Mabel: Yes
HH: Where will you be punished? What will happen to you if you do not tell the truth?
[No answer]. (*Morning Bulletin* 1908, 4)

It is impossible to know what Mabel must have been thinking at the time, but given the circular examination, perhaps she was wondering why the judge was asking her exactly the same question he had earlier, when she had already told him she would go to Hell if she lied. Even though Mabel had given what would otherwise have been a satisfactory answer at the outset of her interrogation, Justice Power only allowed her to give unsworn evidence after she promised to tell the truth.

Whether Mabel—or any child witness for that matter—actually believed they would go to Hell if they lied is unknown. Religious belief was a fluid concept for the courts. Legislation permitted adults to give evidence by affirmation and to accept evidence even where a witness was sworn and later found to not believe in a Christian God. The need for child witnesses to hold religious beliefs to give sworn testimony was debated at length in the 1931 High Court case of *Cheers v Porter* ((1931) 46 CLR 521). William Cheers was convicted of larceny on the unsworn testimony of nine-year-old Robert. The boy had been unable to satisfy the court that he understood the nature of the oath. Larceny, however, was not one of the offences included in s 418 *Crimes Act 1900* (NSW) allowing the unsworn testimony of a child. Rather than losing Robert's testimony, the judge accepted the child's unsworn testimony pursuant to s13(1)(i) of the *Oaths Act 1900* (NSW). This provision allowed witnesses to circumvent the need to swear an oath where they objected to taking an oath, were objected to as being incompetent or appeared incompetent to take an oath. Such witnesses could make a declaration instead (*Oaths Act 1900* (NSW) s 13(1)(i)).

In a split decision (3–2), the High Court refused to grant Cheers special leave to appeal against his conviction. The majority found Robert had been rightly permitted to give unsworn evidence. They found the intention of the New South Wales legislature in drafting s 13(1)(i) was to prevent the loss of testimony through religious unbelief or disbelief of any witness, including a child (*Cheers v Porter* (1931) 46 CLR 521 per Evatt J.). The minority (Dixon and McTiernan JJ) found s 13(1)(i) of the *Oaths Act 1900* (NSW) was limited to witnesses who had the capacity to form a belief, but instead were deliberately disbelieving or holding other religious views. Children who did not understand the nature of an oath, they argued, were not in this category. The decision in *Cheers v Porter* provides a comprehensive discussion of the historical development of the law on oaths. All the judges noted the long-held concerns in English and Australian law that witnesses should not necessarily be rejected because of their religious beliefs and opinions. Tasmania, Queensland and Victoria had provisions within their oath legislation confirming evidence would not be rendered inadmissible on account of the failure of the witness to hold religious beliefs, or beliefs outside of the Christian faith (see for e.g. *Oaths Act 1889* (Tas) s 5). As far as child witnesses were concerned, however, even after 1931 and the decision in *Cheers v Porter* ((1931) 46 CLR 521), the testimony of many children appears to have been lost on account of the child's failure to satisfy the oath test.

A powerful demonstration of the extent of judicial discretion where child witnesses were concerned, and the inconsistencies in its application, is found in the trial of William Fisher in 1941. This was a high-profile case in which Fisher was charged with murdering a three-year-old girl in Sydney's Centennial Park. Two children—Sylvia, aged eleven and Joe, aged thirteen—were key prosecution witnesses. Both were questioned on their understanding of the oath. Despite there only being two years between them in age, the trial judge, Justice Maxwell, questioned Sylvia extensively. He asked her *twenty-five* questions, including questions about her knowledge of God, who taught her about the oath (nuns), when she had learnt about the oath (two weeks earlier) and how she got to Sunday School from her house (she walked). Sylvia was eventually sworn (State Records NSW: Court Reporting Office, NRS 2714, Central Criminal Court transcripts, Criminal F to H. [6/2135], *R v William Fisher*, 29 September 1941, 9–10). Joe, on the other hand, was asked only *eight* short questions, none of which concerned religious education. Before being sworn, Joe simply confirmed if he lied in court, he would be sent to gaol (State Records NSW: Court Reporting Office, NRS 2714, Central Criminal Court transcripts, Criminal F to H. [6/2135], *R v William Fisher*, 29 September 1941, 31).

The trial transcripts don't indicate why Justice Maxwell questioned the two children in this way. Joe may have appeared more confident and comfortable in the courtroom environment, so the judge did not feel the need to ask as many questions as he did of Sylvia. The differences in age could also have played a part. But the intensity of Sylvia's examination compared to Joe's may be attributed to gender, demonstrating the heightened suspicion about female child witnesses previously described in Chapter 2 with respect to the work of criminologist Hans Gross (Adam et al. 1934, 1949, 1962). Fisher's trial and the evidence of these two children is discussed further in Chapter 5.

A further example of how judicial discretion impacted upon child witnesses and the oath test is found in a 1946 murder trial in Queensland. Eight witnesses were called, including the victim's fourteen and ten-year-old daughters. At the committal hearing, the eldest was reported to have sworn on the Koran (*Truth* 1946, 20). Her sister was also reported in the press as having told the court she knew she "would be sent to the reformatory" if she lied, to which Justice Douglas replied she would be punished in some way. He allowed the child to give her evidence. The girls' father was found guilty of murdering their mother and sentenced to life in prison (*Townsville Daily Bulletin* 1946, 3). This one case is hardly representative of child witness cases generally but provides further evidence of the way religion could be dealt with by members of the judiciary.

The Consequences of Failing the Oath Test

There were three alternatives for children who failed to convince the court they understood the nature of the oath. First, the child's evidence was not received at all. Second, in cases where unsworn evidence legislation applied, the child was examined as to their capacity to give unsworn testimony. If they failed this secondary test, their evidence would not be received. Third, where the child was permitted to give unsworn testimony, legislation usually required such evidence to be corroborated by the sworn testimony of another witness before an offender could be convicted. An absence of corroboration often rendered the child's unsworn testimony, although heard by the court, redundant. These corroboration rules are considered in Chapter 7.

The absence of a child's testimony would significantly raise the stakes for the Crown by making it much harder for them to prove their case, but it did not necessarily mean the only possible result would be an acquittal. The case of *R v Sparkman*, in 1930, discussed in Chapter 3, where the girl's identification evidence was placed in front of the jury through the testimony of the police officer, was one such case where the child was not permitted to give evidence. Despite not having heard the child's testimony directly, the jury found the defendant guilty (*R v Sparkman* (1930) 31 SR (NSW) 80). That same year, in *R v Lynch*, the judge refused to allow a child witness to give evidence ((1930) 30 SR (NSW) 420). Percy Lynch had been charged with raping an eleven-year-old girl. In questioning the child on her understanding of the oath, the Chief Justice asked her forty-two questions. She told the court her name and age, describing those living in her home, the Catholic school she attended and the religious instruction she had received from the school nuns. The child explained the nuns had taught her about God, and she understood the need to tell the truth and the consequences of a lie. The questions continued in much the same vein, all referring to what it meant to tell the truth and to tell a lie. In addition to Street CJ's extensive examination, a doctor gave evidence the child had a "mental age of eight years" (State Records NSW: Court Reporting Office, NRS 2714, Central Criminal Court transcripts. [6/1514] Criminal—I-O, *Rex v Percy Matthew Lynch*, 23 June 1930, 2). The Chief Justice decided the girl could not be sworn, nor give unsworn testimony (State Records NSW: Court Reporting Office, NRS 2714, Central Criminal Court transcripts. [6/1514] Criminal—I-O, *Rex v Percy Matthew Lynch*, 23 June 1930, 2).

If a child failed the oath test, there was still a chance they would be permitted to give unsworn testimony if the offence was included in relevant legislation. In *Lynch,* rape was not one of the offences for which unsworn testimony of a child could be received under the New South Wales legislation. Lynch had been charged pursuant to *Crimes Act 1900* (NSW) s 63. The offences for which unsworn testimony could be received were set out in s 418 of the same Act and referred only to those contained within sections 67–81 inclusive. These included carnal knowledge (and attempt) offences as well as buggery, bestiality and indecent assault on *males* of any age. Lynch's case was also prior to the High Court's broad interpretation of the NSW *Oaths Act* in *Cheers v Porter* ((1931) 46 CLR 521). The trial proceeded without the girl's evidence. This was, however, a rare case in which the evidence was clear the girl had been assaulted and Lynch—who admitted to being with the child—was the only one who had an opportunity to commit the offence. As in *Sparkman* ((1930) 31 SR (NSW) 80), the jury found Lynch guilty of rape and the court sentenced him to death (*R v Lynch* (1930) 30 SR (NSW) 420). The conviction was overturned on appeal on account of consent not being raised at the trial as required under *Criminal Appeal Act 1912* (NSW) s 63. A sentence of ten years imprisonment was substituted in lieu of the death sentence.

Unsworn Testimony

Regarded as an aide "to guide the tribunal," unsworn testimony was thought to carry "much danger that children giving [it] might erroneously state things that would incriminate somebody" (*R v Smith* (1901) 26 VLR 683, per Madden CJ at 686). A child's competence to give *un*sworn evidence depended upon their capacity to understand the gravity of the trial process and their obligation to tell the truth (*R v GW* (2016) 258 CLR 108). To determine such capacity, all states, except for South Australia, adopted what was frequently referred to as the "sufficient intelligence" test. Victoria, Western Australia and Queensland already had this test in their legislation, in some form, prior to the turn of the twentieth century (*Crimes Act 1890* (Vic) s 33(1); *Criminal Law Amendment Act 1892* (WA) s 4; Child Protection Act 1896 (Qld) s 7). New South Wales introduced it in 1900 (*Crimes Act 1900* (NSW) s 418) and Tasmania in 1910 (*Evidence Act 1910* (Tas) s 128). Queensland introduced a general test for unsworn testimony well after the other states via the *Evidence Act 1977* ((Qld) s 9).

The precise terms of the sufficient intelligence test varied from state to state. In Western Australia, for example, s 101 of the *Evidence Act 1906* provided:

> in any civil or criminal proceeding…where any child of tender years…does not in the opinion of the Court, …understand the nature of an oath, the evidence of such child may be received, though not given upon oath, if in the opinion of the Court…such child is possessed of sufficient intelligence to justify the reception of the evidence, and understand the duty of speaking the truth. (*Evidence Act 1906* (WA) s 101)

Tasmania followed Western Australia, adopting similar terms when amending s 128 of its *Evidence Act 1910* (Tas). Whereas Tasmania's previous provisions had been restricted to children under seven years of age, from 1910 they applied to "any child of tender years."

In practice, what it meant to be "sufficiently intelligent" was left to the discretion of the judicial officer. Judicial officers were trusted to use their instinct and experience without any scientific or agreed method defined in case law or statute. As late as 1989, in the case of *R v Harding*, the judge had little guidance on the issue but nevertheless thought a "sufficiently intelligent" child was one who had the "capacity to remember"(*R v Harding* [1989] 2 Qd R 373, 374). In that case, a seven-year-old girl had witnessed the murders of two women two years earlier when she was only five years old. She was permitted to give unsworn testimony. Defence counsel objected, arguing "no ordinary child of seven years and four months could reasonably be possessed of sufficient intelligence to justify the reception of evidence of an event so far in the past" (*R v Harding* [1989] 2 Qd R 373, 373). The Queensland Court of Appeal disagreed, finding the magnitude of the events could remain vivid in the child's memory "for some years despite her youth" (*R v Harding* [1989] 2 Qd R 373, 373).

Age does not necessarily appear to have been an issue for many judges when assessing a child's "intelligence" in this context. Cases indicate variances, even within the same jurisdiction. At a trial in 1923 in New South Wales, for instance, Acting Judge Ralston decided that at five years old, the child witness was too young to understand the nature of an oath, but she was "sufficiently intelligent" to understand the need to tell the truth. Ralston accepted her evidence (*R v Eade* (1923) 24 SR (NSW) 117, 118). In 1940, a different judge elsewhere in the state decided an eight-year-old girl was deemed not sufficiently intelligent to give evidence (*Dubbo Liberal and Macquarie Advocate* 1940, 2). Howsoever judges were assessing this notion of "sufficient intelligence," it was with considerable reliance upon, and faith in, each judge's capacity to assess the child witness appropriately.

The judicial discretion to determine which children should be permitted to give evidence had its limits. There were occasions when judicial officers were bound by the legislation. A Victorian case from 1959 illustrates an occasion when such limitations forced the Court of Appeal to make a decision it thought highly unsatisfactory. The defendant was tried at Melbourne general sessions for serious sex offences against a twin brother and sister who were twelve years old at the time (*R v Giles* [1959] VR 583). Both children had given unsworn testimony pursuant to s 403(1). The defendant had been convicted on all counts. He appealed on grounds the jury should have been discharged after a juror made an audible adverse comment about him.

It was during the hearing of this appeal that an anomaly in relation to the drafting of the unsworn testimony provisions was identified. Of the eight charges against the defendant, two were in relation to committing one act of buggery upon each child. Every aspect of the offending against each child had been identical—what was done to the brother was also done to the sister. Both children had given evidence pursuant to s 403 of the *Crimes Act 1957* (Vic), which allowed children to give unsworn testimony in certain cases. As the court found out during the appeal, however, with respect to charges of buggery, s 403 only permitted *boys* under fourteen years to give such evidence. Due to the way the section had been drafted, girls could not give unsworn evidence in relation to the same offence. The wording of s 403 at the time was:

> 403. (1) Where upon the hearing before a justice of a charge of rape or of attempting to rape or of unlawfully and carnally knowing or of attempting or assaulting with intent unlawfully and carnally to know or of indecently assaulting any girl or of any offence such as is described in sections *sixty-eight or sixty-nine of this Act against any boy under the age of fourteen years* [emphasis added]; or where upon the trial of any person for any of such offences the girl or boy in respect of whom the offence is charged to have been committed or any other child of tender years who is tendered as a witness does not in the opinion of the court or justices understand the nature of an oath, the evidence of such girl or boy or other child of tender years may be received though not given upon oath if in the opinion of the court or justices (as the case may be) such girl or boy or other child of tender years is possessed of sufficient intelligence to justify the reception of the evidence and understands the duty of speaking the truth. (*Crimes Act 1957* (Vic) s 403)

Section 403 applied to offences including s 68 of that Act, which referred to buggery offences "with any person under the age of fourteen years" (s 68 *Crimes Act 1957* (Vic)). Thus, the provision defining the crime made no distinction as to gender. Section 403, however, did appear to make such a distinction. Chief Justice Herring commented that it was "quite obvious" s 403 was intended by the legislature to "operate quite generally" for boys as for girls. Nevertheless, the court interpreted s 403 literally and set aside the guilty verdict on this count. The appellant's sentence was amended to remove the punishment for the buggery offence against the girl and was reduced from seven years to five years (*R v Giles* [1959] VR 583, 585).

The Victorian Attorney-General referred the case to the Victorian Statute Law Revision Committee, who recommended s 403 section be "corrected" (Victorian Statute Law Revision Committee 1960, 4). The committee further noted simply extending s 403 to include the offence of buggery against girls would not be sufficient. Section 23 of the *Evidence Act 1958* (Vic) provided for the unsworn testimony of children under seven year of age in relation to any offence, repeating the terms of s 50 of the *Evidence Act 1890* (Vic). Had the girl in this case been under seven years of age, rather than twelve, her unsworn testimony on the buggery charge would have been acceptable, pursuant to s 23. There was, therefore, some inconsistency between s 23 of the *Evidence Act 1958* (Vic) and s 403 of the *Crimes Act 1957* (Vic). The committee took this opportunity to make general recommendations on the procedures for receiving the evidence of children. They first recommended s 403 of the *Crimes Act 1957* (Vic) and s 23 of the *Evidence Act 1958* (Vic) be consolidated to allow children under fourteen years to give unsworn testimony in all proceedings. They further recommended the phrase "has no knowledge of God or of any belief in religion or a future state of rewards and punishments" be replaced with the phrase "does not…understand the nature of an oath" (Victorian Statute Law Revision Committee 1960, 4–5). These recommendations were implemented a few months later in the *Evidence (Children) Act* 1961 (Vic).

As loaded as the term is for twenty-first-century sensibilities, the "sufficiently intelligent" test was not overly difficult to satisfy. Children of all ages, cultural backgrounds (including Indigenous children) and levels of education are found to have passed the test. It offered courts a way to circumvent the strict application of the common law test while still being able to receive the child's testimony. As simple as the test was, children could still fail it. At a committal hearing in 1935, a nine-year-old boy told the police magistrate he had never been to school. He had never heard of God. He did not know what an oath was. He did not know whether it was right or wrong to tell a lie and he did not know what happened to boys who lied (*Townsville Daily Bulletin* 1935, 7). From this report, it is impossible to discern whether the child was nervous or being defiant—or whether his background had not given him the opportunity to learn the required answers to the magistrate's questions. Regardless, the magistrate found the boy was not "possessed of sufficient intelligence and appreciation of the duty on him to tell the truth" and thus refused to accept his evidence (*Townsville Daily Bulletin* 1935, 7).

An Artificial Oath Test—Educating Child Witnesses on the Nature of the Oath

The superiority of sworn testimony in Australian criminal courts during the twentieth century was undeniable. Despite creating the opportunity for more child witnesses to give evidence in the early part of the century, the unsworn testimony legislation was often limited according to the age of the witness, the offence being tried and the need for corroboration. In all respects, it was preferable for children to be sworn. This preference led to some intriguing examples of pragmatism in the nation's criminal courtrooms.

In 1921, Joseph Eade had pleaded guilty to indecently assaulting a four-year-old girl at Maitland in New South Wales and was sentenced to two years' imprisonment (*The Maitland Daily Mercury* 1921, 2). Within weeks of his release, Eade was back before the court in October 1923, this time in Newcastle, on trial for indecently assaulting a five-year-old girl. At the trial, Acting Judge Ralston had decided the girl was too young to understand the nature of an oath. He was satisfied, nevertheless, that she was sufficiently intelligent to understand the need to tell the truth. Ralston received her evidence unsworn. Eade was convicted and sentenced to five years' imprisonment (*The Wyalong Advocate and Mining, Agricultural and Pastoral Gazette* 1923, 12). In December 1923, the New South Wales Court of Appeal upheld the conviction (*R v Eade* (1923) 24 SR (NSW) 117). Four months later, in April 1924, the High Court quashed it due to an absence of corroboration (*Eade v R* (1924) 34 CLR 154). Corroboration is considered in Chapter 7. Where required, corroboration imposed an almost impossible barrier to any conviction in child sex offence matters. In Eade's case, a retrial was ordered (*The Maitland Weekly Mercury* 1924, 11).

At this retrial in June 1924, Judge Hamilton allowed the girl to swear an oath, thereby circumventing the need for her evidence to be corroborated. Eade was convicted again. In sentencing him, Judge Hamilton said he was "quite satisfied" with the verdict (*The Maitland Weekly Mercury* 1924, 11). It is worthwhile reflecting upon the possible reasons for this change. Did Judge Hamilton have a lower threshold for the child to pass the oath test than Acting Judge Ralston who, only nine months before, had decided the girl was too young to be sworn? Was Hamilton, who had sentenced Eade in relation to the 1921 offence, more motivated to secure a conviction? Could the child have received sufficient religious instruction since the first trial?

That the girl received training in answering the oath test is a distinct possibility. Not only is there evidence judicial officers and legal professionals used such unorthodox measures so children could satisfactorily demonstrate their understanding of the oath; there is evidence the practice was often carried out with the court's knowledge and tacit approval. A Victorian manual of evidence, published in 1889, referred to the case of *R v Mullan* where a witness under the age of seven failed the oath test, "the Crown not having availed itself of the opportunity to postpone the trial and enable the child to become acquainted therewith" (Leader 1889, 82).

A case referring to such a practice is found in the 1892 decision of the Victorian Chief Justice Higinbotham in *R v Gregg* ((1892) 18 VLR 218). The Chief Justice expressly referred to the practice of instructing child witnesses in the nature of the oath. This case was one of the first to come before the Victorian Supreme Court after the introduction of the unsworn testimony provisions in the state's *Evidence Act 1890* and *Crimes Act 1890*. The child had failed the oath test at trial but had been permitted to give unsworn testimony. Applying the relevant statutory provisions, the court was forced to quash the defendant's conviction due to a lack of evidence corroborating the child's unsworn testimony. In arriving at this decision, Chief Justice Higinbotham issued a scathing assessment of the new legislative reforms and criticised the Crown's approach in this case. He said:

> [t]here have been and there are means, independent of the statute, by which a child of tender years may be instructed in the nature of an oath, and may be educated to give testimony which is admissible in law for the purpose of vindicating the law in cases of this kind. (*R v Gregg* (1892) 18 VLR 218, 221)

Justice Hood agreed with the Chief Justice that a retrial be ordered. He noted:

> ...it is quite probable that by the time the case is again tried the child, who is eight years of age and intelligent, may have been instructed in the nature of an oath, so as to be sworn and give evidence in the ordinary way. (*R v Gregg* (1892) 18 VLR 218, 224)

While none of the judges cited any case law in support of this practice of instructing children on the oath, there is evidence in newspapers prior to the decision in *Gregg*, and subsequently, which confirms widespread application of such practice in numerous states. In Rockhampton, in 1910, for example, a Supreme Court judge was not satisfied an eight-year-old boy understood the difference between a truth and a falsehood. Rather than discharging the accused, the judge adjourned the trial for two weeks so the boy could be "instructed on the nature of the difference" (*Maryborough Chronicle, Wide Bay and Burnett Advertiser* 1910, 3).

Similarly, in a case in Queensland in 1916, a report in Brisbane's *Telegraph* described an argument in the District Court between the judge, Sir Arthur Rutledge, and defence counsel, Mr. Macrossan. The child, a five-year-old girl, had not satisfied the court she understood the nature of the oath. Macrossan objected to the child giving evidence. Rutledge recounted the experience of one of his colleagues, Judge Macnaughton, who, after the child failed the oath test, had adjourned a matter and ordered the Salvation Army to instruct the child on the nature of the oath. When the child was subsequently brought back before the court (the report does not detail the length of the adjournment), Judge Macnaughton was satisfied the Salvation Army had done its job and allowed the girl to be sworn. Mr. Macrossan maintained his objection to the child giving evidence, despite Rutledge's roundabout suggestion as to how to resolve the problem of the child in this case not understanding the nature of the oath. Rutledge said to Macrossan:

> You want to make this law that any man could tamper with that child, and that he could have no evidence given against him, if the child was not theologically fit to give evidence as to the nature of an oath and her moral relation to the Almighty? (*The Telegraph* 1916, 3)

Mr. Macrossan stood firm, maintaining his argument that the law was what it was and ought to be applied accordingly. After further argument and examination of the child's mother as to her daughter's religious education (to which Mr. Macrossan said such evidence from the mother was irrelevant), the judge recalled the child. He was more specific this time with his examination.

> "Can you tell me," asked his Honour of the child, "where good people: go when they die?"
> The child: "To heaven."
> "Where do bad people go when they die?"
> "Down to hell."
> "Is a person who comes into court, and tells lies a good or bad person?"
> "A bad person."
> His Honour said he did not think he had sufficiently examined the child before. He then decided to allow the oath to be administered. (*The Telegraph* 1916, 3)

A practice which essentially involved coaching a witness clearly had the potential to threaten the fairness of the accused's trial. Defence counsel in a case in the Victorian Supreme Court in 1894 raised such concerns. The child in question was a five-year-old girl. The judge expressed reservations about such a young child swearing an oath. The prosecutor, Mr. Smythe, assured him a church minister had "taught the child the nature of an oath" and she was "intelligent for her years." The child was brought into the court by her mother, but she was "too nervous and frightened" to answer the judge's questions (*Bendigo Advertiser* 1894, 4). Mr. Smythe had previously informed the court there was no corroborative evidence in this case, as would be required if the child gave unsworn testimony. The case would all come down to the child's evidence—and whether her testimony was sworn or unsworn (*Bendigo Advertiser* 1894, 4).

Smythe asked for an adjournment, citing *R v Gregg* ((1892) 18 VLR 218) as precedent for instructing child witnesses in the practice of swearing an oath. He argued it was in the interests of justice that such an application was granted. Defence counsel, Mr. Fedden, objected. Fedden argued any delay would be unfair to his client. He noted the committal hearing had been held on 26 October 1894, some six weeks prior "and surely there had been sufficient time since then to instruct the girl if she were capable of receiving instruction at all." Mr. Fedden argued the new legislation permitting unsworn testimony "was passed for the purpose of meeting cases like this one and it appeared to him that [an adjournment] was like evading the Act." The judge granted the application "in the interests of justice," noting in *R v Gregg* the court had ordered a retrial for the purposes of instructing the child on the oath, even though no application had been made by the Crown for such a purpose (*Bendigo Advertiser* 1894, 4).

This practice of coaching children to pass the oath test appears to have been more common in the later years of the nineteenth century, when the unsworn testimony legislation did not exist or had only recently been passed. Aside from the few examples mentioned above, there is little evidence of it continuing far into the twentieth century, perhaps as more defence barristers began following the approach of Mr. Fedden in objecting to the coaching of child witnesses, given the existence of statutory unsworn testimony provisions in many cases.

Opposition to the Oath Test

Given the lengths to which courts would go to ensure children could give sworn testimony, it is not surprising to find considerable evidence of opposition to the oath test being administered to children. Judges and magistrates were the most vocal in this regard. In 1886, for example, the *Goulburn Evening Penny Post* reported on an exchange between Judge Forbes and defence barrister, Mr. Williamson, who was testing a child on her understanding of the oath:

> *Mr. Williamson*: Surely, your Honour, I can ask the witness whether she knows where she will go to when she dies if she tells a lie?
> *Judge Forbes*: Do you know?
> *Mr. Williamson*: Oh well…
> *Judge Forbes*: I don't think you do, or anyone else.
> *Mr. Williamson*: But the law allows us to anticipate.

> *Judge Forbes*: You would be satisfied, I suppose, if the child said, "If I tell the truth I will go to Heaven, and if I tell a lie I will go to Hell."
> *Mr. Williamson*: Yes.
> *Judge Forbes*: It is all claptrap – absurd. (*Goulburn Evening Penny Post* 1886, 6)

In Queensland in 1907, Magistrate Ranking queried the utility of oaths generally. Suggesting it was "useless" to administer the oath to the eleven-year-old girl before him, Ranking said "I sometimes wonder whether the oath should not be done away with altogether. Many witnesses seem to regard it as a thing of no moment whatever." A solicitor present replied, "Some would not tell the truth no matter how many oaths they took" (*Queensland Times, Ipswich Herald and General Advertiser* 1907, 4). The journalist reporting on this case observed the child had given her evidence "with clearness and obvious truth, and it would, in her case… have apparently made no difference whether the oath was taken or not" (*Queensland Times, Ipswich Herald and General Advertiser* 1907, 4).[2]

Well into the twentieth century, judicial officers continued to express their reservations about children swearing an oath. Perth's Justice Robert Burnside appears to have objected strenuously to the requirement. In Perth in 1916, Burnside remarked children should not have to swear an oath that even adults did not understand (*Truth* 1916, 3). In 1921 he engaged in a lengthy debate with a barrister over the expectation that children should demonstrate their understanding of the oath.

> *Mr Dwyer (to the child)*: Did you make an oath at the Midland Junction trials— No.
> You didn't know what it meant? — No.
> Do you know now? — Yes.
> What? — Kissing the Book.
> What else does it mean?
> *His Honour*: Does it mean anything else?
> *Mr. Dwyer*: Who has been coaching you up to what an oath means?— Daddy
> Do you know what will happen to you if you said what wasn't true? — No.
> You haven't even an idea?— No

(wonderingly)
His Honour (smiling): Well, now, Mr. Dwyer, what's the answer to your little riddle? – Oh, spiritual sanctions.
What?— Spiritual sanctions!
His Honour: There must be an awful lot of spiritual sanctions around this court, then! An English Judge said recently that the amount of perjury that went on was enough to close the doors of the court. I candidly confess that you astonish me by asking a girl of nine what it all means when no intelligent man could answer. Men get into this box; some hold up their hand, some blow out a light, some cut off the head of a cock, and others kiss the book. Not yet have I had the pleasure of convicting a person for perjury, but still I have heard perjury in this court until I am tired of listening to it (*Truth* 1921, 11).

In 1926, an article by an anonymous judge, published in Sydney's *Evening News*, referred to the "Digest of the Law of Evidence" written by Mr. Justice Stephen, which said oath test questions were "little calculated to increase respect either for religion or for the administration of justice." The unnamed judge went on to suggest it should be sufficient for a court to determine the extent to which the child understands it is "a wicked and disgraceful thing" to lie, "for which he may be punished" and for the child to "simply promise to speak the truth" (*Evening News* 1926, 6). In a 1934 case, this time in Victoria, eight-year-old Jack told the court he would go to Hell if he lied, to which Judge Foster replied, "There is no Hell. It's a shame children are taught such things" (*Western Argus* 1934, 19). In response to the outcry that followed this statement, particularly from the Catholic Church, Foster explained he had been trying to spare the child from the mental anguish he himself had suffered as a child, believing there was a fire he might be sent to (*Nambucca and Bellinger News* 1934, 5). As an eleven-year-old witness was about to be sworn in a 1906 case in Victoria, the defence counsel protested on the grounds the child "has not said where she will go if she tells a lie." The police superintendent reportedly "raised a laugh at counsel's expense" by responding "Why you wouldn't know yourself" (*Geelong Advertiser* 1906, 2). Similarly, in 1935, in New South Wales, Judge Curlewis said he would like to see a judge cross-examined on the nature of an oath, admitting "I'm afraid I would not pass" (*Daily Advertiser* 1935, 1).

Opposition to the oath test also came from outside the judiciary. The Victorian Attorney-General, Mr. Albert Bussau, for example, was reported in the Melbourne *Argus* in 1935 to have expressed his intention to take up the issue of the oath with the Crown. Mr. Bussau wanted children to be able to give evidence without the need to take an oath. The practice of questioning them on their understanding of Heaven or Hell, he said, "was invidious. The purpose of the court was to arrive at the truth" (*The Argus* 1935, 9). Nothing appears to have come of Mr. Bussau's comments. Others thought the need to question children on religion was redundant, when most children would be in awe of the judge and likely to tell the truth on that basis (*The Argus* 1935, 9). A Melbourne journalist in 1906 suggested oaths were not part of ordinary life, and it was unlikely parents would instruct children as to their nature "on the horrible hypothesis that someday their little ones will be criminally assaulted" (*The Argus* 1935, 9). The potential impact of the test was not lost on the journalist, who wrote:

> While every man should have a chance for his liberty or his neck, the present unsatisfactory state of the law in regard to child witnesses should be amended as soon as possible, lest some abnormal beings come to think that they are comparatively safe in indulging their loathsome propensities. (*The Argus* 1935, 9)

Reforming the Competency Test in the Late Twentieth Century

Comments similar to those above were made throughout the twentieth century and came from various sources both within and outside the legal profession. There was, however, considerable reluctance to initiate change. In 1975, the Queensland Law Reform Commission recommended the adoption of a general provision for the receipt of unsworn testimony of children, like those that had been in force for nearly a century already in Western Australia and Tasmania (Queensland Law Reform Commission, *The Law Relating to Evidence* (Report No 19,

November 1975)). The Queensland Parliament declined to make the recommended changes.

The late 1970s also saw the beginnings of a subtle shift in how judges approached the task of swearing children. In 1977, in the Queensland matter of *R v Brown*, for example, the Court of Appeal was called upon to consider the requirement for children to have a belief in God to swear an oath. The trial judge had allowed two girls, aged eleven and twelve, to give sworn testimony without first questioning them on their religious beliefs. Acting Chief Justice Wanstall thought this effectively resulted in the girls' testimony going before the jury with the "appearance of testimony sanctioned by oath, when in reality the conscience of neither...was bound by the ceremony performed" (*R v Brown* [1977] Qd R 220, 222). Nevertheless, His Honour went on to discuss a recent decision where the English Court of Appeal had said it was "unrealistic not to recognise that, in the present state of society, amongst the adult population the divine sanction of an oath is probably not generally recognised." Instead, the court thought the test should be whether the child had a "sufficient appreciation of the solemnity of the occasion and the added responsibility to tell the truth ... over and above the duty to tell the truth"(*R v Hayes* [1977] 1 W.L.R 234 cited by Wanstall ACJ in *R v Brown* [1977] Qd R 220, 225). The Queensland appellate court accepted the girls' sworn testimony had been properly received and dismissed Brown's appeal.

From the mid-1980s to the end of the twentieth century, capacity and competency issues with respect to child witnesses underwent substantial reforms via legislative amendments. Starting in 1985, New South Wales repealed s 418 *Crimes Act 1900* and amended its *Oaths Act* to include a new competency test in s 33 (*Oaths (Children) Amendment Act 1985* (NSW)). The amendments allowed children to make a declaration, if they could demonstrate to the court they understood the duty to tell the truth *in court* (*Oaths (Children) Amendment Act 1985* (NSW) s 33). The terms in which the new s 33 was drafted became a central issue in the infamous Mr. Bubbles (Seabeach Kindergarten) case, where charges against two staff members and an owner of the child care centre were dismissed after a magistrate decided the child witnesses could not give evidence pursuant to the new s 33 (*The Canberra Times* 1990, 4).

The children had, in the magistrate's opinion, been unable to demonstrate an understanding of what it meant to tell the truth *in court*—as opposed to elsewhere. This provision was amended shortly after, in 1990 (*Oaths (Children) Amendment Act 1990* (NSW) s 33). During the second reading speech in Parliament, the Hon. E. P. Pickering said the requirement for children to demonstrate they understood the significance of court proceedings was "ill-conceived and unjustified" (New South Wales, *Parliamentary Debates,* Legislative Council, 28 November 1990, 10948). He referred to psychological research and opinion that children under six years of age, such as those in the Mr. Bubbles case, would not have the capacity to understand the significance of court proceedings but would have the capacity to tell the truth. Providing the clearest indication of the changing views towards child witnesses at this time, Pickering argued:

> There appears to be no correlation between an understanding of the duty to tell the truth and the reliability of evidence. Every day in our courts adults with sound understanding of the duty to tell the truth are found to be not "credible" or "reliable" or are "unfortunately mistaken" - descriptions which are often euphemistically used for "lying their heads off." So it is not an understanding of the duty to tell the truth which ensures that honest evidence will be given. (New South Wales, *Parliamentary Debates,* Legislative Council, 28 November 1990, 10948 (The Hon. E. P. Pickering))

The new 1990 provisions were more extensive than the 1985 amendments and drafted with the problems of the previous section in mind. Now, where a child was to give a declaration, the court was required to tell the child of the need to tell the truth, and a child's evidence would not be received if they were unable to satisfy the court they understood the difference between the truth and a lie, or were unable to respond rationally to questions. The section also introduced a presumption that child witnesses would understand the difference between truth and a lie and would be able to respond rationally to questions (*Oaths (Children) Amendment 1990* (NSW) sch 1). The wording of the declaration was also changed. Whereas the 1985 form required the child to promise to tell the truth (*Oaths (Children) Amendment 1985* (NSW) sch 10), in

1990 the declaration required the child to state they would "not tell lies in this court" (*Oaths (Children) Amendment 1990* (NSW) sch 10).

In the same year, 1990, the Law Reform Commission of Western Australia highlighted problematic aspects of the oath test in a discussion paper for its review of the *Evidence of Children and Other Vulnerable Witnesses*. The commission expressed concern that the references to religious belief in the oath test were unfair towards child witnesses who had no religious education, and second, the legislative provisions that allowed for unsworn testimony still relied upon the discretion of judges and was "not a very scientific or reliable method of determining a child's capacity" (Law Reform Commission of Western Australia, *Evidence of Children and Other Vulnerable Witnesses* (Discussion Paper, 1990) 7). Children, however, were still being questioned on their understanding of the oath well into the 1990s and beyond (Schultz 2003, 199). Table 4.2, on the following page, summarises the legislative reforms governing the competency of child witnesses from 1985 to the end of the twentieth century.

New psychological research contributed to understanding that a child's inability to convey understanding of concepts like "truth" and "promise" did not necessarily mean they would make a poor witness. Further, research suggested having children "promise to tell the truth" increased the likelihood they would tell the truth (Lee et al. 2010). In 1995, Federal Parliament passed the *Evidence Act* (*1995* (Cth)). This Act was intended to form the basis of a uniform evidence law for all Australian states and territories. It was immediately adopted by New South Wales in its *Evidence Act 1995* (NSW). This legislation abolished the presumption of incompetency (*Evidence Act 1995* (Cth) s 12). Other states, however, were not as quick as New South Wales to take up the idea of a uniform evidence law. In 1997, the Australian Law Reform Commission (ALRC) recommended that all states introduce a presumption of competency for the evidence of children as per the *Evidence Act 1995* (Cth) and the *Evidence Act 1995* (NSW) (Australian Law Reform Commission and Australian Human Rights and Equal Opportunity Commission, *Seen and Heard: Priority for Children in the Legal Process* 1997, Recommendation 98, par 14.64). Except for New South Wales, the other states and

Table 4.2 Summary of statutory reforms to the competency of child witnesses

	SA	NSW	Tas	Vic	WA	Qld
Act	*Evidence Act (Amend't) Act 1988*	*Oaths (Children) Amendment Act 1985*	*Evidence Amendment (Children and Special Witnesses) Act 1995*	*Crimes (Sexual Offences) Act 1991*	*Acts Amendment (Evidence of Children and Others) Act 1992*	*The Criminal Code, Evidence Act and Other Acts Amendment Act 1989*
Receipt of unsworn testimony	child has reached level of cognitive development…to understand and respond rationally to questions and give intelligible account of his/her experiences AND promises to tell the truth and appears to understand the obligations entailed by that promise	child makes declaration instead of oath where sufficiently intelligent and understands duty of speaking truth (promises to tell the truth at all times in this court)	if judge satisfied child able to give intelligible account of events observed or experiences	understands duty to speak truth and capable of responding rationally to questions about facts in issue, s 8	if child understands serious matter AND obligation to tell truth able to give intelligible account of events observed or experiences 1992s 106C	s 61 and Evidence Act 1977 (Qld) s 9 court explains to child duty of speaking truth, shall receive evidence unless satisfied child not sufficiently intelligent to give reliable evidence

	SA	NSW	Tas	Vic	WA	Qld
Removal of "tender years"	under 7 years	under 12 years	under 14 years, to give evidence on oath s122B	under 14 years unsworn testimony otherwise under 17 years	under 12 years unsworn testimony otherwise child under 18 years	under 12 years

territories that passed uniform evidence legislation (Tasmania, Norfolk Island, Victoria, the ACT and the Northern Territory) did not follow the ALRC's recommendation until after the start of the twenty-first century (*Evidence Act 2001* (Tas); *Evidence Act 2004* (Norfolk Island); *Evidence Act 2008* (Vic); *Evidence Act 2011* (ACT); *Evidence (National Uniform legislation) Act 2011* (NT)). While not agreeing to adopt the uniform evidence laws, Queensland introduced a presumption of competency in 2003 (*Evidence Act 1977* (Qld) s 9; *Evidence (Protection of Children) Amendment Act 2003* (Qld) s 57).

Some teething problems with the new approach to competency, and child evidence more broadly, were raised almost immediately in the 1990s (*Lau* (1991) 58 A Crim R 390; *Hoogwerf* (1992) 63 A Crim R 302; *Revesz* (1996) 88 A Crim R 253). A matter not addressed in the legislation was the impact pre-recorded hearings might have on the procedure for assessing a child's competency. Competency testing had previously taken place in the courtroom, on the day of the trial. Questions were now raised about when competency testing should take place, given video evidence would be recorded well before a jury was empanelled and perhaps before a different judge to the one who would hear the trial (Jackson 2003, 202).

Conclusion

Children began the twentieth century dogged by the presumption they were incompetent to give evidence of any description. Instead, they had to satisfy the court they were competent to give sworn testimony. For much of the century, the "oath test" involved questioning children as to their belief in—or at least knowledge of—God and the punitive consequences attached to lying according to the Christian faith. Even before the twentieth century began, there was opposition to this form of testing children. In addition to calls for reform voiced throughout the twentieth century, some courts adopted unorthodox methods to enable children to pass the test. Towards the end of the century, such artificial means of preparing child witnesses for their court appearance were abandoned as a modern, more secular judiciary reinterpreted the oath test in accordance with expectations of a more secular society. The real changes occurred through statutory reforms of the 1980s and 1990s. These changes were introduced to combat the difficulties children had with giving testimony—sworn and unsworn. Notably, legislatures and the judiciary both began to place more weight on the psychological research demonstrating the capacity of children to tell the truth and less weight on a child's religious education.

For children who had passed the oath test or at least been deemed "sufficiently intelligent" to give unsworn testimony, the toughest tests were yet to come. Child witnesses now faced the daunting ordeal of giving their evidence in often crowded courtrooms and, most difficult of all, undergoing the examination and cross-examination process.

Notes

1. For discussion of the place of religion in and secularisation of Australian society in the twentieth century, see, for example: Swain, Shurlee. 2005. "Do You Want Religion With That? – Welfare History in a Secular Age." *History Australia* 2 (3): 1–79. Or Melleuish, Gregory. 2014. "A Secular Australia? Ideas, Politics and the Search for Moral Order in Nineteenth and Early Twentieth Century Australia." *Journal of Religious History* 38 (3). https://doi.org/10.1111/1467-9809.12076.
2. Similar legislation was introduced in Canada via the *Canada Evidence Act* (*Canada Evidence Act* S.C. 1893 c 31 s 25; Lee, Lindsay, Talwar and Bala 2010).

References

Adam, John, J. Collyer, Norman Kendal, and Hans Gross.1934, 1949, 1962. *System der Kriminalistik, Criminal Investigation Practical Textbook for Magistrates, Police Officers and Lawyers.* London: Sweet & Maxwell.

The Age (Melbourne). "A Jury's Finding." July 17, 1897.

Age of Majority Act 1972 (WA).
Age of Majority Act 1973 (Tas).
Age of Majority (Reduction) Act 1971 (SA).
An Act to Amend the Law as to Oaths 1889 (Tas).
The Argus (Melbourne). "Child Witnesses." July 16, 1935.
The Argus (Melbourne). "Indecent Assault." July 24, 1897.
Australian Law Reform Commission and Australian Human Rights and Equal Opportunity Commission. 1997. *Seen and Heard: Priority for Children in the Legal Process*, Vol. 84.
Barrier Miner. "Immoral Children." April 20, 1904.
Bendigo Advertiser (Vic: 1855–1918). "The Protection of Little Girls." December 5, 1894.
Brunsgard v Jennings [1974] WAR 36.
Cairns Post. "A Child Witness." October 11, 1929.
Canada Evidence Act S.C. 1893.
The Canberra Times (ACT: 1926–1995). "Dowd Hits Back Over Mr. Bubbles." August 7, 1990.
Cheers v Porter (1931) 46 CLR 521.
Child Protection Act 1896 (Qld).
Attorney-General's Reference No 2 of 1993: Re R v Mansell (1994) 4 Tas R 26.
Crimes Act 1900 (NSW).
Crimes Act 1957 (Vic).
Crimes Act 1890 (Vic).
Criminal Appeal Act 1912 (NSW).
Criminal Law and Evidence Amendment Act 1891 (NSW).
Criminal Law Amendment Act 1885 (UK).
Criminal Law Amendment Act 1892 (WA).
Criminal Law Consolidation Act 1876 (SA).
Daily Advertiser (Wagga Wagga, NSW: 1911–1954). "Nature of Oath." May 21, 1935.
The Dubbo Liberal and Macquarie Advocate (NSW: 1894–1954). "Aged Man Gaoled." November 21, 1940.
The Dubbo Liberal and Macquarie Advocate (NSW: 1894–1954). "Obligation of Court Oath Puzzles Two Young Girls." December 14, 1943.
Eade v R (1924) 34 CLR 154.
Evening News (Sydney, NSW: 1869–1931). "The Child Witness." December 30, 1926.
Evening News (Sydney, NSW: 1869–1931). "The Immorality Scare." August 17, 1885.

Evidence Act 2011 (ACT).
Evidence Act 1995 (Cth).
Evidence Act 2004 (Norfolk Island).
Evidence Act 1995 (NSW).
Evidence Act 1977 (Qld).
Evidence Act 2001 (Tas).
Evidence Act 2008 (Vic).
Evidence Act 1890 (Vic).
Evidence Act Amendment Act (No. 2) 1976 (WA).
Evidence (Children) Act 1961 (Vic).
Finkelstein, Ray. 2011. "The Adversarial System and the Search for Truth." *Monash University Law Review* 37 (1):135–144.
Geelong Advertiser (Vic: 1859–1929). "An Intelligent Witness." March 24, 1906.
Goulburn Evening Penny Post (NSW: 1881–1940). "Novel Definition of an Oath." February 16, 1905.
Goulburn Evening Penny Post (NSW: 1881–1940). "The Oath." February 20, 1886.
Green, Bruce. 1992. "The Whole Truth – How Rules of Evidence Make Lawyers Deceitful." *Loyola of Los Angeles Law Review* 25: 699–710.
Henning, Terese. 1995. "Case and Comment *Attorney-General's Reference No. 2 of 1993; Re Mansell*." *Criminal Law Journal* 19: 100–105.
Hoogwerf (1992) 63 A Crim R 302.
Independent (*Footscray*). "Alleged Indecent Offence." August 23, 1913.
Jackson, Hal. 2003. "Child Witnesses in the Western Australian Criminal Courts." *Criminal Law Journal Sydney* 27 (4): 199–210.
Langbein, John. 1978. "The Criminal Trial Before the Lawyers." *University of Chicago Law Review* 45 (2): 263–316.
Lau (1991) 58 A Crim R 390.
Leader, William. 1889. *A Manual of the Law of Evidence – With Copious References to the Victorian Statutes and Leading Cases*. London: Sweet and Maxwell.
Lee, Kang, R.C.L Lindsay, Victoria Talwar, and Nicholas Bala. 2010. "The Competency of Children to Testify: Psychological Research Informing Canadian Law Reform." *The International Journal of Children's Rights* 18 (1): 53–77.
The Maitland Daily Mercury (NSW: 1894–1939). "Maitland Quarter Sessions." July 26, 1921.

The Maitland Weekly Mercury (NSW: 1894–1931). "A Re-Trial." June 21, 1924.

Maryborough Chronicle, Wide Bay and Burnett Advertiser (Qld: 1860–1947). "English Courts." May 15, 1937.

Maryborough Chronicle, Wide Bay and Burnett Advertiser (Qld: 1860–1947). "Indecently Dealing." February 23, 1910.

Melleuish, Gregory. 2014. "A Secular Australia? Ideas, Politics and the Search for Moral Order in Nineteenth and Early Twentieth Century Australia." *Journal of Religious History* 38 (3). https://doi.org/10.1111/1467-9809.12076.

Minors (Property and Contracts) Act 1970 (NSW).

Morning Bulletin (Rockhampton, Qld: 1878–1954). "Swearing a Child Witness." August 19, 1908, 4.

Nambucca and Bellinger News. "Judge's Reasons." October 19, 1934.

New South Wales, *Parliamentary Debates,* Legislative Council, 28 November 1990, 10948 (The Hon. E. P. Pickering).

Oaths Act 1867 (Qld).

Oaths Act 1889 (Tas).

Oaths Act Amendment Act 1884 (Qld).

Oaths (Children) Amendment Act 1985 (NSW).

Oaths (Children) Amendment 1990 (NSW).

Queensland Law Reform Commission. 1975. *The Law Relating to Evidence* (Report No 19, November 1975).

Queensland Times, Ipswich Herald and General Advertiser. "The Value of an Oath." July 16, 1907.

R v Gregg (1892) 18 VLR 218.

The Register (Adelaide, SA: 1901–1929). "A Precocious Boy." February 28, 1905.

Revesz (1996) 88 A Crim R 253.

Robb, James C., and Lynda J. Kordyban. 1989. "The Child Witness: Reconciling the Irreconcilable." *Alberta Law Review* 27 (3): 327–353.

R v Brasier (1779) 168 E.R 202.

R v Brown [1977] Qd R 220.

R v Campbell [1956] 2 QB 432.

R v Eade (1923) 24 SR (NSW) 117.

R v Giles [1959] VR 583.

R v GW (2016) 258 CLR 108.

R v Harding [1989] 2 Qd R 373.

R v Hayes [1977] 1 WLR 234.

R v Lynch (1930) 30 SR (NSW) 420.
R v Smith (1901) 26 VLR 683.
R v Sparkman (1930) 31 SR (NSW) 80.
R v Whitehead (1897) 3 ALR 140.
Schultz, Karen. 2003. "The Need for Competence Tests: Queensland Judicial Perspectives on Non-Accused Child Witnesses in Criminal Proceedings." *University of Queensland Law Journal* 22 (2): 199–223.
Smith, F.B. 1976. "Labouchere's Amendment to the Criminal Law Amendment Bill." *Australian Historical Studies* 17 (67): 165–173.
State Records NSW: Court Reporting Office, NRS 2714, Central Criminal Court transcripts Criminal F to H. [6/2135], *R v William Fisher*, 29 September 1941.
State Records NSW: Court Reporting Office, NRS 2714, Central Criminal Court transcripts. [6/1514] Criminal—I-O, *Rex v Percy Matthew Lynch*, 23 June 1930, 2.
Stead, Thomas. "The Maiden Tribute of Modern Babylon." *The Pall Mall Gazette (London)* July 4–13, 1885.
Swain, Shurlee. 2005. "Do You Want Religion With That? – Welfare History in a Secular Age." *History Australia* 2 (3): 1–79.
The Telegraph (Brisbane, Qld: 1872–1947). "Child Witnesses." July 5, 1916.
Townsville Daily Bulletin (Qld: 1907–1954). "Life Sentence in West End Murder." November 13, 1946.
Townsville Daily Bulletin. "Richmond Murder Case. Startling Answers. By Child Witness." January 31, 1935.
Truth (Brisbane, Qld: 1900–1954). "Child's Graphic Story: Mother's Alleged Murder." September 15, 1946.
Truth (Brisbane, Qld: 1900–1954). "The Nature of an Oath." June 12, 1921.
Truth (Perth, WA: 1903–1931). "A Uniformed Ruffian." September 9, 1916.
United Kingdom *Hansard* HC Deb vol 300 col 754, 763 (31 July 1885) [Electronic Version].
Victorian Statute Law Revision Committee. *Evidence From Children* (Report, 1960).
Weekly Times (Melbourne). "Profligacy Exposed." August 22, 1885.
Western Argus (Kalgoorlie, WA: 1916–1938). "You Will Go to Hell." October 9, 1934.
The Law Reform Commission of Western Australia. *Evidence of Children and Other Vulnerable Witnesses Project No. 87* (Discussion Paper, 1990).
The Wyalong Advocate and Mining, Agricultural and Pastoral Gazette (NSW: 1900–1928). "Indecent Assault." October 12, 1923.

5

"And the Kiddie Was at Home": The Courtroom Environment

During a trial in Queensland's Supreme Court in 1936, a young girl was called to the stand. Described in the press as "crying bitterly," Justice Brennan declared the child was "terrified."

> 'Will her evidence be reliable in her present state?' he asked.
> 'It is a pity there is not another way of dealing with a case of this kind instead of bringing little kiddies into court. It must leave a terrible mark on a child's mind forever to have to come into court like this.' (*Maryborough Chronicle, Wide Bay and Burnett Advertiser* 1936, 5)

Justice Brennan's observations pre-date, by about half a century, the research that does, indeed, demonstrate the potential for courtroom procedure to traumatise child witnesses (Ellison 2002, 12). Not only was the potential harm—the "terrible mark left on a child's mind forever"—a

This chapter has been adapted significantly from the 2017 article Blewer, Robyn. 2017. "Making Kiddies at Home in Court: Supporting Child Witnesses in Twentieth-Century Australian Courtrooms." *Law & History* 4 (1): 62–87. Reproduced with permission.

R. Blewer, *Child Witnesses in Twentieth Century Australian Courtrooms*, Palgrave Histories of Policing, Punishment and Justice, https://doi.org/10.1007/978-3-030-69791-4_5

concern for Brennan; so too was the administration of justice. The child's distress raised questions in the judge's mind of whether her evidence would be reliable. The prosecutor conceded the girl was crucial to the Crown's case. He agreed with Justice Brennan, admitting under the circumstances he had no choice but to enter a *nolle prosequi*—an application to the court made by the Crown indicating they would not be proceeding with that indictment (*Criminal Code 1899* (Qld) s 563). The accused was discharged.

In its 1997 report *Seen and Heard: Priority for Children in the Legal Process*, the Australian Law Reform Commission (ALRC) claimed "the legal system has traditionally given little support and preparation to child witnesses" (Australian Law Reform Commission and Australian Human Rights and Equal Opportunity Commission 1997, vol. 84, par 14.90). Justice Brennan's views, and others like it in this chapter, suggest otherwise. The Australian Law Reform Commission's position may have been informed by the lack of legislation or case law mandating support and preparation for young witnesses. Nevertheless, as preceding chapters of this book have already shown, the legal process could be quite pragmatic—creative even—in making sure the evidence of children was received. Just because support and preparation of child witnesses did not appear in legislation or case law, this did not mean it was not happening. This chapter examines the courtroom environment and how children were supported through the prosecution process. There was widespread awareness among the legal profession, the judiciary and the public that courtrooms could be terrifying and harmful places for children, and a variety of adaptations to ordinary courtroom practice were made to prevent, or at least limit, the potential for harm. Children frequently sat, for example, with parents or relatives, or next to judges or magistrates, to give their evidence, and often in closed courtrooms. Relatives provided support in court. Young witnesses held favourite toys while seated in the witness box. In one case, a child sat on a juror's knee for at least part of her testimony (*Truth* 1925, 14). New South Wales and Western Australia allowed some offences against children to be heard in their less formal Children's Courts, where the parties might sit around a table, rather than in a traditional courtroom (*Mirror* 1940, 4; *State Children's Act* 1907 (WA), s 19). For most of the century, informal methods of support were justified on the basis that they were necessary to secure justice—but they were also evidence of a wider understanding of the plight of the child witness in court (*Scott v Scott* [1913] AC 417; *R v Smellie* (1919) 14 Cr App R 128; *R v Hamilton* (1930) 30 SR (NSW) 277). The decision to implement such measures was, however, a discretionary one. What support, if any, child witnesses were afforded in court depended on judicial officers choosing to adopt such a course, and the cooperation of others in the courtroom. The result was that support was given in an ad hoc, inconsistent manner.

From the 1980s onwards, a significant body of new legislation revealed a shift in how the law perceived witnesses generally. The concept of the "fair trial" was broadened to include fairness to the witness as well as the accused. The law—both legislation and case law—became increasingly concerned with the needs of child witnesses (*R v West* [1992] 1 Qd R 227). Supportive measures by the end of the century were not just about securing justice but also about recognising that the courtroom environment could be harmful to child witnesses, just as Brennan J had surmised in 1936.

To examine the nature of the support offered to child witnesses, this chapter is divided into three parts. It first considers the complexities of the adversarial courtroom and the difficulties faced by child witnesses appearing in them. The second part examines practical, "common sense" measures, rarely opposed by prosecutors and defence representatives, taken by courts to support child witnesses. The final part of the chapter considers more controversial methods of support, namely closed courts and shielding children from the accused's view, which threatened central precepts of the common law.

Child Witnesses and the Adversarial Courtroom

The combative nature of adversarial courtrooms is not amenable to receiving the testimony of children (Spencer and Flin 1990, 80). Reliance on oral evidence, the inexorable belief in the use of cross-examination, and the presence of jurors and the public, all signify a system concerned with robust testing of evidence and transparent processes, but also reveal a system that is entirely adult centred (Ellison 2002, 12–14). Child witnesses, sitting with their feet dangling from the chair, frequently barely able to see over the witness box, their tiny voices often inaudible to those in the room, forced to speak before commonly crowded galleries, will always appear out of place. Their presence in courtrooms has long challenged the "moral legitimacy" of this adult courtroom environment and adversarial process (Mulcahy 2011, 84).

Knowing how, if at all, courts accommodated child witnesses in this environment illuminates the challenges faced by the law and children alike when children were required to participate in the adjudication process. Where the evidence of a child was vital to such a process, but the child appeared upset or nervous, or struggled to answer questions, courts needed a way to respond. In many cases, they responded by discontinuing the proceedings and discharging the accused. Many, though, responded by acknowledging the difficult position in which the child had been placed, and attempted to support the child accordingly.

Locating evidence of the precise nature of the support given to child witnesses presents a methodological challenge. The last quarter of the twentieth century saw a significant increase in legislation regulating courtroom practice. Prior to this, however, case law and legislation were seldom concerned with the internal environment of courts. Similarly, treatises, manuals and textbooks described the law and how it should be applied but did not describe what was taking place inside courtrooms on a daily basis (Fisk and Gordon 2011, 526; Hay 1984, 8). For the first half of the twentieth century, transcripts of court proceedings were not produced as consistently or with the same accuracy as they are today. Further, scientific studies of child witnesses were scarce prior to the late twentieth century. Even depositions and judge's notebooks rarely describe what was occurring inside the courtroom (Freedman 2011; Tanenhaus and Bush 2007, 1075).

Newspaper reports are an especially valuable source on courtroom practices. Press reports provide evidence of the social practices and emotional responses at play in courtrooms, particularly in the first half of the century. Importantly, they provide contemporaneous, albeit mediated, reports of cases involving child witnesses and often recount how these witnesses negotiated the courtroom environment. Children were, for example, variously described as "timid," "confident," "intelligent," "vague," "lucid," "shrewd," "crying," "composed," "naughty," "fearless," "frightened" and "hostile." Of course, newspaper reports are not without their limitations. It is impossible to determine whether cases were reported because they were exceptional or representative (Simpson 2004, 68). Where possible, information contained within newspaper reports has been verified using case law, legislation, archival material and trial registers such as *The Prosecution Project Database,* and relevant case citators such as Austlii, Lexis Advance Casebase and Westlaw. In any event, these reports provide a valuable source of knowledge about the nature of information the public were receiving in relation to the machinations of the criminal justice process.

"Common Sense Methods" of Making Little Kiddies at Home

On the hottest day in Melbourne in 1923, as the temperature reached 41 degrees Celsius, an iceberg was melting in the middle of the city. Chief Justice Sir William "Iceberg" Irvine was presiding over a trial at Melbourne's Criminal Court (*The Advertiser* 1923, 12). He was called "Iceberg" on account of his ordinarily cold, ice-like, manner (*The Tocsin* 1904, 8; *Westralian Worker* 1908, 1). On this day Irvine was described as "a towering and impressive figure," who "relaxed his stern dignity" and "beamed" at a six-year-old girl as she gave her evidence while standing on a chair next to him (*The Advertiser* 1923, 12). At the appropriate time, the court crier lifted the little girl from the judge's bench and carried her to the dock, where she confidently identified the accused. The journalist reporting on the case observed "as the child was the principal witness against the prisoner, the case was one in which judicial procedure gave way to common sense methods" (*The Advertiser* 1923, 12).

As far as this journalist was concerned, it was appropriate for Chief Justice Irvine to support the child as he had done. The notion that it was simply "common sense" for a court to accommodate a child witness in this way is indicative of attitudes towards the prosecution process and children more generally in the early twentieth century. There was no suggestion such a measure was inappropriate, unfair or potentially unjust, even though it had been noted the court had departed from ordinary "judicial procedure." The child's evidence was needed. It was necessary to adapt ordinary procedure accordingly.

The level of support given to children depended on the apparent age and maturity of the child, their manifestation of distress, the extent to which such factors threatened the continuation of the hearing and the willingness of the judicial officer to accommodate the child. A five-year-old girl was permitted to give evidence at the Sydney Coroner's Court while sitting on her mother's knee (*The Richmond River Herald and Northern Districts Advertiser* 1938, 2; *The Central Queensland Herald* 1938, 22). In other cases, children were reported to have given their evidence while standing next to the jury (*The Daily News* 1907, 3), with a support person next to them (*Goulburn Herald* 1903, 2), or sitting in the witness box holding a soft toy (*Healesville Guardian* 1956, 3). No objections appear to have been made in relation to any of these simple measures of accommodating child witnesses. Older children aged eleven and over ordinarily appeared in the witness box. One witness, aged sixteen, was permitted to give evidence from a chair on the floor of the courtroom on account of her being injured and physically unable to sit in the witness box (*Western Star* 1949, 1). Those who were found to have sat next to the judge were aged ten years and under. In 1954, a fourteen-year-old complainant was reported as crying and refusing to answer questions. Had she been younger, she may have been moved to sit next to the magistrate. In this case however, no concessions were made on account of her distress. Indeed, she was treated as a hostile witness (*Mirror* 1954, 5).

Judicial officers were not the only ones to show concern for child witnesses. In Chapter 3, the case of Mary Ryan was considered in the context of police investigations. Mary had been charged with murdering her newborn baby (Queensland State Archives Item ID95466, *R v Mary Ryan*). Her three daughters, Bridget, thirteen, Margaret, ten and Mary, eight, had been interviewed at length by Acting Sergeant Leslie. At their mother's committal hearing, held at the City Police Court in Brisbane, Mr. J. P. Forde, a local solicitor, appeared alongside the prosecutor and defence counsel to "watch the interests of the defendant's children who were witnesses in the case" (*The Brisbane Courier* 1900, 6).

The evidence of the three girls was that their mother had wrapped the baby in rags, placed it next to a log in the backyard and then asked her eight-year-old daughter, also called Mary, to use the "fire stick" from the kitchen to set fire to the rags. Young Mary testified she had done as her mother demanded, thus starting the fire that killed the baby (*The Age* 1900, 6; *Queensland Times, Ipswich Herald and General Advertiser* 1900, 2). Bridget and Margaret gave evidence they had watched Mary carry out their mother's instructions without attempting to stop her, even though they had known what Mary was doing was wrong (Queensland State Archives Item ID95466, Depositions and Indictments).

In these circumstances, with the girls effectively incriminating themselves by admitting they had stood by while Mary killed their sibling, the importance of Forde's appearance in the interests of the girls is obvious. When young Mary began to tell the court she had started the fire that would eventually kill her baby brother, Forde formally requested the young girl be cautioned. Police Magistrate Ranking denied the request, as he thought Mary was unlikely to be charged even if she did incriminate herself (*The Brisbane Courier* 1900, 6).

While the depositions for this matter indicate where Mr. Forde intervened on behalf of the children, the press reports give more details of other support shown to the girls. Defence counsel, Mr. O'Shea, was cross-examining young Mary at 4.30 pm one afternoon. He made an application for the court to rise for the day, earlier than usual, on the basis that Mary "had been so long under examination it would be a fair thing" to do. Magistrate Ranking agreed, remarking the child must have been tired by that point (*The Brisbane Courier* 1900, 6). Whether Mary was tired or not, the early adjournment appears to have been based on a view of what was "fair" to the child generally, rather than in response to her demeanour. The following day, after young Mary completed her testimony, her mother was committed to stand trial.

Mary Snr's trial was held at the Brisbane Supreme Court in June 1900 (Queensland State Archives Item ID95466, *R v Mary Ryan*). The girls were again called to give evidence, but this time no one appeared in their interests, as Mr. Forde had for the committal hearing. Instead, prior to the commencement of the trial, Mary, Margaret and Bridget were each issued Letters Patent by the Queensland Governor, pardoning and releasing them from any offences to which they may have admitted while giving evidence at the committal or in the forthcoming trial (Queensland State Archives Item ID95466, Letters Patent for Mary Ryan's daughters, Mary, Margaret and Bridget, 28 May 1900). The combination of informal measures of support as well as the formal Letters Patent in this case are indicative of a legal system with the capacity, and in this case the willingness, to prepare and protect these children using various methods.

In the 1913 matter of Cecil Banks, the South Australian Supreme Court in Adelaide similarly employed a variety of measures to support a five-year-old girl, Stella. Stella was described as "sobbing bitterly" when called to the stand (*The Journal* 1913, 1). To "console" and "pacify" her, Justice Buchanan had Stella sit on his knee rather than in the witness box, but she continued to cry. The press reported "the presence of onlookers frightened" her (*Daily Herald* 1913, 3). We have no way of knowing if this was the case but, nevertheless, the judge ordered anyone in the room without a personal interest in the case to leave. Then, with the help of some "judicious questioning" from Justice Buchanan and the barristers standing next to the bench rather than at the bar table, the little girl gave her evidence. Banks was convicted and sentenced to six months' imprisonment with hard labour (*Daily Herald* 1913, 3).

While Stella struggled to cope with the courtroom environment, other children showed little or no difficulty negotiating such surroundings, but were supported, nonetheless. Support for a child witness during the trial of Clifford Healy in 1940 again reflected an attitude (of the court and the press alike) that it was simply "common sense" to make the child comfortable in the courtroom. "Hollywood itself could hardly have presented a situation more dramatic," declared Perth's *Mirror*, reporting on the trial (1940, 4). Sitting with Magistrate Schroder around a long table was the "poorly dressed, weak chinned" defendant. He sat across the table from the child witness, "a little seven-year-old girl confidently and intelligently telling a sordid story." The tale of this trial even had a hero—Detective-Sergeant Harry Jackson—who, it was reported:

> rose to heights as a prosecutor in the way he handled his child witness. A seven year old might have been so easily awed by her surroundings. But Jackson took off his hat, lifted her onto a chair, beckoned her mother into an adjacent one and the kiddie was at home. (*Mirror* 1940, 4)

Supporting children with a view to making them "at home" in the courtroom was a priority for the Crown when preparing for a murder trial in Sydney in 1941. In August, William Fisher, a sixty-five-year-old printer, had been charged with the murder of a three-year-old girl who, according to reports, had been sexually assaulted and strangled. The case had attracted intense media attention and public outrage over the tiny child's violent death (*Narandera Argus and Riverina Advertiser* 1941, 2). A few weeks later, during the coroner's court hearing, the girl's father and some members of the public gallery were reported to have repeatedly called out to the accused during the proceedings (*Truth* 1941, 18). Groups of women had demonstrated outside the court, some reportedly doing so in a "hostile fashion" (*Warwick Daily News* 1941, 1). Fisher was committed to stand trial.

In the week prior to the trial, in September—less than eight weeks after the child died—two children who would be key witnesses participated in a dress rehearsal intended to give them "court confidence" (*National Advocate* 1941, 5; *The Daily News* 1941, 18). Eleven-year-old Sylvia and thirteen-year-old Joe were expected to give evidence they had seen Fisher with the little girl on the day she went missing. The competency of both children to give evidence was considered earlier, in Chapter 4. Given the tense atmosphere surrounding the case and the centrality of Sylvia and Joe's testimonies to the trial, the prosecutor presumably did not want to risk either child being unable to give evidence on account of their being intimidated or overwhelmed by the courtroom environment. None of the press reports of Sylvia and Joe's earlier appearance in the coroner's court suggest either child was upset or unable to give their testimony. The dress rehearsal reflected a broader awareness that courtrooms could be foreign, perhaps frightening, environments for children and the desirability of preparing and supporting the children.

The transcripts of the trial reveal Fisher's defence counsel attempted to make an issue of the practice run. Sylvia was cross-examined on the circumstances of the rehearsal. She confirmed the courtroom had been like the one she was in at the time (during the trial) and that someone had sat where the judge was sitting now, and she had been asked questions. Joe was also cross-examined on the same issue. Upon re-examination, he confirmed he had previously given evidence in the coroner's court (State Records NSW, *R v William Fisher*, 29 September 1941, 12–13). Counsel addresses to the jury were not transcribed, so it is not possible to say what the defence made of this dress rehearsal. The cross-examination suggests, however, they at least wanted to raise a suspicion the children's evidence had been rehearsed. Joe's re-examination suggests the Crown, in turn, wanted to confirm the evidence the children were giving at trial was consistent with that they had given in the coroner's court—and thus the practice run was, as had been earlier reported, to give the children "court confidence." Whatever was made of the rehearsal, Fisher was convicted and sentenced to death (*Truth* 1941, 27), later commuted to life imprisonment (*The Sydney Morning Herald* 1941, 9).

Notwithstanding an awareness of the potentially stressful and harmful effect of the courtroom environment on child witnesses, there were few indications coming from the legal profession in the mid-twentieth century that formal reforms were considered desirable or necessary. The legal system, courts and legislatures alike appeared content to retain the status quo, leaving it to judicial officers to decide whether and how to support child witnesses. Towards the end of the century, however, such informal measures were being viewed with increased suspicion. Myers examined the issue of support for child witnesses in the United States during the late 1980s and early 1990s (Myers 1996). Two cases in that study employed measures to support child witnesses that were strikingly similar to those in the cases discussed above. In *State v Palabay* (1992), the Hawaii Court of Appeals found a twelve-year-old witness should not have been allowed to hold a soft toy while in the witness box without the prosecution having "first demonstrated a compelling justification" (844 P.2d 1 (1992) in Myers 1996, 411). The appellate court acknowledged the discretion a trial judge had to "allow special measures aimed at putting young children at ease," but found they should not be employed without the court first determining "the compelling necessity for the special measures." Myers also cites the Superior Court of New Jersey decision in *State v Michaels* (1993), which criticised the trial judge for his zealous approach to making the child witnesses feel "at ease so that their testimony might be obtained" (264 N.J. Super. 579 (1993) at 615). The Superior Court found the trial judge went too far in allowing a young child witness to sit on his knee while testifying, playing ball with the children and encouraging and complimenting them. In so doing the judge had "failed to recognise he could be perceived as crossing the line between an impartial judge and the prosecution" (*State v Michaels* 264 N.J. Super. 579 (1993) at 615). These two cases sit uneasily with examples given earlier in this chapter, where children held soft toys or sat with the judge—even, in Cecil Banks' case, where Stella sat on Justice Buchanan's knee without objection from counsel. The differences illustrate how supportive measures could be interpreted late in the twentieth century as threatening the accused's fair trial, whereas earlier in the century, in Australia at least, the same measures were interpreted as common-sense departures from ordinary judicial procedure, necessary to ensure a trial proceeded. These cases demonstrate the fine line between supporting child witnesses and compromising the accused's right to a fair trial.

When Pragmatism Met Principle

Occasionally, supportive measures did raise objections from defence counsel and other sources, involving more serious and obvious threats to the administration of justice than the above cases. The principle of open justice has always been a fundamental feature of common law legal systems (Bosland and Gill 2014, 482). Countless commentators and lawyers, from Hale to Blackstone and Bentham, have considered the significance of this principle. Bentham went as far as to claim that publicity was "the very soul of justice" (Bentham 1843, 314). Similarly, the opportunity to directly confront one's accuser has long been considered a central principle of the common law (Ellison 2002, 66).

As the twentieth century progressed, the tension between principles like open justice and the right to confront accusers and the desirability of supporting child witnesses continued.

Cecil Banks' case in 1913, where Stella sat on Justice Buchanan's knee, provides an opportunity to explore the application of the principle of open justice in more detail. At the outset of the trial, the prosecutor made an application for the court to be closed "in view of the nature of the case." Having read the depositions in preparation for the trial, Justice Buchanan refused the application, having decided the case was not one that warranted closing the court. The trial began in open court with the public in attendance. It was only in response to Stella's continued distress that Buchanan subsequently made the order to exclude the public from the courtroom (*Daily Herald* 1913, 3).

Notwithstanding its centrality to the common law, the principle of open justice has never been absolute (*Scott v Scott* [1913] AC 417, per Haldane [LC], at 437). Case law and legislation provided exceptions to closed courts and were used to restrict the application of the open-justice principle in Australian courtrooms throughout the twentieth century. South Australia's *Criminal Law Consolidation Amendment Act 1885,* for example, empowered judicial officers to exclude the public from hearings or trials relating to "rape or other offences against females, or unnatural offences" (*Criminal Law Consolidation Amendment Act 1885* (SA) s 13). Judges could choose to close the court or leave it open to the public. It would have been applicable to Cecil Banks' case, which makes Justice Buchanan's initial refusal to close the court all the more compelling. His Honour's refusal to close the court raises important questions about the exercise of judicial discretion in these cases, and the subsequent implementation of legislation in the late-twentieth century that removed such discretion and made closed courts mandatory. In refusing to close his court, Justice Buchanan may have been guided by a very recent Privy Council decision. *Scott v Scott* [1913] AC 417 confirmed "...it may well be that justice could not be done at all if it had to be done in public...The question is by no means one which...can be dealt with by the judge as resting in his mere discretion as to what is expedient. The latter must treat it as one of principle, and as turning, not on convenience, but on necessity" (*Scott v Scott* [1913] AC 417, 438). *Scott* emphasised the law's only objective in closing courts was the administration of justice—not because of the nature of the evidence expected to be heard. The prosecutor in *Banks* had asked for a closed court on account of the evidence. Buchanan J refused this application, and only exercised his discretion to exclude the public when Stella's distressed state threatened the administration of justice by threatening the continuation of the trial.

Closing courts in view of the nature of the evidence, rather than any perceived threat to the administration of justice, would become an issue some years later in Western Australia in 1926, when Alfred Florance was charged with indecently assaulting a young girl at Fremantle. Perth's *Mirror* referred to a "movement" to have the case heard *in camera* on account of the evidence expected to be heard. The *Mirror* claimed "every decent-minded member of the community will hope for the sake of the child witnesses that an *in camera* hearing is decided on" (1926, 3). As far as the *Mirror* was concerned, it was the interests of the child witness, not the administration of justice, that should have been the priority in the case. The need for such a decision was avoided as Florance's committal hearing took place in the Fremantle Children's Court, which was always closed to the public. Section 19 of the *State Children's Act 1907* (WA) permitted cases against children, as well as those committed by children, to be heard in the Children's Court—and thus *in camera*.

Closing courtrooms for the hearing of children's testimony, while certainly not routine, was not uncommon. Excluding the public from these hearings was rarely opposed. Such a decision only appears to have formed the basis of one appeal, which came before the courts a few years after the Florance case in Western Australia. In 1930 in New South Wales, the defendant, Hamilton, had been charged with indecently assaulting his fifteen-year-old stepdaughter. There was no suggestion the girl was upset or unable to give her evidence while the public was present. Judge Coyle nevertheless ordered spectators to leave the courtroom during her testimony. The *Truth* noted prior to making the formal order, His Honour had informally asked the public to leave but had been ignored. He took the "drastic step" of ordering the court to be cleared (*Truth* 1930, 1). The trial proceeded, and the jury found Hamilton guilty. He was sentenced to seven years' imprisonment.

Hamilton appealed his conviction on several grounds, including Coyle's decision to clear the courtroom. Richard Windeyer, K. C., represented Hamilton at the trial and the appeal. Windeyer argued because the trial had taken place in a closed court, his client had "not been tried by a properly constituted court" (*Truth* 1930, 1). The Court of Criminal Appeal agreed. On this ground alone, it upheld Hamilton's appeal, quashed his conviction and ordered a retrial (*R v Hamilton* (1930) 30 SR (NSW) 277). The *Truth* reported Judge Coyle had cleared the court in the interests of the child witness "to save her from a gaping, morbid-minded crowd" (1930, 1). Judge Coyle's own explanation of his decision-making process was referred to in the Court of Criminal Appeal's subsequent judgment. Explaining his thought process to the appellate court, Coyle maintained he had closed the court to "prevent the morbid section of the community ... from listening to most unpleasant details" (*R v Hamilton* (1930) 30 SR (NSW) 277). By the judge's own admission then, his orders were made to prevent the public from hearing the evidence, not in the interests of the child witness—or even in the interests of justice.

Judge Coyle admitted that in making these orders he had pushed the limits of his powers, telling the Court of Criminal Appeal "in order to do a great right in the interests of decency, [I] did what was only a little wrong" (*Truth* 1930, 1; *Evening News* 1930, 7). The Court of Criminal Appeal disagreed with Judge Coyle, finding his actions were, in fact, very wrong. Chief Justice Street confirmed the principle of open justice was "so clear upon authority that I do not think it is necessary to refer to the authorities [meaning case law] in any detail" (*R v Hamilton* (1930) 30 SR (NSW) 277 at 278). The Chief Justice cited the authorities of *Scott v Scott* [1913] A.C 417 and *The King v The Governor of Lewes Prison* [1917] 2 KB 254, but otherwise did not discuss them. Hamilton was subsequently retried at the Darlinghurst Sessions and acquitted (*National Advocate* 1930, 5). Despite quashing Hamilton's conviction so emphatically, the court nevertheless noted Judge Coyle's "praiseworthy motive" and appeared to regret having to make the decision they did (*National Advocate* 1930, 5). They expressed a hope the legislature would look at amending the law to give judges the discretion to exclude the public "in these cases" (*R v Hamilton* (1930) 30 SR (NSW) 277 at 278). The Court of Criminal Appeal's call was ignored. It was not until 1981, fifty years later, that New South Wales introduced legislation to routinely close courtrooms in criminal matters involving the testimony of child witnesses (*Crimes (Sexual Assault) Amendment Act 1981* (NSW) sch 1). South Australia followed in 1988, making it mandatory for all persons present to leave the courtroom for the evidence of a child in sexual offences. Significantly, this amendment also made provision for a person providing "emotional support for the child" to remain in the court (*Evidence Act Amendment Act 1988* (SA) s 8(1)(b)).

The process for Queensland to move from open to closed courts for the hearing of child witness testimony was also a lengthy one. In 1933 a case known as "The Tarragindi Outrage" gained considerable press and public attention. The defendant was charged with one count of rape and another of attempted rape upon a sixteen-year-old girl. While the press did not identify the girl, they did report the sordid details of her evidence. The headlines alone give an indication of the testimony she gave: "Screaming Girl Fights Frantically Against Her Attacker" and "Pathetic Tale of Victim – "I Cried Out, Help! Help! But No One Came" (*Truth* 1933, 17; *The Week* 1933, 24). The very public nature of this hearing, and extensive press reporting of it, motivated the Queensland Justices Association to write to the state's Attorney-General, expressing their concerns about the procedure for receiving children's testimony. Arguing in favour of closed courtrooms and limits on publishing details of the testimony of children, the Association claimed the attention cases like "The Tarragindi Outrage" received resulted in crowded courtrooms. Showing concern for child witnesses generally, the justices argued it was "quite wrong to permit a child's welfare to be endangered simply so that a section of the public should have its taste gratified" (Queensland Justices Association 1933).

It was a decade after "The Tarragindi Outrage" and the Justices Association's letter before Queensland amended its *Justices Act 1886* (s 71A) to provide for *in camera* hearings for sexual offences against children (*Criminal Code Amendment Act 1945* (Qld) s 15). Not everyone was pleased with such reforms, with opposition to the closure of courts from a variety of sources. The press, in particular, were not happy. They argued sex offenders should not be afforded the "privilege of anonymity" and publicity was necessary to deter such crimes (*Truth* 1946, 15).

The principle of publicity was not the only problematic issue during the twentieth century. The accused's right to confront their accuser was also a subject of debate, and an issue the law took a considerable length of time to resolve. This was so even where—or perhaps because—early twentieth-century case law allowed for children to be shielded from the view of the accused where necessary to secure justice. Being in sight of and near the accused has been recognised in contemporary research as a source of considerable stress for child witnesses (Cashmore 1990, 228). It is a problem that is not necessarily new to the law, though. The English Court of Appeal considered it in 1919 in *R v Smellie* ((1919) 14 Cr App R 128). At trial the accused, charged with neglecting and ill-treating his eleven-year-old daughter, was ordered to sit on stairs leading to the dock so as not to intimidate the child as she gave her evidence. The accused was convicted but appealed on several grounds. He argued he was entitled to be within sight and hearing of any witness; that the effect on the mind of the jury of seeing him sit on the stairs was incalculable; and, finally, the effect of the witness not seeing the accused was heightened in this case, because his daughter was more likely to lie in her evidence without the restraining influence of her father's presence (*R v Smellie* (1919) 14 Cr App R 128). Lord Coleridge delivered the Court of Appeal's decisive judgment in a one sentence, repeated here in its entirety:

> If the judge considers that the presence of the prisoner will intimidate a witness, there is nothing to prevent him from securing the ends of justice by removing the former from the presence of the latter. (*R v Smellie* (1919) 14 Cr App R 130)

The decision reflects the view of the court a few years earlier in *Scott v Scott* ([1913] AC 417) where again, the law confirmed judges were empowered to do what was necessary to secure the ends of justice. *Smellie* ((1919) 14 Cr App R 128) was not applied, or even referenced, in any reported decision in Australia until 1992 in the Queensland case of *R v West*, which concerned a nineteen-year-old complainant being declared a "special witness" by the trial judge, who ordered a screen be placed in the courtroom between the witness and the accused (*R v West* [1992] 1 Qd

R 227). There, the court applied the decision in *Smellie*, but indicated securing the ends of justice involved balancing the needs of the witness with those of the accused. Achieving such balance, the court held, did not necessarily involve the "complete elimination of prejudice against the accused" (*R v West* [1992] 1 Qd R 231).

"It's a Pity There Is not Another Way"—Calls for Reform

As noted at the outset of this chapter, in 1997 the Australian Law Reform Commission concluded the traditional legal system had done little to support child witnesses. It is worth thinking about how and why they arrived at such a conclusion. Despite child witnesses not appearing often in legislation or case law throughout most of the twentieth century, this chapter has demonstrated there was, nevertheless, widespread awareness of the challenges child witnesses regularly faced when attending court—and the challenges they presented for the courts.

Awareness led to frequent calls for reform to existing procedures. In 1926, for example, Mr. Walter Hutley, a former President of the South Australian State Children's Council, appeared before South Australia's Law Reform Commission. A press report of Hutley's evidence reported he had argued children were "awed and frightened by the atmosphere" in court and "fuller and truer facts would be obtained…by women justices" (*The Register* 1926, 11). Echoing the arguments made in relation to women police officers—that women were more suited to dealing with women and children in court—Mr. Hutley suggested women justices could take evidence of children in relation to sexual offences and then "submit such evidence to the court" (*The Register* 1926, 11). Such recommendations were not implemented.

There appear, however, to have been some informal changes made to courtroom procedure at this time in South Australia. In 1926, for example, the Women Justices Association of Australia welcomed reforms allowing child witnesses to leave the courtroom immediately after giving evidence, rather than having to remain at the back of the room for the duration of the trial (*The West Australian* 1926, 11). At the organisation's national conference that year, South Australian representative, Mrs A. K. Goode, encouraged all members to spend time in courtrooms in their states. She drew their attention to the law that required witnesses to remain in the courtroom after giving evidence, describing how she had seen many children forced to listen to "much that was repulsive to the young mind" (*The West Australian* 1926, 11). South Australia had amended this practice to now have children removed from the courtroom after their evidence was concluded. This reform does not appear in any legislation in South Australia but is still indicative of a system prepared to make informal amendments, in this instance, to existing practice and procedure.

Women's organisations continued to call for changes to the existing process for taking evidence from children throughout the twentieth century. In 1930 the Australian Federation of Women Voters, like the Women Justices in 1926, called for the establishment of specialist courts for offences against children. These courts, they proposed, would have one magistrate and two justices of the peace, one of whom would be female. The Federation argued having three judicial officers on the bench would be more like a trial by jury rather than a judge-only trial (*The Age* 1930, 16). No such reforms were introduced. In 1933 the National Council of Women voiced concerns offences against children were not reported because of the associated publicity that surrounded such cases. They were also concerned children were being called on to give statements and evidence repeatedly, which might prevent them from forgetting the incident. They argued the interests of children had to be considered in the criminal justice process (*Townsville Daily Bulletin* 1933, 4). Such recommendations were not implemented.

In Western Australia in 1934, the Women's Service Guild called on the state's Minister for Justice, John Willcock, to implement legislation to close courts while children were giving evidence. The Guild acknowledged the necessity in some cases for children to give evidence in court, but argued that "it is equally essential to safeguard the child from the dreadful psychological effects of the publicity afforded by the present system…" (*The West Australian* 1934, 22). The Minister did not heed the Guild's call, preferring to maintain the existing system of allowing judges to close courts in exceptional circumstances. In 1950, the Country Women's Association (CWA) called for substantial changes to existing courtroom procedures. Like the Federation of Women Voters, the CWA called for the establishment of specialist courts for sexual offences. Their design for such courts included policewomen or other women providing support to the children; a supreme court judge and jury with the same judicial powers as ordinary supreme court justices; all courtroom personnel to wear civilian clothes, as the wigs and gowns tended to "terrify" children; and the dispensation of ordinary legal formalities. Beyond these reforms, the CWA also called for children's court magistrates to be empowered to issue harsher penalties to sexual offenders; the evidence of children in ordinary courts be held *in camera*; and sex offenders be admitted to an institution for the term of their natural lives (*The West Australian* 1950, 21). Again, such reforms were not implemented.

Women lawyers, too, argued for reform of existing practice. An article appearing in the *Telegraph* in Brisbane in 1941 pitted female and male colleagues against each other in a battle reflecting the tension existing between the interests of the child and the interests of the system (and the tension between the gender roles) (1941, 7). The female lawyers identified the dangers of the present system being the "mental effect" on children of giving evidence in court. Like the National Council of Women some years earlier, they feared parents often chose not to report offences for fear of having their children called to give evidence in court. Such a choice might increase the risk offenders would go free to commit further offences. On the other hand, male lawyers claimed it was a "necessary evil" for children to be called as witnesses and any psychological damage to the child was the "lesser evil in the interests of justice" (*The Telegraph* 1941, 7). The precise identity of these lawyers, and the context of their debate, is unclear. Their words, however, mirror the concerns raised concurrently by women's organisations, contributing evidence to the discourse of reform gaining momentum around the middle of the twentieth century.

Public debates like that of the men and women lawyers of Queensland raised awareness of the practices and procedures for children to give evidence, particularly in relation to sexual offences. This, in turn, led to the establishment of a government inquiry. In 1944, the Queensland "Committee of Inquiry Regarding Sexual Offences" considered the plight of child witnesses. The committee attributed the underreporting of offences committed against children to parents' reservations about children giving evidence in court (*The Courier-Mail* 1944, 3). Such findings provide an Australian context for the same point made by Holly Brewer in her research on child witnesses in the United States and United Kingdom, namely that public knowledge of, and dissatisfaction with, the procedure for children to give evidence in court often impacted upon the criminal justice process by defining which matters were heard before the legal system had considered, or even been made aware of, the case (Brewer 2005, 159). The Queensland "Committee of Inquiry Regarding Sexual Offences" acknowledged the complexity of the courtroom environment. They disagreed, however, on what changes would be appropriate. Committee member and psychiatrist, Professor John Bostock, expressed concern over the harm such an environment could do to an already traumatised child, while Justice Macrossan was concerned reforms could compromise the accused's right to a fair trial. Fellow committee member, Mrs. Constance Bevan, President of the League of Women Voters, called for the establishment of specialist courts to hear matters involving sexual offences against children (*Cairns Post* 1944, 4). In this one example we see the quite different approaches of medicine, law and social reformers. While there were some reforms introduced following this inquiry, specialist courts were not included. Courtrooms were closed to the public, however, for the hearing of charges of sexual offences against children.

Some decades after Queensland's inquiry, the final report of the 1977 *Royal Commission on Human Relationships* paid considerable attention to the problems of children appearing as witnesses in sexual offence trials. The 1977 Commission specifically noted "concern about the child's role in legal prosecutions is not new" (Commonwealth of Australia, *Royal Commission on Human Relationships* (Final Report 1978), vol. 5, 215). It cited a fifty-year-old 1925 report of the United Kingdom, *Departmental Committee on Sexual Offences Against Young Persons*, which criticised the protracted prosecution process for forcing the child witness "to remember what, in its own best interests, it should be allowed to forget" (*Command Paper 2561* (London: HMSO, 1925): 27. Cited in Commonwealth of Australia, *Royal Commission on Human Relationships* (Final Report 1978) vol. 5, 215). The Royal Commission noted despite such longstanding awareness of the problematic nature of children testifying in court, "little has been done to alleviate the position of the child victim in the criminal justice system" (vol. 5, 216). This observation foreshadows the conclusion drawn by the Australian Law Reform Commission in 1997 that the traditional legal system had done little to support children in court.

The Reforms of the 1980s Onwards

The 1977 *Royal Commission on Human Relationships* was the first substantial report to recognise the shift in understanding children and the impact the legal process might have on children's overall well-being, particularly their capacity to recover from trauma. Acknowledging the tension between the interests of the child and the rights of an accused, the Commission outlined the need to protect child witnesses through minimum participation in trials "without unduly hampering the defence" (Commonwealth of Australia, *Royal Commission on Human Relationships* (Final Report 1978) vol. 5, 220). In what looks very much like the contemporary ground rules hearing process, the Commission recommended pre-trial conferences to "establish the best modus operandi for the conduct of the trial" (vol. 5, 220). During these proposed hearings, it was anticipated parties might agree to dispense with a child's court appearance altogether by accepting his or her written statement (as the Queensland women lawyers had suggested over thirty years earlier). The Commission made no mention of the use of physical screens or other in-court mechanisms to shield the child from the view of the accused. Instead, where the physical presence of a child witness was required at trial, they recommended confrontation between the accused and the child be completely avoided by the accused being excluded from the courtroom for the duration of the child's testimony, provided his or her counsel remained in the court. To facilitate this, the Commission thought it entirely possible and appropriate for the judge to be made aware at the pre-trial conference of any proposed defence, "if necessary, in the absence of the prosecutor" (Commonwealth of Australia, *Royal Commission on Human Relationships* (Final Report 1978) vol. 5, 220). This recommendation for pre-trial conferences does not appear to have been implemented, at least formally.

Even though the idea of pre-trial hearings was not adopted in practice, from the publication of the Commission's report in 1978 to the end of the twentieth century, reforms to child witness courtroom procedures were introduced at an ever-increasing pace. For an issue that had garnered little legislative, judicial or academic attention for the preceding decades, if not centuries, from the mid 1970s onwards, the legislation passed, the judicial decisions made, and the research conducted heralded extensive changes to courtroom procedure. Suddenly, or so it seemed, the eyes of the law had been opened to the plight of child witnesses and it became imperative that they be protected from the harm courtrooms posed. Table 5.1 on the next page identifies and summarises those changes.

A few observations can be made about the data in Table 5.1. Closed-circuit television technology was adopted rapidly (Australian Law Reform Commission, *Report 63—Children's Evidence: Closed Circuit TV* (Report No 63, 1992), 1). The use of this technology quickly became the dominant method for dealing with the evidence of children. It obviated the need for children to appear in the courtroom, allowing them to provide their evidence in a way Justice Brennan could only have imagined in 1936 when he expressed a yearning for an alternative to "bringing little kiddies into court" (*Maryborough Chronicle, Wide Bay and Burnett Advertiser* 1936, 5). Concerns were raised the adoption of video and closed-circuit procedures would be thought of as a panacea for all child witness-related problems and other problems associated with cross-examination, competency testing and the reliability of children as witnesses might be overlooked (Cashmore 1990, 249). The additional reforms noted in Table 5.1 would suggest otherwise. The separation of the accused from the child, the provision of support persons in court and the closure of courts had nothing to do with technological innovations but were introduced as additional measures to support child witnesses.

Table 5.1 Summary of legislative reforms for support of child witnesses from 1975

	SA	NSW	Tas	Vic	WA	Qld
Closed courts	*Evidence Act Amendment Act (no 3) 1984* NB: *Evidence Act Amendment Act 1988* s 3—court must close for child witness	Crimes (Sexual Assault) Amendment Act 1981 see also *Crimes (Child Assault) Amendment Act 1985*	no express provision by end of 20thC. NB: *Evidence Amendment (Children and Special Witnesses) 1995*—CCTV for all children unless court orders otherwise	*Crimes (Sexual Offences) Act 1991*	no express provision by end of 20thC. NB: *Acts Amendment (Evidence of Children and Others) Act 1992* pre-trial hearings -only persons auth. by judge	*Criminal Law (Sexual Offences) Act 1978*
Video/CCTV evidence	*Evidence (Vulnerable Witnesses) Amendment Act 1993*	*Crimes (Child Victim Evidence) Amendment Act 1990* New s 405D *Crimes Act 1900*	*Evidence Amendment (Children and Special Witnesses) 1995*	*Crimes (Sexual Offences) Act 1991*	*Acts Amendment (Evidence of Children and Others) Act 1992*	*Criminal Code, Evidence Act and Other Acts Amendment Act 1989* s 63 for u12

(continued)

Table 5.1 (continued)

	SA	NSW	Tas	Vic	WA	Qld
Support person in court	*Evidence Act Amendment Act 1988*	*Evidence (Children) Act 1997*	*Evidence Amendment (Children and Special Witnesses) 1995*	*Crimes (Sexual Offences) Act 1991*	*Acts Amendment (Evidence of Children and Others) Act 1992*	*Criminal Code, Evidence Act and Other Acts Amendment Act 1989* s 63 for u12
Exclusion of/separation from defendant	*Evidence (Vulnerable Witnesses) Amendment Act 1993*	*Crimes (Child Victim Evidence) Amendment 1990*		*Crimes (Sexual Offences) Act 1991*	*Acts Amendment (Evidence of Children and Others) Act 1992*	*Criminal Code, Evidence Act and Other Acts Amendment Act 1989* s 63 for u12

Another observation that can be made about the legislation passed in the 1990s is the language of the *Evidence (Children) Act 1997* (NSW) compared to the other states. NSW adopted a rights-based approach. Section 27, for example, says "[c]hildren have a right to presence of a supportive person while giving evidence." Section 29 says children have a "right to alternative arrangements for giving evidence when accused is unrepresented." The legislation drafted by other states did not adopt such an approach, preferring instead to say children are "entitled" to supportive measures (*Acts Amendment (Evidence of Children and Others) Act 1992* (WA) s 106E(1); *Evidence Act Amendment Act 1988* (SA) s 5). Dr Macdonald, member for Manly, moved the matter of child sexual assault as a matter of public importance in NSW Parliament on 20 November 1997, saying "I seek to push the boundaries for the judicial system...The system needs a major overhaul...The current system is anachronistic and does not work: it fails our children" (NSW Legislative Assembly, Parliamentary Debates, 20 November 1997, Dr Macdonald (4.15 pm)). The legal effect of rights language was negligible, particularly as the word only appears in the title of the relevant section rather than in the substantive body of it. It is a notable attempt, though, to frame the reform as a children's rights issue following the 1989 United Nations Convention of the Rights of the Child, as well as the Australian Law Reform Commission Issues Paper 17, *Speaking for ourselves: Children and the legal process—Kids Issues Paper* (ALRC and HREOC 1996; Chaaya 1998, 262–278).

Conclusion

One cannot help but wonder what Justice Brennan would think, were he to enter a contemporary courtroom to see a child giving evidence today. What would the members of the Australian Federation of Women Voters, the National Council of Women and the Women's Services Guild think if they walked into a criminal courtroom today to see a child giving evidence via a remote video-link? They might be amused to see their recommendations being implemented nearly a century after they had first suggested them. Perhaps they would be bitterly disappointed to find what was so obvious to them all those decades ago was only now being recognised by the justice system as appropriate, or even necessary. When the Australian Law Reform Commission said the traditional legal system had done little to support children in court, they were right. This chapter demonstrates how many calls for reform were disregarded. But they were wrong, too. Notwithstanding a lack of legislative reform over the century, there is substantial evidence supportive measures were implemented informally and pragmatically.

The appetite for reform of courtroom procedure continues apace in the twenty-first century. An expanding body of research demonstrating the significant impact courtroom environments can have on child witnesses, as well as concerns raised on more than one occasion by the Royal Commission into Institutional Responses to Child Sexual Abuse (McClellan 2006, 2015) have led to legislative reforms across the country (Zajac et al. 2012; Li 2012; Jackson 2003; Cossins 2006, 299; 2009, 68; Lindsay et al. 1997). Among many reforms introduced more recently are the *Statutes Amendment (Vulnerable Witnesses) Act 2015* (SA) (s 7(2)(a)(i)—amends the *Evidence Act 1929* (SA)), which allow for children and vulnerable witnesses to give evidence in informal surroundings. New South Wales has introduced a specialist child sexual offence evidence programme through the *Criminal Procedure Amendment (Child Sexual Offence Evidence Pilot) Act 2015* (NSW), passed in November 2015. In August 2016, the Victorian Law Reform Commission published its report, *The Role of Victims of Crime in the Criminal Trial Process*, containing comprehensive recommendations for amendments to existing procedures relating to child witnesses (Victorian Law Reform Commission, *Role of Victims of Crime in the Criminal Justice Process* (August, 2016) ch 8, 213). Its intermediary pilot programme began in July 2018. South Australia, Victoria and New South Wales are in the process of trialling, or have introduced, specialist courts for sex offences in 2017. Queensland has also introduced changes to its courtroom procedures for the prosecution of child sexual offence charges (*Criminal Code (Child Sexual Offences Reform) and Other Legislation Amendment Bill 2019* (Qld)). Changes to the courtroom environment are just one part of the child witness story, though. Despite such significant changes to courtroom procedures, child witnesses must still undergo the traditional examination and cross-examination process, and the issue remains of how the law treats the evidence of children.

References

Acts Amendment (Evidence of Children and Others) Act 1992 (WA).

Australian Law Reform Commission and Australian Human Rights and Equal Opportunity Commission. *Seen and Heard: Priority for Children in the Legal Process*, vol. 84 (Report No 84, 1997).

Australian Law Reform Commission and Australian Human Rights and Equal Opportunity Commission. *Speaking for ourselves: Children and the legal process – Kids Issues Paper* (Issues Paper No 17, 1996).

Australian Law Reform Commission. *Report 63 – Children's Evidence: Closed Circuit TV* (Report No 63, 1992).

Bentham, Jeremy. 1843. *The Works of Jeremy Bentham*, vol. 4. Edinburgh: William Tait.

Blewer, Robyn. 2017. "Making Kiddies at Home in Court: Supporting Child Witnesses in Twentieth-Century Australian Courtrooms." *Law & History* 4 (1): 62–87.

Bosland, Jason, and Jonathan Gill. 2014. "The Principle of Open Justice and the Judicial Duty to Give Public Reasons." *Melbourne University Law Review* 38: 482–524.

Brewer, Holly. 2005. *By Birth or Consent: Children, Law, and the Anglo-American Revolution in Authority.* Chapel Hill: University of North Carolina Press.

Cairns Post (Qld: 1909–1954). "Court Procedure." April 14, 1944.

Cashmore, Judy. 1990. "The Use of Video Technology for Child Witnesses." *Monash University Law Review* 16: 228–250.

Chaaya, Michael. 1998. "Children's Evidence in Sexual Abuse Cases: The Need for a Radical Reappraisal." *Current Issues in Criminal Justice* 9 (3): 262–278.

Commonwealth of Australia. *Royal Commission on Human Relationships*, vol. 5 (Final Report, 1978).

Cossins, Anne. 2006. "Prosecuting Child Sexual Assault Cases: Are Vulnerable Witness Protections Enough?" *Current Issues in Criminal Justice* 18 (2): 299–317.

Cossins, Annie. 2009. "Cross-Examination in Child Sexual Assault Trials: Evidentiary Safeguard or an Opportunity to Confuse." *Melbourne University Law Review* 33 (1): 68–104.

Crimes (Child Assault) Amendment Act 1985 (NSW).

Crimes (Child Victim Evidence) Amendment Act 1990 (NSW).

Crimes (Sexual Assault) Amendment Act 1981 (NSW).

Crimes (Sexual Offences) Act 1991 (Vic).

Crimes Act 1900 (NSW).

Criminal Code (Child Sexual Offences Reform) and Other Legislation Amendment Bill 2019 (Qld).

Criminal Code Amendment Act 1945 (Qld).

Criminal Code, Evidence Act and Other Acts Amendment Act 1989 (Qld).

Criminal Law (Sexual Offences) Act 1978 (Qld).

Criminal Law Consolidation Amendment Act 1885 (SA).

Criminal Procedure Amendment (Child Sexual Offence Evidence Pilot) Act 2015 (NSW).

Daily Herald (Adelaide, SA: 1910–1924). "Indecent Assault." November 19, 1913.

Ellison, Louise. 2002. *The Adversarial Process and the Vulnerable Witness.* Oxford, UK: Oxford University Press.

Evening News (Sydney, NSW: 1869–1931). "No Closed Doors." May 9, 1930.

Evidence (Children) Act 1997 (NSW).

Evidence (Vulnerable Witnesses) Amendment Act 1993 (SA).

Evidence Act 1929 (SA).

Evidence Act Amendment Act (No 3) 1984 (SA).

Evidence Act Amendment Act 1988 (SA).

Evidence Amendment (Children and Special Witnesses) 1995 (Tas).

Finnane, Mark, Andy Kaladelfos, Alana Piper, Yorick Smaal, Robyn Blewer, and Lisa Durnian, et al. *The Prosecution Project Database.* https://prosecutionproject.griffith.edu.au/prosecutions (version 1, 17 July 2016).

Fisk, Catherine, and Robert W. Gordon. 2011. "Foreword: "Law As…" Theory and Method in Legal History." *University of California Irvine Law Review* 1 (3): 519–540.

Freedman, Estelle B. 2011. "'Crimes which Startle and Horrify': Gender, Age, and the Racialization of Sexual Violence in White American Newspapers, 1870–1900." *Journal of the History of Sexuality* 20 (3): 465–497.

Goulburn Herald (NSW: 1881–1907). "Tragedy at Queanbeyan." August 26, 1903.

Hay, Douglas. 1984. "The Criminal Prosecution in England and Its Historians." *The Modern Law Review* 47 (1): 1–29.

Healesville Guardian (Lilydale, Vic: 1942–1954). "Ex-Jockey for Trial on Serious Charges." January 27, 1956.

Jackson, Hal. 2003. "Child Witnesses in the Western Australian Criminal Courts." *Criminal Law Journal Sydney* 27 (4): 199–210.

Justices Act 1886 (Qld).

Li, Elaine Yi. 2012. "Children and Jury in Court." *Cross-Sections: The Bruce Hall Academic Journal* VIII: 131–144.

Lindsay, R. C. L., Joanna D. Pozzulo, Wendy Craig, Kang Lee, and Samantha Corber. 1997. "Simultaneous Lineups, Sequential Lineups, and Showups: Eyewitness Identification Decisions of Adults and Children." *Law and Human Behavior* 21 (4): 391–404.

Maryborough Chronicle, Wide Bay and Burnett Advertiser (Qld: 1860–1947). "Nolle Prosequi Entered." February 14, 1936.

McClellan, Peter. 2006. "Who Is Telling the Truth? Psychology, Common Sense and the Law." *The Australian Law Journal* 80 (10): 655–666.

McClellan, The Hon Justice Peter. "Professional Knowledge and Judicial Understanding." Keynote address, 14th Australasian Conference on Child Abuse and Neglect (Auckland, 31 March 2015).

Mirror (Perth, WA: 1921–1956). "Little Girl of 7 Alleges Man's Shocking Conduct." January 13, 1940.

Mirror (Perth, WA: 1921–1956). "Florance Case." July 31, 1926.

Mirror (Perth, WA: 1921–1956). "Girl Denies She Told Police of Alleged Offence." February 6, 1954.

Mulcahy, Linda. 2011. *Legal Architecture: Justice, Due Process and the Place of Law.* London: Routledge.

Myers, John E.B. 1996. "A Decade of International Reform to Accommodate Child Witnesses." *Criminal Justice and Behavior* 23 (2): 402–422.

Narandera Argus and Riverina Advertiser (NSW: 1893–1953). "William Fisher Committed for Trial." September 5, 1941.

National Advocate (Bathurst, NSW: 1889–1954). "Child's Death." October 1, 1941.

National Advocate (Bathurst, NSW: 1889–1954). "Terrible Charge." July 16, 1930.

New South Wales, Parliamentary Debates, Legislative Assembly 20 November 1997, Dr Macdonald (4.15 pm).

Queensland Justices Association, 7 June 1933, Queensland State Archives, Item ID8688, Legal papers.

Queensland State Archives, Queensland State Archives Item ID95466, Depositions and Indictments. *R v Mary Ryan.*

Queensland State Archives, Queensland State Archives Item ID95466, Depositions and Indictments. Letters Patent for Mary Ryan's daughters, Mary, Margaret and Bridget, issued 28 May 1900.

Queensland Times, Ipswich Herald and General Advertiser (Qld: 1861–1908). "Suspicion of Murder." March 6, 1900.

R v Hamilton (1930) 30 SR (NSW) 277.

R v Smellie (1919) 14 Cr App R 128.

R v West [1992] 1 Qd R 227.

Scott v Scott [1913] AC 417.

Simpson, Antony E. 2004. "Popular Perceptions of Rape as a Capital Crime in Eighteenth-Century England." *Law and History Review* 22 (1): 27–70.

Spencer, John R, and Rhona H. Flin. 1990. *The Evidence of Children: The Law and the Psychology.* Oxford: Blackstone.

State Children's Act 1907 (WA).

State Records NSW: Court Reporting Office, NRS 2714, Central Criminal Court transcripts, Criminal F to H [6/2135], *R v William Fisher*, 29 September 1941, 12–13.

Statutes Amendment (Vulnerable Witnesses) Act 2015 (SA).

Tanenhaus, David S., and William Bush. 2007. "Toward a History of Children as Witnesses." *Indiana Law Journal* 82 (4): 1059–1075.

The Advertiser (Adelaide, SA: 1889–1931). "A Chief Justice and a Child Witness." February 22, 1923.

The Age (Melbourne, Vic: 1854–1954). "Woman's Interests." May 14, 1930.

The Age (Melbourne, Vic: 1854–1954). "Queensland." February 27, 1900.

The Brisbane Courier (Qld: 1864–1933). "Alleged Murder at North Pine." February 27, 1900.

The Central Queensland Herald (Rockhampton, Qld: 1930–1956). "Evidence Given by Child." January 20, 1938.

The Courier-Mail (Brisbane, Qld: 1933–1954). "Tighter Laws Urged to Cut Sex Crimes." October 26, 1944.

The Daily News (Perth, WA: 1882–1950). "Child Witnesses Dress Rehearsed." September 30, 1941.

The Daily News (Perth, WA: 1882–1950). "Conspiracy Charge." September 10, 1907.

The Journal (Adelaide, SA: 1912–1923). "A Serious Charge." November 18, 1913.

The King v The Governor of Lewes Prison [1917] 2 KB 254.

The Register (Adelaide, SA: 1901–1929). "Children in the Courts." March 20, 1926.

The Richmond River Herald and Northern Districts Advertiser (NSW: 1886–1942). "Horrible Case." January 21, 1938.

The Sydney Morning Herald (NSW: 1842–1954). "Death Sentence Commuted." December 31, 1941.

The Telegraph (Brisbane, Qld: 1872–1947). "Views Differ on Children in Court." May 31, 1941.

The Tocsin (Melbourne, Vic: 1897–1906). "State Galleries." December 8, 1904.

The Week (Brisbane, Qld: 1876–1934). "Tarragindi Outrage." April 26, 1933.

The West Australian (Perth, WA: 1879–1954). "Children as Witnesses." September 21, 1934.

The West Australian (Perth, WA: 1879–1954). "Letters to the Editor." September 20, 1950.

The West Australian (Perth, WA: 1879–1954). "Women Justices." August 7, 1926.

Townsville Daily Bulletin (Qld: 1907–1954). "Women's Protest." June 12, 1933.

Truth (Brisbane, Qld: 1900–1954). "Behind-Doors Justice…" May 19, 1946.

Truth (Brisbane, Qld: 1900–1954). "Tarragindi Outrage." April 30, 1933.

Truth (Brisbane, Qld: 1900–1954). "Tiny Girl's Ghastly End: Father Decries Aged Accused in Court." September 7, 1941.

Truth (Sydney, NSW: 1894–1954). "Child Witness Sits on Juror's Knee." September 20, 1925.

Truth (Sydney, NSW: 1894–1954). "Closed Courts." May 25, 1930.

Truth (Sydney, NSW: 1894–1954). "Old Man Found Guilty of Strangling Tiny Tot." October 5, 1941.

United Kingdom, *Committee on Sexual Offences against Young Persons, Command Paper 2561,* (London: HMSO, 1925): 27. Cited in Commonwealth of Australia, *Royal Commission on Human Relationships*, vol. 5 (Final Report, 1978).

Victorian Law Reform Commission, *Role of Victims of Crime in the Criminal Justice Process*, August, 2016.

Warwick Daily News (Qld: 1919–1954). "Child's Murder." September 2, 1941.

Western Star (Roma) (Toowoomba, Qld: 1948–1954). "Latemore Committed for Trial at Next Sittings of Criminal Circuit Court in Roma on Hit-Run Charges - Victim Gives Her Evidence in Plaster." August 19, 1949.

Westralian Worker (Perth, WA: 1900–1951). "'Iceberg' Irvine." July 17, 1908.

Zajac, Rachel, Sarah O'Neill, and Harlene Hayne. 2012. "Disorder in the Courtroom? Child Witnesses under Cross-Examination." *Developmental Review* 32 (3): 181–204.

6

"What the Nipper Said Was True": Examination

It is one thing for a child to demonstrate their capacity to give evidence, or to cope with the courtroom environment. They still need to tell their story. They still must be able to speak, to hear and understand questions, and to respond to those questions. For all the reforms to witness procedure considered in the previous chapters, oral testimony remains the primary method for courts to receive a child's evidence, and cross–examination is still the primary method of testing a child's evidence. Even with the reforms that have allowed for pre-recorded evidence and the acceptance of police interviews as evidence-in-chief, the spoken word is still central to the adversarial trial (Cossins 2009, 68).

This chapter begins with a brief overview of the oral tradition and the challenges examination could present for witnesses, before considering the roles of prosecutors and defence counsel in examining and cross-examining witnesses. Carrying the burden of proving the Crown's case in a way deemed fair to the accused was difficult enough for prosecutors, who were often shouldered with additional burdens when calling a child witness. Children who simply did not understand what was required of them, or who were unable to swear an oath or were intimidated by the

R. Blewer, *Child Witnesses in Twentieth Century Australian Courtrooms*, Palgrave Histories of Policing, Punishment and Justice,
https://doi.org/10.1007/978-3-030-69791-4_6

courtroom environment frequently further challenged the prosecutor. The decisions prosecutors had to make were not simple. Should they seek permission to treat a difficult witness as hostile? Should they effectively give up and discontinue a matter altogether where a child was unable to give evidence—or should they take the risk of carrying on in the absence of that testimony? These decisions could have significant consequences for the child, the defendant and the administration of justice.

At the other end of the bar table, defence counsel had their own, equally challenging concerns. They carried the responsibility of defending the accused and their client's right to test the Crown's case. This could literally be a matter of life and death for the defendant. Traditionally lauded as "the greatest legal engine ever invented for the discovery of truth" (Wigmore, as cited in Spencer and Flin 1993, 270), cross-examination is celebrated by the common law still. Cross-examination of children receives considerable attention in research conducted from the late twentieth century onwards (Spencer and Lamb 2012; Cossins 2009; Bowden et al. 2014). Awareness of the problems of cross-examining children is evident, though, for much of the twentieth century. Defendants are found to have instructed their counsel not to cross-examine the child witness. Some are found to have avoided it where they were representing themselves—and even where it would likely have resulted in their acquittal. In 1930 the Australian Federation of Women Voters called for reforms to existing procedure (*The Age* 1930, 1). They wanted all questions from the prosecutor and defence to be put to child witnesses through the court instead of being questioned directly by the barristers or defendant. Nothing came of this proposal at the time. Instead, throughout the twentieth century children were required to give their evidence orally, beginning with examination by the prosecutor. Now, in the 2020s, intermediary schemes like that envisaged by the Australian Federation of Women Voters are becoming commonplace.

The final part of the chapter considers reforms to the cross-examination of children during the last quarter of the twentieth century and beyond. Even though there was considerable enthusiasm for casting aside old methods of interviewing children, of testing their competency and for adopting modern technology to facilitate the process, examination and cross-examination remained largely impervious to reform.

The defendant's right to cross-examine children personally was abolished during these decades, but otherwise there was extraordinarily little change. Despite knowing the dangers to a child of participating in this process, it seems the system did not dare entertain thoughts of a different way of dealing with the evidence of children other than via this adversarial process.

The Oral Tradition

The common law adversarial system's reliance upon the oral testimony of witnesses in the twentieth century is said to have been the result of a decision in England in the thirteenth century to adopt the jury trial as the preferred means of administering criminal justice (Bronitt and Mares 2004; Hostettler and Turney 2008). Given oral testimony replaced the trial by ordeal, this was a sensible move. Eight hundred years or so on, however, the common law was still grappling with some of the more problematic aspects of relying on the spoken word, including, importantly, whether this was the best way of arriving at the truth (Steffen 1988, 799; Wilson et al. 2005).

In the late eighteenth century, legal scholar and barrister, Sir Geoffrey Gilbert, concerned with what would be the "best evidence" available for a trial, argued the best evidence would be written documents. Oral testimony was the least desirable form of proof in his view (Langbein 1996, 1194). Jeremy Bentham, however, disagreed with Gilbert and instead declared oral testimony of witnesses in court superior to all other forms of evidence. Bentham called witnesses "the eyes and ears of justice" (Bentham in Magner 1995, 68). While Bentham and Gilbert were arguing over the best source and mode of evidence, trial procedures in England were in a "state of flux" (May 2003, 1983). Examination of witnesses was then, in the 1700s, as it had been long beforehand, a matter for the judge. It was judicial officers who examined the accused who, precluded from being represented in court, otherwise had to speak on his or her own behalf (Struve 2008, 443). Judicial officers "dominated the examination of witnesses while parties played only a modest role in the interrogative process" (Landsman 1990, 1150). At this time, the primary objective of criminal trials was to give the accused an opportunity to respond to the charges against him or her (Langbein 2005, 30). Defendants were effectively forced to prove their innocence. Public prosecutors were expected to exercise restraint in response to the power imbalance that existed between themselves as legal practitioners and the accused. By the end of the nineteenth century oral testimony was still the preferred form of evidence—only by this time it was lawyers, not judges, who dominated court proceedings (Langbein 2005; Radzinowicz 1948; May 2003). The adversarial trial had evolved to become a battle between two competing sides.

In this new adversarial environment, the potential for the examination process to be problematic was recognised. Limits were placed on particular forms of questioning witnesses. In South Australia, for example, questions deemed "irrelevant" and "vexatious" were restricted from 1888 (*Evidence Further Amendment Act 1888* (SA) s 2). When considering what was relevant or irrelevant, questions attacking the character and credibility of the witness were to be particularly scrutinised by the court (*Evidence Further Amendment Act 1888* (SA) s 3). The following year, in 1889, Tasmania passed legislation allowing witnesses to refuse to answer questions intended to injure their character, or which were indecent or scandalous, intended to insult or annoy or involved unnecessary imputations (*The Evidence Act 1889* (Tas) ss 3–6). Victoria followed suit in 1890 (*Oaths and Evidence Act 1890* (Vic) s 9, ss 11–12), and Western Australia in 1906, where the relevant provisions were contained within a part of the *Evidence Act 1906* (WA) titled "Protection of Witnesses." New South Wales introduced limits in 1922 (*Evidence (Amendment) Act 1922* (NSW) s 3). These provisions recognised the potential for examination, and cross-examination particularly, to be challenging, if not harmful, to witnesses, at least in terms of their reputation. They were drafted, however, in terms that gave judges substantial discretion. Section three of the *Evidence (Amendment) Act 1922* (NSW), for example, said the court:

> shall have a discretion to disallow the question, if in its opinion the matter is so remote in time, or of such a nature that an admission of its

truth would not materially affect the credibility of the witness. (*Evidence (Amendment) Act 1922* (NSW) s 3)

It was not difficult for defence counsel, wanting to create doubt about a child's testimony, to convince a judge that questioning a young girl about whether she had been wearing lipstick was necessary in fairness to the accused (*Williamstown Chronicle* 1954, 4; Featherstone and Kaladelfos 2016). So too was questioning a witness about their reputation or sexual history justified on the basis they were relevant to issues of consent or credibility (Commonwealth of Australia, *Royal Commission on Human Relationships* (Final Report, 1978, vol 5, 189). Historians Lisa Featherstone and Andy Kaladelfos have considered the prosecution of sex crimes, including those against children, in the 1950s and identified the examination process as particularly problematic (Featherstone and Kaladelfos 2016; Zajac et al. 2017, 237). Similarly, historian Jill Bavin-Mizzi's study of the testimony of girls in sexual assault trials demonstrated the fine line girls walked between appearing too knowledgeable of matters related to sex and appearing too innocent to describe the offence accurately (1995, 29). Questions, it was argued, would help expose the "dishonest, mistaken or unreliable witness" and uncover inconsistencies and inaccuracies in the witness's evidence (Ellison 1999, 35). Even though these legislative reforms of the late nineteenth and early twentieth centuries were aimed at protecting witnesses from the potential harm associated with a public cross-examination, the accused's entitlement to a fair trial remained the primary concern of the court and took precedence over the rights or interests of witnesses (Mason 1995, 7).

A common criticism of the examination process made by scholars and practitioners is the use of a question-and-answer form of examining witnesses, rather than focusing on the narrative (Mason 1995, 7). But having witnesses tell their story has never been the objective of the adversarial trial. Indeed, finding the truth is not even the objective (Eades 2008, 210; Finkelstein 2011, 136; Green 1992, 699). Witnesses are there to assist the parties to the litigation (Plater 2006, 111). The importance of the oral testimony of witnesses, including children, was summed up by the Australian High Court in 1987, in *Butera v Director of Public Prosecutions for the State of Victoria*, where Chief Justice Mason and Justices

Brennan and Deane declared oral evidence gives a trial "the atmosphere which, though intangible, is often critical to the jury's estimate of the witnesses" (*Butera v. Director of Public Prosecutions for the State of Victoria* (1987) 76 ALR 45 at 50).

Prosecutors

As lawyer and legal scholar, Dr. David Plater has observed, the role of the prosecutor has erroneously been described as one of a "partisan persecutor bent on securing the conviction of an accused" (Plater 2006, 111). The role of the prosecutor could more accurately be described as that of a quasi-judicial "minister of justice" who, in prosecuting criminal offences on behalf of the state, must do so with detachment and fairness (Plater 2006, 111). For most of the twentieth century, where cases involved the testimony of child witnesses, the burden of proving the Crown's case was arguably an even heavier one than it is now. Prosecutors needed child witnesses to pass the oath test. They needed the child to be physically, emotionally and mentally capable of giving evidence in a courtroom and recounting events that were likely traumatic for them and thus difficult to speak about in front of a room full of strangers. Prosecutors might have had little or no knowledge or warning of how a child might struggle with the process until the hearing had begun and the child was called. To bring a child witness into a courtroom, while often vital to the administration of criminal justice, also presented a risk for the prosecution.

In 1944, during a trial in Newcastle, New South Wales, a nine-year-old girl was giving her evidence. When the prosecutor indicated he had no further questions for the child, the young girl said, "I am not finished yet" (*Newcastle Morning Herald and Miners"* 1944, 6). What did she mean? There are several ways her comment could be interpreted. It could have been an indication she did not understand the process and had more to say about the events in question. This makes sense. Children, particularly as young as nine, would be unlikely to understand the nature of adversarial trials, and whether the prosecutor had all the evidence they wanted from the child and did not want her to continue. The prosecutor may have known whatever else she wanted to say was inadmissible. The child may simply have not understood this and was struggling to comprehend why she had been stopped in the middle of her story. Defence counsel took a different view. They used the girl's comment to argue she must have rehearsed her evidence, for how else could she have known she was not finished? This argument was successful. In summing up the case for the jury, the judge said the child was a "precocious young miss, probably named after a film star, and determined to carry on tradition by acting a part" (*Newcastle Morning Herald and Miners* 1944, 6). In another case in New South Wales in June 1903, a prosecutor asked five-year-old Hilda to identify the defendant. He asked her if she could see "the man." Hilda confirmed she could see him. "Where?" She did not know. Unable to get an answer from the girl, the prosecutor painstakingly went through each man in the courtroom, including those in the public gallery. "Was it I? Was it that man up there? Was it any of the men at the back there?" Little Hilda could not say. Finally, he obtained permission from the magistrate to lead the witness, saying to her directly as he pointed to the accused, "You see that man there? Is that the man?" "Yes!" (*The Daily News* 1903, 1).

While Hilda no doubt frustrated the prosecutor to the point where he asked for permission to lead her, an alternative way for prosecutors to deal with difficult child witnesses was to seek permission to treat the child as a hostile witness (*Mirror* 1945, 16; 1954, 5). Treating a witness as hostile carried significant risks. It could be at odds with the prosecutor's obligation to present the case fairly, especially where it appeared the prosecutor was trying to get the witness to change their evidence (Gans and Palmer 2014, 42). It could also give a jury the impression the prosecutor was being unfair to the child. For most of the twentieth century, however, prosecutors were under no obligation to treat child witnesses fairly. Their obligation in bringing the case on behalf of the state was to do what was necessary to prosecute the charge in a way that was impartial and fair to the accused.

A 1913 case from New South Wales exemplifies the dilemmas prosecutors faced in treating children as hostile witnesses. On 7 February 1913, Mr. Charles Duchatel, a Sheriff's Officer, was travelling in a sulky with his son when he saw a man by a creek with a young girl. Based on what he had seen, Duchatel told his son to go to the nearby hotel and ring the police while he would chase after the pair. After catching up to them, the girl told Duchatel her name was "Cissie" and the man was her father. The man had then run away. Sergeant Sheehy attended the scene and took nine-year-old Millie (which was her real name) to confront the suspect, John Rope. In front of Rope and Sheehy, Millie made a statement and Sheehy arrested Rope (*National Advocate* 1913, 4). Rope was charged with indecently assaulting Millie. At the committal hearing, Millie repeated her allegations (*The Bathurst Times* 1913, 3). Rope was committed to stand trial.

Millie was subsequently called to give evidence at the Rope's trial at the Bathurst Quarter Sessions on 20 February 1913. She stepped into the witness box and was questioned by Acting Judge Hamilton on her understanding of the oath. She told His Honour that if she did not "kiss the book she would tell lies" and "if she did not tell the truth…she would be put in the 'burny' fire." Millie confirmed she had been to Sunday School and "knew it was wrong not to tell the truth," whereupon the judge commented: "She knows more than we do." After being sworn, Millie's examination began in a mild, encouraging manner. "Come on Millie and tell us all about it" said the prosecutor, Mr. J.N. Mason (*National Advocate* 1913, 4). Millie denied saying the accused interfered with her and denied she had told Sergeant Sheehy this (*National Advocate* 1913, 4). She told the court she had undressed herself and Mr. Rope had been across the other side of the creek. Millie was reported to have "invariably replied" to Mr. Mason's questions by saying "No, that man did not interfere with me" (*National Advocate* 1913, 4).

This was not the answer Mason expected. He sought permission to treat Millie as a hostile witness. Rope's defence counsel objected, but the judge remarked "[e]ither she or Sergeant Sheehy is telling lies, and we must try and find out who it is." Throughout what was reported as a "rigorous" cross-examination by Mason, Millie denied "again and again" she had been told not to say anything about the accused. At the conclusion of the Crown case, Rope's defence barrister, McIntosh, asked Judge Hamilton to direct the jury to acquit the accused on the basis there was no evidence Rope had indecently assaulted Millie. Hamilton declined the application, saying the jury "were the best judges" of the evidence. Judge Hamilton summed up the proceedings for the jury, telling them the case was one of the most extraordinary cases he had come across in his years of criminal court experience. Hamilton observed that the girl's initial allegations had been made immediately after the offence, when there had been no chance of anyone attempting to induce her to lie—but then Millie's evidence at the trial had contradicted what she had said prior to Rope's arrest. Rope was acquitted but, perhaps indicating the jury thought the true verdict ought to be otherwise, the jury foreman asked that Mr. Duchatel be commended for his actions in chasing down Rope on the day in question (*National Advocate* 1913, 4).

Another example of a prosecutor treating a child as a hostile witness was found in a committal hearing in Western Australia in 1945. A thirteen-year-old complainant was not providing the testimony police prosecutor, Detective Sergeant Triat, was expecting from her. The girl had been called to give evidence of an alleged indecent assault committed upon her by a thirty-seven-year-old soldier, who had been living with her family at the time. With "tears trickling down her cheeks," she told Triat she could not remember what had happened. "…But it was so long ago." Permitted to treat the child as a hostile witness, Triat said "Look here; you know very well what happened. The quicker you tell us, the quicker we'll get it over." The girl was reported to have then "told her story begrudgingly" (*Mirror* 1945, 16). At the end of that hearing, the defendant was committed to stand trial. He subsequently pleaded guilty to the offence as charged and was sentenced to twelve months' imprisonment. Of course, there would be many reasons for a defendant to plead guilty. In this case, however, whether the defendant's plea was motivated by a desire to obviate the need for the thirteen-year-old girl to give evidence again at trial is worth considering. He does not appear to have received any concessions in pleading guilty. The charge he pleaded to was not a lesser charge, nor was the sentence more lenient for that time. In his sentencing remarks, the judge—in a public courtroom—called the child a "precocious type" who had given her "encouragement and her full consent" to the offence. Had the defendant exercised his right to a trial, rather than plead guilty, it was highly likely he would have been acquitted given the girl's "hostile" demeanour at the committal, coupled with a judge who had decided the girl was precocious. And yet he pleaded guilty and received a twelve-month prison sentence.

For most of the twentieth century there was little change to how prosecutors dealt with children in court. It was only in the 1990s the role of the prosecutor was reimagined as far as their relationship with child witnesses was concerned. In its 1997 *Seen and Heard* report, the Australian Law Reform Commission recommended prosecutors at federal, state and territory levels do more to meet child witnesses before trials "to establish a rapport" and inform the child of the trial procedure (Australian Law Reform Commission, *Seen and Heard: Priority for Children in the Legal Process* (1997), vol 84, par 14.93). The Commission noted the steps Western Australia, New South Wales and parts of Queensland had already taken since 1990 in this regard (par 14.94). The adoption of video technology at the end of the twentieth century had a marked impact on the prosecutor's role at trial. Pre-recorded police interviews with children were admissible as evidence-in-chief in most states from the late 1990s (see for e.g *Evidence (Children) Act 1997* (NSW) s 11). This reform highlighted the importance of the police interview and their skills as interviewers. It also had the effect of reducing the prosecutor's contribution to the examination process (Westera et al. 2017, 253). While prosecutors appeared supportive of the use of video-taped interviews as evidence-in-chief, they have since reported reservations with respect to the impact videos might have on juror engagement, the relative informality of the interview in comparison with the courtroom, technical problems, reduced preparedness of the child for cross-examination and, importantly, the quality of the questioning and skills of the interviewer (Burrows and Powell 2014, 386).

Cross-Examination

Compared to prosecutors, who have more or less always been a part of the criminal trial process, defence barristers are a much more recent addition to the adversarial courtroom. Their presence in court was only widely accepted from the mid-to-late eighteenth century, but the increasing professionalisation of public prosecutors and the tendency for some Crown witnesses to employ unfair trial tactics often left defendants in a vulnerable position in court. This, in turn, led judicial officers to increasingly allow defence counsel to assist the accused in court (Langbein 2005, 110). Judges would call upon barristers sitting in the back of the courtroom, either waiting for their matter to come on or with nothing to do but watch the proceedings. Those men would have to step up to the bar table, whether they wanted to or not, and assist the defendant. This is what is now known as the cab rank rule for barristers. In this sense, the presence of defence counsel is about access to justice. Allowing defence counsel into criminal courtrooms was, however, according to John Langbein, the "fateful step" that "sent our procedure down the path toward what would become the adversary criminal trial" (Langbein 2005, 106). Since taking this "fateful step," cross-examination has become a fundamental part, indeed the defining feature, of the adversarial trial.

The *Evidence Act 1995* (Cth) defines cross-examination simply as the "questioning of a witness by a party other than the party who called the witness to give evidence" ("Dictionary – Other Expressions," pt2 s 2). The Australian law dictionary meaning of cross-examination, however, is "the questioning of an opponent's witness in order to show the unreliability of the witness's evidence-in-chief or to obtain concessions which support the cross-examiner's case" (Mann 2013). American judge and scholar, John Wigmore, famously lauded cross-examination as the "greatest legal engine ever invented for the discovery of truth," but also pointed out lawyers could use it to "make the truth appear like falsehood" (Wigmore in Bowden et al. 2014, 560). The idea that cross-examination is undertaken with the objective of showing the unreliability of a witness's evidence-in-chief, or to even make the truth appear like a falsehood, suggests the potential for such a process to be stressful, if not harmful, to the person being cross-examined. This has been particularly acknowledged in the context of child witnesses.

Eleven-year-old William was cross-examined in 1953 on his credibility and reported to have commenced "sobbing bitterly when admitting his aunt and uncle had taught him to tell lies since he was a little boy" (*Morning Bulletin* 1953, 4). As important as the cross-examination process is to the adversarial trial, contemporary research has demonstrated it causes children the most stress in terms of their participation in the prosecution process (Spencer and Lamb 2012; Cossins 2009; Bowden et al. 2014). Described as a form of "legitimated bullying," some legal scholars have argued cross-examination of children gives an accused "an illegitimate advantage" (Cossins 2009, 69; Bowden et al. 2014, 539). Counsel have been known, for example, to exploit a child witness's minor inconsistencies as to dates, locations and particular events to create doubt in the minds of jurors (Zajac et al. 2017, 236). This is still happening today, despite research showing such inconsistences tend to show children are being truthful, or at least that inconsistencies are not proof of dishonesty or lies (Zajac et al. 2012, 194). In employing traditional language of "putting to" a child a particular version of events, counsel can confuse a child who does not understand the adult-oriented criminal justice processes. Cross-examination has been proven to result in inconsistent and inaccurate evidence, with the potential to cause victims of crime further trauma (Cossins 2009, 74; Bowden et al. 2014, 550). Zajac, O'Neill and Hayne have identified several problematic questioning techniques frequently employed by examiners, such as challenging a child's credibility, asking leading or suggestive questions, and asking questions regarding highly specific or peripheral details (Zajac et al. 2012, 181).

The adversarial trial is inherently one of strategy. There is evidence defence barristers have long employed various tactics to undermine child witnesses during their cross-examination. In a case in 1913, the defendant had been charged with exposing himself to two little girls. At the committal hearing, one of the girls was cross-examined on a "number of points intended to prove that the police had made up her statements by leading questions." The child responded by answering "yes" to almost every question from the defendant's barrister. The prosecutor, Mr. Brown, was reported to have drawn "the attention of the Bench to the trend of the cross-examination in drawing out such answers." The magistrate agreed the girl's answers "served to show how dangerous such evidence was" (*Independent* 1913, 1). It is not clear to what the magistrate was referring in calling this evidence dangerous—whether the practice was successfully drawing out the dangers of police writing statements for children; or the barrister's strategy was dangerous in the effect it was having on the child, who was agreeing to everything asked of her; or whether the practice was drawing out the child's lies. The other girl, nine, gave evidence that corroborated her friend's. She was "emphatic" the defendant was the man who had exposed himself to them. At the conclusion of the hearing, the magistrate told the court he believed the children were telling the truth, but the evidence was not sufficient to commit the defendant to stand trial (*Independent* 1913, 1).

Drawing on, if not exploiting, common attitudes towards women and girls was a frequent—and frequently successful—strategy used by defence counsel throughout the century. A girl in 1919, in response to leading questions, admitted knowing it would be wrong to go with the defendant to his room, but said she did not know it would be wrong to meet him on the hill (*Geraldton Guardian* 1919, 3). Girls as young as nine years old were cross-examined on their reputation for going with boys (*The Daily News* 1910, 3), for not screaming at the time of an offence (*Truth* 1915, 5), and for wearing lipstick (*Williamstown Chronicle* 1954, 4). A press report of a trial in Queensland in 1926 does not refer to the cross-examination of the child in question but does give an idea of the narrative the defence barrister built throughout the case. Beginning with his opening address to the jury, the barrister said this case would show to the jury there was a need for laws to protect men from "certain young women," just as there was a law to protect girls. In his closing address to the jury, the barrister drew attention to the girl's clothing at the time of the attack, and commented she looked older than her real age. The defence barrister reminded the jury

> it was difficult to tell the ages of women these days...It seemed that the older they got the shorter they wore their skirts. The old toast had been change[d]. Instead of saying "the Ladies, God Bless [sic] them," they now said, "the Ladies, God Dress Them." The girl in question looked to be more than 17 years, and spoke as if she were older. Apparently she wanted cave men handling and did not get it. (*Daily Standard* 1926, 1).

The jury found the defendant not guilty (*The Prosecution Project Database* Trial ID #46403, Sidney Cameron 1926).

Exploiting inconsistencies, however minor, in a child's testimony was another common theme in cross-examinations of children. The approach often served to reinforce commonly held assumptions about the capacity of children to fantasise or lie. The case of Myrtle Slape, in Adelaide in

1917, illustrates this point very well. Slape was charged with ill-treating her stepdaughter, Rosa, aged eight. The defendant was German, so the reports of the case need to be read with the climate of the First World War in mind. Nevertheless, at the trial in the Police Court, the prosecutor said the evidence would show "unparalleled ferocity on the part of one human being to another" (*The Advertiser* 1917a, 9). Eight-year-old Rosa gave evidence she was beaten every day, burned with the iron, had her head bumped against the wall and was struck on the head with a hairbrush. Rosa was described as in a "highly strung, nervous condition" while giving evidence in court, where she stood next to Miss C.E. Dixon, one of the justices of the peace on the bench. Counsel had "considerable difficulty" in taking the child's evidence. There were frequent adjournments "because the child fretted." During her cross-examination, Rosa was questioned about having told her father she had hit her eye on the bed stand, and that the iron had fallen off the stand and connected with her hand. When her cross-examination was finished "the child collapsed into the arms of Miss Dixon." The prosecutor said he "would not subject her to re-examination until she had thoroughly recovered" (*Daily Herald* 1917, 3).

While Rosa rested, the trial continued with other witnesses. Medical evidence verified the physical injuries, including the extensive burns to Rosa's hands and face. The child's aunt gave evidence she had seen the child with bruises and black eyes on at least five occasions and that the defendant, Rosa's stepmother Myrtle Slape, had said to her "I will beat her when and where I like" (*The Advertiser* 1917a, 9). Slape, in her defence, claimed the child's injuries were all results of accidents, aside from one whipping issued in chastisement. While the other witnesses were giving their evidence, Rosa had fallen asleep. "It would be too much for anyone's feelings to awaken her," said the prosecutor, Mr. Smith (*Daily Herald* 1917, 3). Slape was found guilty by the magistrates on the bench and fined £50 plus £25 costs.

Slape appealed against her conviction and won. In delivering his decision, Justice Murray referred at length to Rosa's cross-examination. The inconsistencies the defence barrister had drawn out of the child were the determining factor in Myrtle's acquittal. Justice Murray noted the "entirely different" accounts of the burning Rosa had given. In her evidence-in-chief, Rosa had testified her stepmother had pushed her into the corner of the room and burned her on the hands and face, while she still had her school dress on. In cross-examination, however, Rosa had said the incident was an accident and she did not have her school dress on (*The Advertiser* 1917b, 7). Justice Murray had initially thought the girl may have been referring to two different occasions, but he was "forced to abandon that idea by her own language." Rosa had spoken only of one burn. This was, Murray said, a "contradiction which showed that the child's evidence was untrustworthy." Myrtle's appeal was upheld, and her conviction quashed (*Daily Herald* 1917, 6). Contemporary research demonstrates inconsistencies like those in Rosa's evidence do not necessarily indicate a particular event did not occur, or a child is lying (Zajac et al. 2012, 194), yet Justice Murray decided the inconsistencies demonstrated the child's testimony could not be trusted.

Prior to this trial, the State Children's Department had commenced action in the Children's Court charging Rosa with being a neglected child. Those proceedings were suspended while the criminal charges against Myrtle Slape were being prosecuted. The matter resumed after Myrtle's successful appeal. The medical evidence from Myrtle's trial was tendered again in this hearing (*Daily Herald* 1918, 3). The Children's Court, however, was not bound by the same rules of evidence as the trial court. The State Department tendered further evidence it argued proved Rosa's treatment at the hands of her stepmother went beyond an acceptable level of "chastisement." According to their records, evidence of Rosa's injuries included:

1. Mark on end of nose (July, 1917).
2. Swollen and bruised left eye (July 19, 1917) caused by bedhead of corks.
3. Burn on wrist (July, 1917).
4. Black bruise upper part of each arm (July 20) caused by father's strapping.
5. Number of bruises on both arms (July 21, 1917).
6. Marks on lip and chin.
7. Mark three inches long below left knee.
8. Big bump on nose and two black eyes in August, 1916.

9. Back of hand much swollen in 1914.
10. Bad cut under left eye in 1914 caused by whip (Mrs. Slape admits this).
11. Wales on her arm from wrist to shoulder in 1912.
12. Bruise on calf of leg, said to have been caused by a spade, in April, 1917.
13. Four or five black eyes, caused on different dates.
14. Horizontal dark bruise across cheek from ear to mouth.
15. Inside of lip bruised (Summer of 1915–1916).
16. Bad bruises on back and shoulder and down to elbow, September 1914.
17. Arm badly marked from hand to elbow about 1913.
18. Bruises on back of legs (1917).
19. Held up for 10 minutes round neck.
20. Marks on leg. July 1, 1917.
21. Frequent beatings heard next door by Mrs. Percival.

(*Daily Herald* 1918, 3)

If the evidence presented at the Children's Court was accurate, it demonstrated this was a case of long-term physical and psychological abuse of a young girl. The strategies described in Myrtle's trial and the other cases above that sought to create doubt over inconsistencies, however small, in a child's testimony were accepted as part of the trial process, and robust testing of the evidence against the accused.

Protecting Children from Cross-Examination

The reporting of Rosa Slape's cross-examination suggests it was an exceptionally trying experience for her. Supportive measures were implemented to minimise trauma to the child, like positioning Rosa next to the female justice while she gave her evidence, and the prosecutor opting to delay Rosa's re-examination. There was, however, no indication that any of the three justices on the bench intervened in the cross-examination specifically. Notwithstanding their considerable discretion to do so, there were very few occasions in the cases studied for this research where judges chose to intervene in the cross-examination of a child. One exception was in 1901, when a magistrate, according to the press, was "forced to speak his mind" about the "unnecessarily severe" cross-examination of a thirteen-year-old-girl. Cross-examining the child on an offence she had allegedly witnessed, the accused's barrister:

> [t]old the child that she was a most inquisitive little girl to pry into what was going on between others in the pawnshop. The child, upon hearing such language burst into tears. She was mercifully told by the bench to stand down, Mr. Paul, JP, adding that she had given her evidence very well indeed. (*The Bendigo Independent* 1901, 2)

Justice Napier was another judge who demonstrated concern for a child witness undergoing cross-examination. During the trial of *R v Kennewell* ([1927] SASR 287) in Adelaide's Supreme Court in 1926, Napier rebuked Mr. Kennewell's counsel, Mr. Rollison, for spending fifteen minutes re-reading the depositions in their entirety to the fifteen-year-old complainant. When Rollison had finished reading, he asked the girl if there was anything untrue in what he had just read. Justice Napier intervened and disallowed the question. Rollison insisted the girl should be made to answer but Napier said it was "not fair to ask [the] witness a question in the form put [by Rollison] after she had been subjected to a harassing cross-examination." Mr. Rollison responded by accusing Justice Napier of "harassing [him] during the whole of [his] cross-examination." His Honour responded, declaring he had adopted what he believed were the "proper judicial means of protecting a witness from such cross-examinations" (*News* 1926, 1).

In *R v Eade* in 1923, Judge Hamilton made his views of the defence barrister's approach clear (*R v Eade* (1923) 24 SR (NSW) 117). Referring to the numerous tense exchanges between himself and defence counsel, Mr. Young, Hamilton said to the jury:

> You must have noticed that I resented the attitude of Mr. Young, but in all probability you do not know Mr. Young as well as I do or you would have appreciated perhaps more than you have done what has taken place…I am sorry to say that Mr. Young has a habit of trying to annoy a judge so as to try and put the jury in antagonism with the judge. The only way I

> see to stop him in that pernicious practice of his is to deal with him with a firm hand. (*Evening News* 1924, 8)

The friction between the judge and the defence barrister, and the suggestion this was a frequent practice of Mr. Young, illuminates the combative nature of adversarial trials. Mr. Young's style had nothing to do with arguing a point of law or testing the evidence in the case but instead, had everything to do with manipulating the jury. Judge Hamilton was clearly taking none of it. In such an environment, whether to intervene or not in cross-examination could be a difficult decision for a judge to make. Contemporary research suggests some judges fear intervening in the cross-examination of a child witness, even where justified, because of the risk it could cause a jury to sympathise with the accused, or at least think the judge was acting partially (Cashmore 2007, 286).

Judicial officers, though, were not the only ones who disapproved of defence counsel cross-examinations of children. A defendant's opinion of his own barrister was reported in 1920. Referring to the impressive child witness, the newspaper reported:

> Even the burglar himself seems to have been filled with admiration of her, for, when he was asked to say anything in mitigation of sentence, he expressed his disgust that his barrister should have tried to discredit her by suggesting she had imagined a great deal - the result of seeing things at cinema theatres. "All I've got to say is that what the nipper said was true," the burglar declared. "She's a sharp girl that. I'm sorry I frightened her. I wouldn't have hurt a hair on her head." (*The Bathurst Times* 1920, 3)

It arguably speaks volumes about cross-examination as a part of the process when a convicted criminal is portrayed as a hero of sorts for attempting to rescue the child's credibility after she had, in his view, been ruthlessly attacked by his barrister who, in turn, is reduced to someone more dishonest and underhanded than the convicted burglar. Counsel's suggestion the child had concocted the story was exposed as a tool to undermine the child's testimony and create doubt, rather than find the truth. For members of the public reading this press report, the description of the barrister would have done little to engender respect for the prosecution process. In another case, in Adelaide in 1931, a forty-seven-year-old man was charged with indecently assaulting a six-year-old girl. The child refused to answer any questions. In all likelihood, the defendant would have been discharged on account of the failure of the child to give evidence. Instead, he was reported to have pleaded guilty "to save the girl the ordeal of cross-examination" (*News* 1920, 6).

Cross-Examination by the Accused

For most of the twentieth century, defendants had a right to cross-examine witnesses personally, including child witnesses. This right stems from the longstanding legal assumption that a "liar will compound in the face of his adversary" (Law Reform Commissioner of Tasmania, *Child Witnesses* (Report No 62, 1990), 20). The right to cross-examine a witness has been repeatedly confirmed in case law as one of the fundamental features of the adversarial process (*Whitehorn v R* (1983) 57 ALJR 809, 810). In the case of the "Ramsay Bush Outrage" in Queanbeyan in 1901, discussed in Chapter 3, Joseph Campbell was charged with criminally assaulting nine-year-old Violet. He had lured Violet and two of her friends, May and Maud, into the bush by promising to help them find baby magpies. Violet gave evidence Campbell had thrown her to the ground, put his hands around her throat and choked her. Violet said her friend Maud had run away, but Campbell had chased her down and brought her back to the scene, threatening to kill Maud if she ran away again. Violet described being assaulted twice, bleeding profusely, and Campbell threatening all the girls not to report the offences. Violet cried while being cross-examined by the defendant "but only for a little while" (*Queanbeyan Age* 1901, 3). Her friend, May, eight, gave evidence in similar terms to Violet's. May was "in the box" for three hours, two of which were under cross-examination by Campbell (*Mudgee Guardian and North-Western Representative* 1901, 2). Campbell was convicted, sentenced to death and later executed (*The Maitland Daily Mercury* 1901, 3).

Two other examples of cross-examination of children by self-represented defendants showed the children, like Violet and May, to have withstood the intense stress of such an examination, at least on the face of it. In one case the child was "subjected…to a long cross-examination…but only reiterated her statements" (*Truth* 1901, 2). In the other case, the defendant had been accused of abducting an eleven-year-old boy and taking him on a journey where they walked from Melbourne to Adelaide, to Broken Hill and on to Queensland, where the police apprehended them fourteen months after their journey began. The defendant argued he had the boy's parents' consent to take him. He cross-examined the boy to demonstrate to the court he had looked after the boy well:

> *The accused*: At Charleville did I not suggest that you should go to school? Did you not then say that they had tried to drown a new boy at the school?
> *Witness*: They did not try to drown him; they just threw him in the river.
> *The accused*: Did I not try at nights to "learn" you how to write, to make pothooks and do sums?
> *Witness*: One night you did.
> *The accused*: What did the people of Charleville say about us?
> *Witness*: They said that I was always clean.
> *The accused*: You had three changes a week and your boots were always clean?
> *Witness*: I cleaned my own boots.
> (*Kalgoorlie Miner* 1924, 5).

These cases where the children were consistent in their testimony and even managed to undermine the defendant's argument provide examples of why defendants, less skilled in the art of examination than the professionals, might have been reluctant to cross-examine children directly. Some self-represented defendants appear to have been mindful of the risks of this process and opted not to cross-examine child witnesses. One defendant in 1937 cross-examined every other witness but the child complainant (*The Charleville Times* 1937, 8). Another chose not to cross-examine two children, eight and six years old. Instead, he informed the court he was not cross-examining them because he regarded both "as too young to be fit to understand and answer any questions" (*Truth* 1916, 3). While this reason may have been the defendant's honest view, it might also have been a strategic decision on his part to draw attention to how young the children were and to cast doubt upon their evidence-in-chief and prevent the children from receiving the sympathy of the jury. Whatever his objective, it failed. The defendant was convicted of indecently dealing with the eight-year-old girl and sentenced to two years' hard labour (*Truth* 1916, 3).

The accused's right to cross-examine witnesses personally was an issue that only garnered critical attention during the 1980s and 1990s. One of the first Australian jurisdictions to consider prohibiting the practice was Tasmania, in 1990. On this occasion, however, the Tasmanian Law Reform Commissioner, Henry Cosgrove QC, declined to recommend any change to the existing rules. He was cognisant of the potential for such confrontation to evoke memories and fears for children, but Cosgrove also thought any fear children exhibited when being cross-examined by the accused "may also stem from the fact that the allegation is false" (Law Reform Commissioner of Tasmania, *Child Witnesses* (Report No 62, 1990), 20). In 1991 the Law Reform Commission of Western Australia published its final report on *The Evidence of Children and Other Vulnerable Witnesses* (Project No 87, April 1991). The Commission recommended the use of intermediaries to cross-examine children where defendants were self-represented. The West Australian Parliament adopted this recommendation in 1992, as did New South Wales in 1996 (*Crimes Amendment (Children's Evidence) 1996* (NSW)). Other states removed the right of the defendant to personally cross-examine children in the same period (*Criminal Procedure Act 1986* (NSW) s 294A; *Evidence Act 1977* (Qld) s 21 N; *Evidence Act 1929* (SA) s 13B(1)(a); *Evidence Act 1958* (Vic) s 37CA(4); *Evidence Act 1906* (WA) s 106G(1)). After more than sixty years, the same reforms the Australian Federation of Women Voters had called for in 1930, when they recommended all questions from the prosecutor and defence be put to child witnesses through the court instead of being questioned directly by the barristers or defendant (*The Age* 1930, 1), were being implemented.

Resisting Reform

In 1990, when the Tasmanian Commissioner made his suggestion a child might be upset during cross-examination because they were lying, there was already a growing body of research demonstrating the potentially harmful effects examination and cross-examination could have on children. In their 1988 study, *Strange Language—Child Victims Under Cross Examination*, Mark Brennan and Roslin E. Brennan analysed twenty-six court transcripts from committal hearings, district and supreme court trials and appeals. This comprised more than 5000 questions and responses. Their analysis of these questions found that all legal professionals in the courtroom, not just defence counsel, used language that confused children and prevented them from giving their evidence "in the most convincing way" (Brennan and Brennan 1988, 5). They found cross-examination was

> a special kind of questioning which is geared tactically to upset the credibility of a witness…a question is not a mere question but a tactical tool deployed on the battleground of credibility; a battleground where the option for negotiation is wrested from the child victim witness. (Brennan and Brennan 1988, 3)

In a further study, Mark Brennan showed child witnesses between six and fifteen years of age "fail to hear as sensible language around half of what is addressed to them during cross-examination" (Brennan 1995, 71). Brennan concluded these results showed child witnesses were being "linguistically discriminated against in a most clear and deliberate way" (Brennan 1995, 73). Research between the late 1970s and the end of the 1990s identified a range of factors contributing to problems children encountered in giving evidence. These included the imbalance of power between the child and the examiner, undeveloped language skills and unfamiliarity with the process (Cashmore 2007; Brennan and Brennan 1988; Spencer and Lamb 2012). By this time, it had been sixty years since the Australian Federation of Women Voters had called for questions to be put to children through the court rather than counsel (*The Age* 1930, 1). It had been over a century since legislatures had acknowledged the potentially fraught nature of the examination process by passing legislation to limit certain types of questions.

Concerns about the impact of the examination process on children were raised at other times during the twentieth century, but recommended reforms rarely contemplated replacing cross-examination of child witnesses with an alternative method of taking and testing their evidence. Speaking in 1944 at the Queensland, "Committee of Inquiry Regarding Sexual Offences" for example, a former police magistrate, Mr. C. D. O'Brien, argued that children giving evidence repeatedly in various interviews and courts, often with lengthy delays between, left them open to subsequent criticism by defence counsel. Children, he claimed, were effectively left in an impossible position. If their stories were consistent, defence counsel would suggest there "had been coaching and collusion." Inconsistencies, on the other hand, gave the cross-examiner an opportunity to argue the child was lying. Mr. O'Brien specifically identified cross-examination, as opposed to any other aspect of the trial process, as a reason "parents shrank from exposing their children to the torments and tortures of" trial. Notwithstanding such views, he was not prepared to argue for an alternative to cross-examining children. Rather, O'Brien argued that judicial officers ought to be given summary power to disallow any question without the right of appeal (*The Courier-Mail* 1944, 4).

In an early study of the impact of examination on child witnesses in England in 1963, Gibbens and Prince (1963, 22) concluded the process could be harmful but they, too, stopped short of calling for the process to be replaced with another. Instead, they suggested careful vetting of cases to identify those where it would be in the child's interests not to prosecute to entirely avoid the process of giving evidence. Gibbens and Prince's study was subsequently referred to at length in the Australian Royal Commission on Human Relationships, published in 1977. The Commission adopted a similar view to Gibbens and Prince and recommended the creation of a tribunal "to assess the competing interests involved in determining whether to prosecute" (Commonwealth of Australia, *Royal Commission on Human Relationships* (Final Report, 1978), vol 5, 217). This tribunal would consist of a judge, *in camera* proceedings, written evidence only, and written submissions by social workers, parents and police outlining their opinions on whether to prosecute. No such tribunals were established at the time. The recommendations reflect, in some ways, the contemporary pre-trial "ground rules hearings," which establish how the examination of child witnesses will proceed. A key difference now, though, is that ground rules hearings proceed on the basis the matter will be prosecuted; thus, the pre-trial hearing is to establish how best to run the trial. This differs to the question initially posed by the Royal Commission, which was to hold a pre-trial hearing to determine whether to even *have* a trial. The Commission seems to have taken an all-or-nothing view of the trial procedure—to decide to run a trial under normal circumstances or abandon the prosecution completely. The Commission expressly rejected a recommendation to adopt the practice in Israel of using "youth examiners" to examine children as an alternative to examination by counsel. This practice, the Commission said, would compromise an accused's "basic protections provided under the law for those accused of crime" (Commonwealth of Australia, *Royal Commission on Human Relationships* (Final Report, 1978), vol 5, 188). The Commission recommended children not give evidence at committal hearings but otherwise advocated retaining the existing system with the implementation of support mechanisms to help witnesses through the process.

Towards the end of the century, some states attempted to place increased controls on the examination process by passing new legislation to limit questioning of witnesses in certain circumstances (*Evidence Act Amendment Act 1976* (SA) s 3; *Evidence Act (No 3) 1976* (Tas) s 2; *Evidence Act* 1977 (Qld) s 2; *Crimes (Sexual Assault) Amendment Act 1981* (NSW) sch 1). On the surface, these provisions appear remarkably like those introduced in the late-nineteenth and early-twentieth centuries, outlined at the start of this chapter, where, for example, judges were permitted to intervene in cross-examinations intended to embarrass the witness. A comparison, however, of the 1922 New South Wales legislation with the new 1981 provisions shows that the court's discretion was substantially reduced in 1981 (*Evidence (Amendment) Act 1922* (NSW) s 3; *Crimes (Sexual Assault) Amendment Act 1981* (NSW) sch 1). The new provisions were more detailed regarding the questions that were prohibited, and the circumstances in which evidence, for example of sexual experience, could be admitted (*Crimes (Sexual Assault) Amendment Act 1981* (NSW) sch 1). While the relevant sections still gave counsel considerable scope to cross-examine a witness on their sexual experience, the legislation only allowed such questions where their "probative value outweigh[ed] any distress, humiliation, and embarrassment…the complainant might suffer as a result of its admission" (*Crimes (Sexual Assault) Amendment 1981* (NSW) sch 1, inserting into the *Crimes Act 1900* (NSW) s 409B). These amendments at the end of the twentieth century demonstrate what little change occurred over the century in cross-examination practices. Once again, the option of looking for alternatives to cross-examination of children was not considered.

West Australian reforms contained within the *Acts Amendment (Evidence of Children and Others) Act 1992* (WA) included a provision for the appointment of a "communication aid." These "aids" would be additional to support persons and would provide "assistance in communicating questions and evidence" to child witnesses under the age of sixteen years (*Acts Amendment (Evidence of Children and Others) Act 1992* (WA) s 106F). The Law Reform Commission of Western Australia described these people as "child interpreters," suggesting "the function of a child interpreter would be analogous to a foreign language interpreter in a case where the witness does not have sufficient understanding of English" (*Evidence of Children and other Vulnerable Witnesses* (Project No 87, April 1991), 91). The section was drafted in very general terms, which appear to have given the judge full discretion to appoint such an aid. No case law or evaluation of the use of communication aids was found during this research but they are still provided for in the state's current legislation (*Evidence Act 1906* (WA) s 106F(2)).

Finally, in 1997 the Australian Law Reform Commission identified concerns with the examination process. Alternatives considered by the Commission included allowing children to give evidence in narrative form rather than question and answer form (*Seen and Heard: Priority for Children in the Legal Process* (1997), vol 84, par 14.115), the use of child interpreters (par 14.113), and specific provisions to assist Indigenous child witnesses and other children with particular needs to effectively communicate with the court (par 14.122). Many of these recommendations are only now being trialled and introduced in Australian courts, over two decades later.[1]

Conclusion

A press report of a case in South Australia in 1912 gave the following description of a child witness:

> [she] pleased all her hearers with the straightforwardness of her answers to the examining counsel. She was the victim of an alleged assault and showed clearly from her evidence that she was as innocent as a child of her tender years should be. Lawyers, police, and hearers in the court expressed admiration for the little one as a witness. Mr. Dashwood, the crown prosecutor was very pleased with the splendid way the child had given her evidence. It was truthful and coincided exactly with her evidence given in a lower court. It was the best evidence he had ever heard from a child witness. (*Daily Herald* 1912, 4)

This "exemplary young witness" sums up the impossibly high bar child witnesses were expected to meet during the examination process during the twentieth century. The girl was "straightforward" in her evidence, suggesting she was able to answer questions in a way that suited the adults in the room. Yet, there is a suggestion at least some of her testimony was child-like enough to convince the court she had not consented to the offence, so her credibility was maintained. Her evidence is described as "truthful," inferring she had not contradicted herself under cross-examination and finally, her evidence had been consistent with that she had given at the committal.

The cases in this chapter show few children to have been so "exemplary." The cases of prosecutors treating adolescents as hostile witnesses, defence counsel accusing children of lying, interfering in other people's business, and reducing child witnesses to tears, have illustrated the long history of problems associated with how courts elicited oral testimony from children. Yet, in the face of opposition to the process and what appeared to be a widespread understanding that oral examination was a less-than-ideal way of extracting evidence from children, the legal system remained committed to it on the basis that anything else risked compromising the fairness of the trial for the accused. The question remains, however, as to whether this process elicits the best evidence from the witness.

Note

1. See *Criminal Procedure Amendment (Child Sexual Offence Evidence Pilot) Act 2015* (NSW); *Criminal Procedure Act 2009*(Vic) part 8.2A, which commenced 28 February 2018; *Evidence (Children and Special Witnesses) Amendment Bill 2020* (Tas); *Statutes Amendment (Vulnerable Witness) Act 2015* (SA); *Criminal Code (Child Sexual Offences Reform) and Other Legislation Amendment Act 2020* (Qld). Western Australia introduced "communication aids" in 1992 via the *Acts Amendment (Evidence of Children and Others) Act 1992* (WA).

References

Acts Amendment (Evidence of Children and Others) Act 1992 (WA).

Australian Law Reform Commission and Australian Human Rights and Equal Opportunity Commission, *Seen and Heard: Priority for Children in the Legal Process* (Report No 84, 1997), vol. 84.

Bavin-Mizzi, Jill. 1995. "Understandings of Justice: Australian Rape and Carnal Knowledge Cases 1876–1924." In *Sex Power and Justice: Historical Perspectives of Law in Australia*, edited by Diane Kirkby, 19–32. Melbourne: Oxford University Press.

Bentham, Jeremy. *Introductory View of the Rationale of Judicial Evidence* (1838–1854), cited in Eilis Magner. 1995. "The Best Evidence - Oral Testimony or Documentary Proof?" *University of New South Wales Law Journal* 18 (1): 68.

Bowden, Phoebe, Terese Henning, and David Plater. 2014. "Balancing Fairness to Victims, Society and Defendants in the Cross-examination of Vulnerable Witnesses: An Impossible Triangulation." *Melbourne University Law Review* 37: 539–584.

Brennan, Mark. 1995. "The Discourse of Denial: Cross-Examining Child Victim Witnesses." *Journal of Pragmatics* 23: 71–91.

Brennan, Mark, and Roslin E. Brennan. 1988. *Strange Language—Child Victims Under Cross-Examination.* Wagga Wagga, NSW: Riverina Murray Institute of Higher Education.

Bronitt, Simon, and Henry Mares. 2004. "The History and Theory of the Adversarial and Inquisitorial Systems of Law." *Legaldate* 16 (3): 1–2.

Burrows, Kimberlee, and Martine Powell. 2014. "Prosecutors' Perspectives on Using Recorded Child Witness Interviews About Abuse as Evidence-In-Chief." *Australian and New Zealand Journal of Criminology* 47 (3): 374–390.

Butera v. Director of Public Prosecutions for the State of Victoria. 1987. 76 ALR 45.

Cashmore, Judy. 2007. "Child Witnesses: The Judicial Role." *Judicial Review* 8 (2): 281–294.

Commonwealth of Australia. *Royal Commission on Human Relationships* (Final Report, 1978), vol. 5.

Cossins, Annie. 2009. "Cross-Examination in Child Sexual Assault Trials: Evidentiary Safeguard or an Opportunity to Confuse." *Melbourne University Law Review* 33 (1): 68–104.

Crimes (Sexual Assault) Amendment 1981 (NSW).

Crimes Act 1900 (NSW).

Crimes Amendment (Children's Evidence) 1996 (NSW).

Criminal Code (Child Sexual Offences Reform) and Other Legislation Amendment Act 2020 (Qld).

Criminal Procedure Act 1986 (NSW).

Criminal Procedure Act 2009 (Vic).

Criminal Procedure Amendment (Child Sexual Offence Evidence Pilot) Act 2015 (NSW).

Daily Herald (Adelaide, SA: 1910–1924). "A Child's Injuries." August 1, 1917.

Daily Herald (Adelaide, SA: 1910–1924). "An Exemplary Young Witness." April 5, 1912.

Daily Herald (Adelaide, SA: 1910–1924). "Stepmother Totally Unfit." January 28, 1918.
Daily Herald (Adelaide, SA: 1910–1924). "The Slape Case." September 20, 1917.
Daily Standard (Brisbane, Qld: 1912–1936). "Women of Wynnum." May 27, 1926.
Eades, Diana. 2008. "Telling and Retelling Your Story in Court: Questions, Assumptions and Intercultural Implications." *Current Issues in Criminal Justice* 20 (2): 209–230.
Ellison, Louise. 1999. "The Protection of Vulnerable Witnesses in Court: An Anglo-Dutch Comparison." *International Journal of Evidence and Proof* 3: 29–43.
Evening News (Sydney, NSW: 1869–1931). "Judge Annoyed." June 12, 1924.
Evidence (Amendment) Act 1922 (NSW).
Evidence (Children and Special Witnesses) Amendment Bill 2020 (Tas).
Evidence (Children) Act 1997 (NSW).
Evidence Act (No 3) 1976 (Tas).
Evidence Act 1906 (WA).
Evidence Act 1929 (SA).
Evidence Act 1958 (Vic).
Evidence Act 1977 (Qld).
Evidence Act 1995 (Cth).
Evidence Act Amendment Act 1976 (SA).
Evidence Further Amendment Act 1888 (SA).
Featherstone, Lisa, and A. Kaladelfos. 2016. *Sex Crimes in the Fifties*. Melbourne: Melbourne University Press.
Finkelstein, Ray. 2011. "The Adversarial System and the Search for Truth." *Monash University Law Review* 37 (1): 135–144.
Gans, Jeremy, and Andrew Palmer. 2014. *Uniform Evidence*, 2nd ed. South Melbourne, VIC: Oxford University Press.
Geraldton Guardian. "Alleged Indecent Dealing." April 3, 1919.
Gibbens, T., and Joy Prince. 1963. *Child Victims of Sex Offences*. London: Institute for the Study and Treatment of Delinquency.
Green, Bruce. 1992. "The Whole Truth—How Rules of Evidence Make Lawyers Deceitful." *Loyola of Los Angeles Law Review* 25: 699–710.
Hostettler, John, and Bob Turney. 2008. *Criminal Jury Old and New: Jury Power from Early Times to the Present Day*. London, UK: Waterside Press.
Independent (Footscray, Vic: 1883–1922). "Alleged Indecent Offence." August 23, 1913.

Kalgoorlie Miner (WA: 1895–1950). "Alleged Child Stealing." August 6, 1924.

Landsman, Stephan. 1990. "From Gilbert to Bentham: The Reconceptualization of Evidence Theory." *Wayne Law Review* 36 (3): 1149–1186.

Langbein, John H. 1996. "Historical Foundations of the Law of Evidence: A View from the Ryder." *Columbia Law Review* 96 (5): 1168–1202.

Langbein, John H. 2005. *The Origins of Adversary Criminal Trial.* Oxford: Oxford University Press.

Law Reform Commissioner of Tasmania, *Child Witnesses* (Report No. 62, 1990).

Mann, Trischa, ed. 2013. *Australian Law Dictionary*, 2nd ed. Melbourne: Oxford University Press.

Maryborough Chronicle, Wide Bay and Burnett Advertiser (Qld: 1860–1947). "Nolle Prosequi Entered." February 14, 1936.

Mason, Anthony. 1995. "Fair Trial." *Criminal Law Journal* 19 (1): 7–11.

May, Allyson. 2003. *The Bar and the Old Bailey, 1750–1850.* Chapel Hill: University of North Carolina Press.

Mirror (Perth, WA: 1921–1956). "Child Witness Couldn't Remember." June 2, 1945.

Mirror (Perth, WA: 1921–1956). "Girl Denies She Told Police of Alleged Offence." February 6, 1954.

Morning Bulletin (Rockhampton, Qld: 1878–1954). "Second Day of Hearing: Detective Questioned in Ferguson Murder Case." September 23, 1953.

Mudgee Guardian and North-Western Representative (NSW: 1890–1954). "The Queanbeyan Outrage." November 4, 1901.

National Advocate (Bathurst, NSW: 1889–1954). "An Extraordinary Case." February 21, 1913.

Newcastle Morning Herald and Miners' Advocate (NSW: 1876–1954). "Child Witness Criticised." July 5, 1944.

News (Adelaide, SA: 1923–1954). "Indecent Assault." April 4, 1931.

News (Adelaide, SA: 1923–1954). "Witness Protected." November 30, 1926.

Oaths and Evidence Act 1890 (Vic).

Pigot, Thomas, Great Britain Home Office, and Great Britain Advisory Group on Video-Recorded Evidence. 1989. *Report of the Advisory Group on Video-Recorded Evidence.* London: Home Office, United Kingdom.

Plater, David. 2006. "The Development of the Prosecutor's Role in England and Australia with Respect to its Duty of Disclosure: Partisan Advocate or Minister of Justice?" *University of Tasmania Law Review* 25 (2): 111–155.

Queanbeyan Age (NSW: 1867–1904). "Police Court." November 6, 1901.
R v Eade (1923) 24 SR (NSW) 117.
R v Kennewell (1927) SA SR 287.
Radzinowicz, Leon. 1948. *A History of English Criminal Law and Its Administration from 1750, Vol. I: The Movement for Reform*. London: Stevens & Sons.
Spencer, John, and Michael E. Lamb. 2012. *Children and Cross-Examination: Time to Change the Rules?* Oxford: Hart.
Statutes Amendment (Vulnerable Witness) Act 2015 (SA).
Steffen, Thomas L. 1988. "Truth as Second Fiddle: Re-evaluating the Place of Truth in the Adversarial Trial Ensemble." *Utah Law Review* 4: 799–845.
Struve, Laura. 2008. "This Is No Way to Tell a Story." *Law & Literature* 20: 423–443.
Tasmania Law Reform Institute, *Facilitating Equal Access to Justice: An Intermediary/Communication Assistant Scheme for Tasmania?* (Issues Paper No 22, May 2016).
The Advertiser (Adelaide, SA: 1889–1931). "Alleged Cruelty to a Child." July 31, 1917a.
The Advertiser (Adelaide, SA: 1889–1931). "Law Courts. A Conviction Quashed." September 20, 1917b.
The Age (Melbourne, Vic: 1854–1954). "Woman's Interests." May 14, 1930.
The Bathurst Times (NSW: 1909–1925). "Small Witnesses." February 9, 1920.
The Bathurst Times (NSW: 1909–1925). "Extraordinary Case." February 21, 1913.
The Bendigo Independent (Vic: 1891–1918). "Child Witness and Lawyer." December 3, 1901.
The Charleville Times (Qld: 1896–1954). "Serious Offence." December 31, 1937.
The Courier-Mail (Brisbane, Qld: 1933–1954). "Child Terrified at Sex Hearings." May 31, 1944.
The Daily News (Perth, WA: 1882–1950). "A Daughter's Charge." January 20, 1910.
The Daily News (Perth, WA: 1882–1950). "Alleged Indecent Assault." June 9, 1903.
The Evidence Act 1889 (Tas).

The Law Reform Commission of Western Australia, *Evidence of Children and other Vulnerable Witnesses* (Project No 87, April 1991).

The Maitland Daily Mercury (NSW: 1894–1939). "Execution of Joseph Campbell." December 20, 1901.

The Prosecution Project Database [PP], https://prosecutionproject.griffith.edu.au/prosecutions. (version 1, 17 July 2016), Trial ID #46403, Queensland Supreme Court [QLDSC], Sidney Cameron, 1926.

The *Prosecution Project Database [PP]*, https://prosecutionproject.griffith.edu.au/prosecutions (version 1, 17 July 2016), Trial ID #2456, Western Australia Supreme Court [WASC], George Simpson, 1910.

Truth (Melbourne ed.) (Vic: 1914–1918). "Indecent Assault Alleged." January 30, 1915.

Truth (Perth, WA: 1903–1931). "A Uniformed Ruffian." September 9, 1916.

Truth (Perth, WA: 1903–1931). "Bestial Blackguard." December 19, 1908.

Westera, Nina, Martine Powell, and Becky Milne. 2017. "Lost in the Detail: Prosecutors' Perceptions of the Utility of Video Recorded Police Interviews as Rape Complainant Evidence." *Australian & New Zealand Journal of Criminology* 50 (2): 252–268.

Whitehorn v R (1983) 57 ALJR 809.

Wigmore, John. *Evidence*, sect. 1367 (Chadbourn rev. 1974), cited in John R Spencer and Rohna H. Flin. 1993. *The Evidence of Children: The Law and the Psychology*, 2nd ed. London: Blackstone Press.

Williamstown Chronicle (Vic: 1856–1954). "Serious Charge Against Man at West Newport." February 26, 1954.

Wilson, Michael, Felicity Nagorcka, and Michael Stanton. 2005. "Stranded Between Partisanship and the Truth? A Comparative Analysis of Legal Ethics in the Adversarial and Inquisitorial Systems of Justice." *Melbourne University Law Review* 29 (2): 448–477.

Zajac, Rachel, Nina Westera, and Andy Kaladelfos. 2017. "A Historical Comparison of Australian Lawyers' Strategies for Cross-Examining Child Sexual Abuse Complainants." *Child Abuse and Neglect* 72: 236–246.

Zajac, Rachel, Sarah O'Neill, and Harlene Hayne. 2012. "Disorder in the Courtroom? Child Witnesses Under Cross-examination." *Developmental Review* 32: 181–204.

7

"Trying to Bend the Law to Fit": Corroboration

If a child witness had demonstrated their capacity to swear an oath or, at least, to understand the need to tell the truth, coped with the courtroom environment, and withstood the pressure of examination and cross-examination, the effect of *what* they said was still constrained by legal principles that continued to question their credibility. Common law corroboration rules were introduced as a way of confirming the credibility of the child witness and affected the testimony of every child witness in one way or another until the end of the twentieth century. Corroboration is generally understood as evidence that confirms a witness's testimony. The requirement for such evidence was originally devised as a response to the evidence of women and children, whose testimony was regarded as lacking the credibility of the sworn testimony of white Christian men (Naylor 1989, 82).

Chapter 4 considered statutory reforms in the late nineteenth century that provided for the receipt of unsworn testimony of children. The effect of these reforms meant a greater number of children were giving evidence in court (Blewer 2020, 277). The application of new corroboration rules accompanying these reforms, however, often made such testimony

R. Blewer, *Child Witnesses in Twentieth Century Australian Courtrooms*, Palgrave Histories of Policing, Punishment and Justice, https://doi.org/10.1007/978-3-030-69791-4_7

redundant, to the extent that the conviction rate decreased (Blewer 2020, 277–278). The twentieth century is characterised by some decidedly creative, and at times controversial, interpretations of the relevant rules of corroboration. By the late twentieth century, the situation had become untenable. The legal principles had developed to a point where they were seemingly inconsistent, unduly complex and unclear. Speaking to the parliament of Western Australia in 1992, the Honourable Peter Foss described how corroboration rules were being applied:

> When it was so plain that the witness was telling the truth, and was a reliable witness, but it looked like the person charged would get off because of the requirement for corroboration, we found the courts would start to use the most extraordinary devices to find corroboration. To a large extent the rules relating to corroboration became weird…we had a strange situation where people were assessing witnesses and trying to bend the law to fit. They did not always succeed because there is a limit on how far judges can go. (*Parliamentary Debates*, Legislative Council, 4 June 1992, 3397–3398)

The weirdness Foss spoke of was largely a result of separate common law rules and statutory rules. At common law, corroboration was not mandatory. Where statute applied, it was. At common law, juries were free to convict on the word of a child alone, if they had been warned by the judge of the dangers of doing so. If statute applied, a defendant could not be convicted without further corroborative evidence that implicated the accused (see for e.g *Crimes Act 1891* (Vic) s 33; *Criminal Law and Evidence Amendment Act 1891* (NSW) s 7). Both approaches—common law and statutory—proved to be problematic for courts throughout the twentieth century.

Like the preceding chapters in this book, opposition to the application of corroboration rules is found throughout the twentieth century. Attempts to reign in its reach were often met, nevertheless, with calls to remember Sir Mathew Hale's famous statement of the eighteenth century that children could easily make allegations of sexual offences that were difficult for an accused to refute (Hale 1736). The converse of Hale's argument is, of course, that while corroboration was a requirement of the law, offences against children would be easy for offenders to commit and difficult for the Crown to prove (Backhouse 2000, 79).

Pre-Twentieth Century Approach to Corroboration

Despite being revered for his views on the ease with which innocent men might be convicted upon the words of a woman or child, Hale "was no apologist [for] sex offenders" (Myers et al. 2002, 36). Rather, he believed such criminals should be dealt with "severely and impartially…with death" (Hale, as cited in Myers et al. 2002, 36). Myers and colleagues suggest Hale's views were not based on distrust of the evidence of women, per se. Rather, in Hale's experience, the very "heinousness" of sexual crimes often led judges and juries to be "overly hastily carried to the conviction" of the accused (Myers et al. 2002, 36). Hale was thus concerned that sexual offences be considered with the caution, care and vigilance they required. The desirability of corroboration was therefore a device intended to protect innocent men but not make a conviction impossible where the evidence proved the accused was guilty. Like many commentators since, Hale understood these clandestine offences against children and the challenge of locating any corroborative evidence. He thought, however, "concurrent circumstances…proved by other witnesses" would be sufficient to confirm the credibility of a child witness (Hale 1736, 634–635, as cited in Lyon and Lamagna 2007, 1034).

In making these observations, Hale was simply reflecting a long history of the common law's reluctance to see an offender convicted upon the word of one witness. The idea that an accused should not be convicted upon the word of one witness has thus always been a feature of the criminal trial. From the eighteenth century, the law on corroboration developed in deference to Hale (Backhouse 2000, 79). It was, however, a complex issue from at least the middle of the eighteenth century. It was a requirement at trials in England in the 1740s, but by the 1780s had become more of an "advisory rule" (Langbein 2005, 206). Around this time, Sir William Blackstone wrote in glowing terms of child witnesses generally, but like Hale, concluded a person should not be convicted on such evidence alone. He suggested "there should be some concurrent testimony, of time, place and circumstances" (Blackstone 1765–1769, 214, as cited in Jackson 2000, 93). It was then left to a jury to decide how much weight this concurrent evidence held.

Following the views of Hale and Blackstone, the common law position in the late nineteenth century was that judges ought to warn juries of the dangers of convicting an accused on the uncorroborated evidence of a child's sworn testimony but, if despite such a warning they still believed the accused to be guilty, they were free to convict (*R v Paul* (1890) 25 QBD 202).

Statutory Reforms

As noted in Chapter 4, concern over the perceived increase in sexual offending against young children coupled with the common law requirement that children could only give evidence if it was sworn, had led most Australian jurisdictions to pass legislation in the nineteenth century permitting the receipt of unsworn testimony of children in certain sexual offence matters. Where such legislation was applicable, corroboration of the child's testimony was mandatory.[1] What was corroborative for the purposes of these statutory provisions, however, was not as straightforward as Hale or Blackstone's descriptions. Taking the *Crimes Act 1891* (Vic) as an example, s 33(2) applied to charges of rape, carnal knowledge and indecent assaults on girls (*Crimes Act 1891* (Vic) s 33). The section stipulated unsworn testimony of children of tender years could be received but must be corroborated by evidence proving the defendant committed the offence, not just evidence that confirmed the child's testimony. This requirement that evidence had to implicate the accused was controversial from the outset. Within a matter of weeks after its enactment, s 33(2) was tested in the Victorian Supreme Court in *R v Gregg* ((1892) 18 VLR 218). This case was also discussed in Chapter 4, where Chief Justice Higinbotham had admonished the prosecutor for not ensuring the child was instructed on how to swear an oath before coming to court. At trial the jury found the defendant guilty. He was sentenced to two years' imprisonment and 20 lashes. Gregg appealed against his conviction. Applying the new provision in s 33(2), the Court quashed Gregg's conviction and ordered a retrial. Chief Justice Higinbotham had been firmly of the view that "forcible evidence" corroborating the child's was found in the statement the girl made to her mother about the offence shortly after it had occurred (*R v Gregg* (1892) 18 VLR 218, 221). The Chief Justice acknowledged, however, that the mother's testimony was not material evidence implicating the accused and thus was not acceptable for the purposes of s 33(2). The judge was not impressed with the effect the reforms would have on cases like this one:

> I am not aware of any kind of corroboratory evidence more satisfactory than that of a female child suffering under a shock of this kind, and indicating by appearance, manner, words, and acts the distress caused by the assault. But under the present law such corroboration can only be given so as to implicate the accused person, if the child knows at the time of the assault the person who has assaulted her, or if some other testimony exists independent of that of the child by which the assailant can be identified ... this provision of the existing law demands, in my opinion, the attentive consideration of the Legislature...especially on account of the failure of justice in many cases arising from the inability of the Court to give effect to the credible evidence of the child in consequence of this particular requirement of corroborative evidence implicating the accused. (*R v Gregg* (1892) 18 VLR 218, 222)

Justice A'Beckett, who had agreed with the initial guilty verdict when he heard Gregg's trial, cited "the immature mental capacity" of children as justification for the new statutory reforms. Justice Hood agreed there was evidence "to support the girl's story and to confirm her credibility" but, like Higinbotham, understood the impact of the new s 33(2), saying:

> I think that the Legislature has in these cases required something more. There must be some other material evidence implicating the accused; that is, something proved altogether apart from the child's story tending to establish the guilt of the prisoner. (*R v Gregg* (1892) 18 VLR 218, 222)

Gregg was retried and acquitted (*The Age* 1892, 5; *The Prosecution Project Database* Trial ID #559765, Edmund Gregg, 1892).

Nearly a decade later, another Victorian case, *R v Smith*, considered the operation of these statutory rules. Taking a contrary approach to that of his predecessor, Chief Justice Higinbotham, Chief Justice Madden approved of the provision in s 33(2) (*R v Smith* (1901) 26 VLR 683). At trial, Smith had been accused of indecently assaulting a five-year-old girl, Eva. Eva and her six-year-old cousin were called as witnesses. The jury found Smith guilty, but Justice Williams reserved questions regarding the interpretation of s 33(2) of the *Crimes Act 1891* (Vic) for the Full Court. Applying the reasoning of the Court in *R v Gregg*, the Full Court upheld Smith's appeal and quashed his conviction (*R v Smith* (1901) 26 VLR 683). The Court found that both children giving unsworn evidence of Smith exposing himself and saying "C'mon Eva" was not sufficient to implicate him in the crime of indecent assault. Chief Justice Madden expressed his support for the statutory provision, noting a child could easily imagine such an offence, and "any man who just happened to be in the vicinity might be convicted" (*R v Smith* (1901) 26 VLR 683, 686).

In December 1901, direct eyewitness testimony perfectly demonstrated the consequences for an accused where there was corroboration of a child's testimony. It was a rare example. William Brooker was tried in Melbourne. He had been charged with sexually assaulting his twelve-year-old daughter, Christina. While being assaulted, Christina had screamed. Her older sister, Emma, had run to Christina's aid and thus witnessed the assault firsthand. Emma, able to swear an oath, corroborated Christina's testimony. Brooker was convicted and sentenced to fifteen years' imprisonment (*The Mildura Cultivator* 1888, 5). The "Ramsay Bush Outrage," committed by Joseph Campbell, discussed in Chapters 3 and 6, was another crime that took place before child witnesses. Two girls gave evidence of having witnessed the offences committed against Violet. Campbell was convicted and sentenced to death (*The Maitland Daily Mercury* 1901, 3). These cases demonstrate the penalties would be severe where corroboration was clear. Such cases, however, were few and far between.

There is evidence that, by the early twentieth century, some time after statutory corroboration rules had been introduced in various states, the new provisions may have been impacting upon the conviction rates given an apparent decrease in conviction rates (Blewer 2020). This decrease was contrary to the intention behind the reform that was intended to increase convictions, but either was not noticed or was noticed but disregarded. Either way, early in the twentieth century New South Wales and Western Australia amended their existing statutory requirements. In 1900, New South Wales expanded the list of offences requiring the corroboration of unsworn testimony of children to include indecent assaults against boys (*Crimes Act 1900* (NSW) s 418). In 1906, Western Australia amended its legislation. The passing of the *Evidence Act 1906* (WA) retained the earlier corroboration provisions in relation to specific offences, but the state also introduced a broader, general requirement for corroboration (*Evidence Act 1906* (WA) s 101). The new provision in s 101 required the unsworn testimony of *any* child of tender years in relation to *any* civil or criminal proceeding be corroborated. Debating this significant provision in parliament, the Attorney-General reminded the members the requirement for corroboration was "not new." Extending legislative requirements for corroboration to all offences involving unsworn testimony of children was necessary, he said, because children "suffered very much from hallucinations and were unreliable" (*Parliamentary Debates*, Legislative Assembly, 9 August 1906, 939).

In making this claim, the Attorney-General may have been influenced by a high-profile Perth trial heard only a few months earlier (*R v Walsh* (1905) 7 WALR 263). A jury had found John Walsh guilty of carnal knowledge of a girl under thirteen. The relevant section of the *Code*, s 185, required corroboration of the child's evidence that implicated the accused, even though the girl gave sworn testimony (*Criminal Code Act 1902* (WA) s 185). There was independent evidence that the girl, nine-year-old Violet, had been seen with Walsh, at his house. Medical evidence established she had been "criminally assaulted or…guilty of some other misconduct" (*R v Walsh* (1905) 7 WALR 263, 264). Violet testified Walsh had threatened to kill her if she told anyone what had happened. When he was arrested, Walsh claimed "It would do me no good to say anything. She is a little hussy who used to come into my bedroom while I was changing my clothing" (*Truth* 1905, 2; *The Daily News* 1905, 11). The jury found Walsh guilty of attempted carnal knowledge, but

Commissioner Roe reserved the question of corroboration for the Court of Appeal.

The Chief Justice delivered his judgment, saying the case demanded the rules of corroboration be "strictly enforced":

> The prosecutrix, according to the evidence, was an exceedingly naughty child, and she gave evidence of acts of which she could not have possibly known unless she had been a party to improper conduct with men … It was incumbent upon the prosecution not only to shew that she did go to the accused's house or was seen in company with the accused, but that she was seen with him under such circumstances as would lead the inference to be drawn that something improper was taking place between them or was going to take place between them. As I pointed out in the course of the argument if they had been seen in an indelicate position, if the accused had been seen enticing the girl into his house or taking her into a room or shutting the door or pulling down the blinds those would be circumstances from which an inference could be drawn, in view of the sworn testimony of the girl, implicating the accused with the offence with which the girl charged him … With regard to the alleged admission of inference to be drawn from the statement of the accused to the constable who arrested him I can see nothing to implicate him in the statement that this girl was "a young hussy." I agree with the accused that she was a young hussy who came into his room when he was changing his clothes … [o]ur experience leads us to conclude where a man is really guilty of an offence he frequently, when called upon to explain, protests his innocence and declares that he knows nothing about it and that the person who is said to have visited his house never came near at all. In this case the accused has not disputed that the young girl came to the house, but he says she was a young hussy and that she came when he was changing his clothes. I am clearly of the opinion that this cannot be taken to be any material evidence tending to implicate the accused in the offence with which he was charged. (*R v Walsh* (1905) 7 WALR 263, 264–265)

The written decision of the Court of Appeal provides an extensive overview of the evidence and the legal principles at stake. Several press articles provide an interesting illustration of approaches to reporting on the evidence of children at the time. At Walsh's committal hearing, *The Northam Advertiser* reported Violet "disclosed a most revolting offence" in a closed courtroom before Walsh was committed to stand trial (1905, 3). Perth's *Daily News* reported on the trial in measured terms: "The evidence of the little girl was to the effect that the accused...had tampered with her several times" (1905, 11). Perth's *Truth* celebrated the Court of Appeal's decision in overcoming the "vixenish viciousness of Violet" (*Truth* 1905, 2). According to this paper, the way nine-year-old Violet gave her evidence was proof of her lies. Reporting her full name, the paper proclaimed:

> Seldom (and it is fortunate for mankind generally that it is so) do children go into the witness-box either as prosecutrix or witness and exhibit such precocious knowledge as did this girl...Worldly and impudent beyond all reason, the girl entered the witness-box and without tremor or tear glibly told a story of Walsh's alleged wickedness, which many a more seasoned female would have shirked. Nor had her story to be wrung from her, as is generally the case with children of tender age. She was, she showed, a willing party to what she alleged had taken place between Walsh and herself, but of course, as is invariably the case, there were no other eyes looking on, nor could she or her parents produce one scrap of corroborative evidence... (*Truth* 1905, 2)

Walsh's case highlighted the problem courts were having in defining the precise evidence required to implicate an accused. A matter that came before the Dubbo Circuit Court in 1906 provides yet another example of the difficulty of defining corroborative testimony implicating the accused. William Carroll was charged with indecently assaulting a girl under fourteen years (*R v Carroll* (1906) 6 SR (NSW) 258). At Carroll's trial he wore boots that "curiously enough" matched prints that had been found at the scene, but were different to the boots he was wearing when arrested shortly after the alleged offence took place (*R v Carroll* (1906) 6 SR (NSW) 258, 259). The jury found Carroll guilty. On appeal, the Chief Justice found the jury must have believed Carroll had worn the boots on the day of the assault, even though he was not wearing them when the police found him shortly after the offence allegedly took place and took him to the scene. Adopting the same reasoning applied in *Walsh*, Carroll's barrister argued that even if the shoe prints belonged to the young man, that could only prove Carroll had been at the scene on the day of the assault, not that he was guilty of it. The Court rejected the submission. The Chief Justice did not think "there could be any stronger corroborative evidence." Carroll's conviction was upheld (*R v Carroll* (1906) 6 SR (NSW) 258, 259).

It is difficult to reconcile the decisions in *Walsh* and *Carroll*. The child visiting Walsh's home was not deemed corroborative; yet Carroll coincidentally wearing shoes in court whose prints matched those allegedly found at the crime scene was considered corroborative evidence implicating the accused.[2] In 1914, the issue made it all the way to the High Court. A jury had found Charles Eather guilty of indecent assault. The five-year-old girl gave unsworn evidence (*R v Eather* (1914) 14 SR (NSW) 280). Both Eather and the child had gonorrhoea. At Eather's trial, Judge Hamilton had interpreted this as material evidence implicating Eather in the commission of the offence. Hamilton saw "…no room for any doubt that the verdict of the jury was a correct one" (*R v Eather* (1914) 14 SR (NSW) 280, 281). Eather appealed unsuccessfully to the New South Wales Court of Criminal Appeal on the ground there was no corroboration. Demonstrating how challenging the issue was, the judges of the Court of Criminal Appeal were split on their decision. Chief Justice Cullen found the evidence of the surrounding circumstances, including the evidence of the disease, sufficiently implicated Eather. Justice Gordon found the evidence was corroborative, and any argument went to the weight of such evidence, rather than whether it was corroborative. Justice Pring, though, disagreed, declaring "when the legislature passed s 418 of the *Crimes Act* they were introducing quite a new principle into the law of evidence…a serious inroad upon the general rules of evidence" (*R v Eather* (1914) 14 SR (NSW) 280, 285).

Eather's application for leave to appeal against the Court of Criminal Appeal's decision to the High Court was refused, but like the Court of Criminal Appeal, the High Court was divided in its decision. Justice Isaacs believed the Court should have heard the appeal because it involved a potentially "fundamental breach" of the law (*Eather v R* (1914) 19 CLR 409, 414). This was simply a decision to refuse leave to appeal to the High Court, and therefore did not require the Court to consider the case beyond deciding whether it would hear the matter.

Justice Isaacs did consider the case more broadly, though. He thought s 418 had been "seriously misinterpreted" by the lower courts because Eather was:

> shown to have been on friendly terms with the girl and her parents, to have been seen speaking to her in the presence of others on innocent occasions, and if those are circumstances implicating a man in a charge of this nature, then no one is safe from the most atrocious accusations that the testimony of a child of limited intelligence can be conjectured to support. (*Eather v R* (1914) 19 CLR 409, 416)

In turn, Chief Justice Griffith set out "to remove any impression that any injustice has been done in this case" (*Eather v R* (1914) 19 CLR 409, 429), saying "I think it right to say that at least a statutory majority of the court take a very different view of the facts from that stated by [Issacs J], and a different view of the law applicable to them" (*Eather v R* (1914) 19 CLR 409, 429).

A few years on, in 1917, in the matter of John Croft, the Western Australian Court of Appeal considered yet another ambiguous aspect of the statutory requirements for corroboration of child witness testimony. Croft was tried in Perth for the unlawful and indecent assault of an eight-year-old girl (*Croft v The King* (1917) 19 WALR 49). The girl and her six-year-old brother both gave unsworn testimony at Croft's trial. Section 101(2) of the *Evidence Act 1906* (WA) required unsworn testimony of children of tender years to be corroborated "by other evidence in some material particular" (*Evidence Act 1906* (WA) s 101). The boy confirmed the evidence of his older sister from the location of Croft's tent. He confirmed they had both gone into the tent; Croft gave him money and sent him to buy lollies; he had left his sister with the accused; he bought lollies and later shared them with his sister. After deliberating for ten minutes, the jury found Croft guilty (*Truth* 1916, 3).

Croft did not appeal the verdict. Given the boy's testimony was unsworn, however, the verdict raised the question of whether his unsworn testimony was capable of corroborating his sister's unsworn testimony. The Attorney-General used his powers under s 21 of the *Criminal Code* to refer the matter to the Court of Appeal (*Criminal*

Code Act 1902 (WA) s 21). He sought their opinion as to whether the brother's unsworn testimony was "evidence in some material particular" as per s101(2). Notwithstanding provision in s 21 for such appeals to be considered "in private," the Court heard the matter in open court, stating the question of corroboration of a child's evidence was a matter of public importance. The court found in drafting s 101, the legislature had intended for the unsworn testimony of a child to only be corroborated by the *sworn* testimony of another witness (*Croft v The King* (1917) 19 WALR 49). The published reasons indicate the Court would let the Attorney-General know of their decision but otherwise, there appears to be no record of Croft's fate.

The High Court revisited s 418 of the *Crimes Act 1900* (NSW) in 1924 in the matter of *Eade (Eade v R* (1924) 34 CLR 154). Eade had been charged with indecently assaulting a five-year-old girl. This was not the first time he had been charged with such offences. In 1921 a jury found Eade guilty of assaulting a different girl. In sentencing Eade, Judge Hamilton said "it had been over 40 years since [I have] heard such an abominable case. [I] could not imagine anything worse than the injury which has been inflicted on the girl. It was too shocking for words" (*Evening News* 1921, 6). In 1924, shortly after being released from prison for his 1921 offence, Eade was on trial for similar offences against another girl. On the evidence of the child and her mother (which the trial judge said corroborated her daughter's), Eade was found guilty and sentenced to five years' imprisonment (*The Wyalong Advocate and Mining, Agricultural and Pastoral Gazette* 1923, 12). The New South Wales Court of Appeal upheld the conviction (*R v Eade* (1923) 24 SR (NSW) 117, 122). The High Court, however, quashed it and ordered a retrial on the basis the mother's evidence did not corroborate her daughter's because it did not implicate Eade (*Eade v R* (1924) 34 CLR 154, 160). All it did was tell the Court "what [the girl] did and said on that occasion" (*Eade v R* (1924) 34 CLR 154, 157). The Court considered the other evidence in the case. There was independent evidence proving the girl purchased some pies subsequently found in Eade's home, but all this did was establish Eade's opportunity to commit the crime, not that he had, in fact, committed the crime. There was some evidence, though, that the majority judges did think could corroborate the girl's unsworn evidence. When he had been questioned by police, Eade had made an unsworn statement denying the allegations. He denied knowing the girl, giving her money for the pies, letting her into his house or knowing how the pies got there (158). In their joint decision, Chief Justice Knox, and Justices Gavan, Duffy, and Starke said:

> Now if a jury be of [sic] opinion that the prisoner's statements are false, then they may properly come to the conclusion that his falsehood indicates that the child's story is true, and that he is telling lies in order to discredit the evidence of the other witnesses because he is unable to account for what they say they saw, in any way consistent with his own innocence. Corroboration may be found in independent evidence or in admissions of the prisoner, or in inferences properly drawn from his conduct and statements. (*Eade v R* (1924) 34 CLR 154, 158)

The Court were saying unsworn denials made by an accused out of court could corroborate the unsworn testimony of a child given in court, if the jury thought the accused had been lying and the girl telling the truth. "Corroboration," the majority judges held, "may be found in independent evidence, or in admissions of the prisoner or in inferences properly drawn from his conduct and statements" (158). A retrial was ordered. Was the High Court looking for a way to bend the law to fit the outcome they, and others, perhaps wanted?

Eade was retried in June 1924. The girl gave evidence—again. Eade was found guilty—again. It was Judge Hamilton who presided over the retrial and sentenced Eade—again, having first sentenced him for the 1921 offence. "I am quite satisfied with your conviction … and I sentence you to 4 ½ years penal servitude" (*The Maitland Daily Mercury* 1924, 6).

"The Reverence of a Rule of Law"—Common Law Practice

At Eade's 1924 re-trial, the girl gave sworn testimony. The common law rules thus applied, not the statutory rules. The requirement for corroborative evidence implicating the accused was circumvented. In comparison with the legislative reforms of the late nineteenth and early twentieth centuries, common law corroboration rules were comparatively straightforward at the start of the twentieth century. But over the next eighty years or so, they became just as confusing as the statutory provisions, if not more so. Like the statutory approach, examining the common law rules reveals inconsistencies and complexities that only increased over time, as judicial officers appear to have followed different lines of precedent and employed different means of bending the law to fit the cases before them. As with statute, the definition of corroboration was ambiguous. In common law cases there were additional challenges relating to the terms of the judicial warning to juries that it was unsafe to convict an accused on the uncorroborated evidence of a child. Arguments were raised about the precise scope of that warning and when it should be issued. Should it be issued with respect to all children, not just unsworn children? Should it be issued only where there was no corroboration, or rather, in every case?

In 1916 the English Court of Criminal Appeal attempted to clarify the common law rules for corroboration in *R v Baskerville* (1916) 2 KB 658. This decision would also apply in Australia. Baskerville had been convicted of sexual offences in relation to two boys. The boys were charged as accomplices to the offence (*Criminal Law Amendment Act 1885* (UK) s 11). According to the law at that time, there was no statutory provision requiring corroboration for such charges. The jury found Baskerville guilty. He appealed on the grounds that the boys' testimony was uncorroborated, and the judge had failed to properly warn the jury they should not find the accused guilty unless there was sufficient corroboration.

The evidence in the case centred on a letter the defendant had written to one of the boys confirming plans for the two boys to meet Baskerville on Sunday at 8 pm, not 7.30 pm "as arranged." At trial the judge had warned the jury "that they ought not to convict the prisoner upon the evidence of the boys unless it was in their opinion corroborated in some material particular affecting the accused" and told them the letter was corroborative (*R v Baskerville* (1916) 2 KB 658, 659). On appeal, the defence argued this letter did not corroborate the boys' oral testimony because it was capable of an alternative interpretation consistent with Baskerville's innocence (*R v Baskerville* (1916) 2 KB 658, 659). Baskerville had given evidence he had invited the boys to his home to help equip them with life skills, and the letter simply confirmed those plans. It did not necessarily implicate Baskerville in the commission of sexual offending. Baskerville's barrister provided a lengthy list of cases demonstrating the development of this line of authority in the common law that appeared to require this additional requirement of evidence implicating the accused. The prosecutor, however, argued the common law corroboration rule only required evidence showing the witness was telling the truth. For this they cited a legal text, Stephen's *Digest of the Law of Evidence* (1914). They further argued there was "abundant corroboration pointing to the prisoner's guilt" and therefore no warning had even been required in the first place (*R v Baskerville* (1916) 2 KB 658, 661).

That two barristers could make such divergent arguments illustrates the confusion around corroboration rules. The Court acknowledged the inconsistencies in judicial decisions over the previous century and attempted to "lay down rules for future guidance" (*R v Baskerville* (1916) 2 KB 658, 667). It confirmed that uncorroborated evidence of an accomplice (in this case the boys) was admissible in court. The Court confirmed that at common law, corroboration was not mandatory but rather it was a "rule of practice" for a judge to warn juries of the danger of convicting on uncorroborated testimony. They confirmed it was at the judge's discretion to advise a jury not to convict upon such evidence—but it was also open to jurors to convict on "unconfirmed evidence" if they wished. The court went on to note this "rule of practice has become virtually equivalent to a rule of law" and acknowledged the growing body of case law where convictions had been quashed because a judge had failed to give such a warning.

Attempting to clarify the definition of corroboration, the Court confirmed that the applicable test was the same as for the statutory provisions. That is, the evidence had to implicate the accused by confirming, in some material particular, the crime had been committed and that it was the accused who had committed it (*R v Baskerville* (1916) 2 KB 658, 667). "It would," they said, "be in high degree dangerous to attempt to formulate the kind of evidence" that would be corroborative (*R v Baskerville* (1916) 2 KB 658, 667). In this case, the jury had received the appropriate warning. They were therefore entitled to convict Baskerville as they had done. Baskerville's appeal was dismissed. As legal scholar Simon Bronitt has noted, this outcome served to confuse the issue more than ever, as courts now set about defining evidence that did, and did not, confirm an accused's guilt (Bronitt 1991, 3037).

The first case considering common law corroboration requirements to go before the Australian High Court after *Baskerville* was *Hargan* in 1919 (*Hargan v The King* (1919) 27 CLR 13). At the Narrabri Quarter Sessions in New South Wales, a jury found Hargan guilty of unlawful carnal knowledge of a girl between the ages of ten and sixteen years (*Hargan v The King* (1919) 27 CLR 13). The girl was fourteen years old and had recently given birth to a child. At the trial before Judge Cohen, she had given sworn evidence; thus, the common law rules for corroboration applied. One press report noted the child "proved to be a most difficult witness, being apparently stupefied with her strange surroundings" (*The North Western Courier* 1919, 2). She nevertheless testified the accused had committed the offence against her. In summing up the case for the jury, Judge Cohen said:

> It has been said that the evidence of the girl herself is uncorroborated. It is my duty to tell you that corroboration is unnecessary; that is, if you believe the girl's evidence, it is not necessary to have corroboration. This case resolves itself into a question of fact. It is for you to say whether you believe the story of the girl or the story of the accused. (cited in *Hargan v The King* (1919) 27 CLR 13, 16)

The jury apparently believed the girl and found Hargan guilty. In his sentencing submissions, Hargan's counsel, Mr. Martin, asked the judge to consider the good character of the accused against the "apparently loose moral habits" of the child and suggested no injury had been done to the girl. He also "drew attention to the unsatisfactory way the girl gave her evidence," to which Judge Cohen responded by noting the accused was a man of forty years of age who had "probably ruined the girl for life" (*The North Western Courier* 1919, 2).

Hargan appealed against his conviction, arguing there was no corroboration of the girl's evidence. He had admitted the girl was at his house on the day in question, but only to clean it. Medical evidence indicated she "had undoubtedly had frequent sexual relations with somebody." On cross-examination, the child admitted her mother had told her what to say about the offence. The Crown argued this was only in respect to what words would be appropriate to describe the offence, and that the girl's evidence should not be interpreted as suggesting the allegations were fabricated. The NSW Court of Criminal Appeal upheld the conviction (*R v Hargan* (1919) 19 SR (NSW) 257, 259).

Hargan then appealed to the High Court (*Hargan v The King* (1919) 27 CLR 13). There, Justice Barton focused on Judge Cohen's summing up for the jury, and that Cohen had not urged or warned the jury to carefully consider the girl's uncorroborated testimony before finding Hargan guilty. Justice Barton cited a long list of English precedents referring to the common law corroboration rules (*R v Graham* (1910) 4 Cr App R; *R v Brown* (1910) 6 Cr App R 24; *R v Pitts* (1912) 8 Cr App R; *R v Severo Dossi* (1918) 13 Cr App R; *R v Warren* (1919) 14 Cr App R, cited in *Hargan v The King* (1919) 27 CLR 13, 16–19). Each of these confirmed the legal principle that where children "of tender years" had given sworn testimony, a warning about the uncorroborated evidence of young children should still be given. Thus, Justice Barton found Judge Cohen had been correct when he said corroboration was "not necessary," but "the question is whether in this case his duty ended there. I do not think it did" (*Hargan v The King* (1919) 27 CLR 13, 19). While Barton agreed with Judge Cohen a jury could convict upon the evidence of "one person against another," he found that in cases like Hargan's, juries should be warned the uncorroborated evidence of the child, although sworn, was "not by itself a very safe basis on which to rest a conviction" (*Hargan v The King* (1919) 27 CLR 13, 19). Cohen, Barton believed, should have advised the jury to weigh up the girl's evidence "with the utmost care" before taking "what is technically the legal course" (*Hargan v The King* (1919) 27 CLR 13, 21). Barton found, in the absence of such a warning, there had been a miscarriage of justice. Justices Isaacs and Rich concurred.

In his decision, Justice Isaacs confirmed there was "no rule of strict law" requiring juries to exercise the caution Justice Barton had suggested. "At most" he said, "it is only a practice, a rule of propriety, which… if disregarded cannot be made a legal ground to quash or set aside a conviction." According to Isaacs, the question was "not of strict law," but of "justice and fairness to the accused" (*Hargan v The King* (1919) 27 CLR 13, 23–24). The practice of warning juries was, however, "so well established as to have…almost the reverence of a rule of law" (*Hargan v The King* (1919) 27 CLR 13, 24). As long as the judge warned the jury to treat a child's sworn testimony with caution where it was uncorroborated, it would be open to the jury to disregard the warning and the lack of corroboration and find the defendant guilty. In this case, even though Judge Cohen had told the jury corroboration was not required if they believed the girl, he had not sufficiently warned the jury of the dangers of doing so. Hargan's conviction was quashed, and no re-trial ordered.

The following year the High Court again considered the common law approach to corroboration in *Hicks v R* ((1920) 28 CLR 36). Hicks had been charged with having carnal knowledge of a girl under ten. The girl, who was eight years old, gave sworn testimony so, as per *Hargan,* corroboration of her evidence was not required. Other evidence proved the accused was in the vicinity at the relevant time and had subsequently given a false account of his whereabouts at the relevant time. Medical evidence proved the child had been "ravished." The jury found Hicks guilty. He appealed to the High Court on several grounds, one of which was the failure of the trial judge to adequately warn the jury on the danger of convicting on the uncorroborated evidence of the girl. The majority judges (Chief Justice Knox and Justices Duffy and Starke) said:

> It seems to us idle, in the face of this evidence, to contend that there was no corroboration of the child's story of the carnal knowledge of her by

> the prisoner. *Hargan's* case has no application to cases in which the sworn evidence of the child is corroborated. (*Hicks v R* (1920) 28 CLR 36, 41)

Simply put, the majority here thought there was obvious corroborative evidence in the false account Hicks gave of his movements on the night. Those lies corroborated the evidence of the child. In those circumstances, no warning about uncorroborated testimony was required. Whether the trial judge had given a warning about uncorroborated evidence was not an issue.

Justices Isaacs and Rich, both of whom had been on the bench for *Hargan* as well, agreed with the majority in *Hicks* on the issue of corroboration (although they ultimately disagreed with the majority on other bases). They explained their position on corroboration more expansively than the majority had. Hicks' counsel had argued there might have been sufficient corroborative evidence of an indecent assault, but there was insufficient corroboration of the offence of carnal knowledge of a girl under ten years. For this, Hicks' counsel argued, there needed to be corroboration "as to the necessary fact of penetration" (*Hicks v R* (1920) 28 CLR 36, 48). The two judges noted the historical approach to corroboration, as per Hale and Blackstone's views that the evidence needed only to confirm a child's credibility. Now, in 1920, they said, the law had changed to bring it "more in accordance with the general attitude of our law towards an accused person" and the need for "fair treatment of the accused" (*Hicks v R* (1920) 28 CLR 36, 48).

While cognisant of the need to be fair to the accused, Justices Isaacs and Rich thought evidence of penetration was not required. They cited the "recent and authoritative" English case of *Baskerville* where the Court had confirmed corroborative evidence would vary depending on the circumstances of the case and that it needed to affect "the accused by connecting or tending to connect him with the crime." It "need not be direct evidence that the accused committed the crime; it is sufficient if it is merely circumstantial evidence" (*R v Baskerville* (1916) 2 KB 658, 667, cited in *Hicks v R* (1920) 28 CLR 36, 49–50). Like the majority, Justices Isaacs and Rich found the evidence in Hicks' case, including "the absence of any evidence even suggesting the presence of another man who could have been the offender," sufficiently implicated Hicks in the commission of the offence as charged (*Hicks v R* (1920) 28 CLR 36, 49–50). Hicks' appeal was dismissed.

This ever-evolving common law approach to corroboration was an issue in the 1922 South Australian matter of *R v Young* ([1923] SASR 35). A jury found Young guilty of sexually assaulting his stepson. Young's defence counsel, Mr. E. Cleland K.C., had argued there was no case for the jury because the child's evidence was uncorroborated. Justice Gordon disagreed (*R v Young* [1923] SASR 35, 47). In summing up the case for the jury, Gordon had pointedly said "[i]n my opinion there is some evidence fit for you to consider as corroboration of the boy's evidence, if you believe it" (*R v Young* [1923] SASR 35, 47). There were three pieces of evidence Justice Gordon thought corroborated the child's. The first was the medical testimony of "recent scars on the boy's anus." Second was evidence of the boy's grandfather coming across the boy and the accused two years earlier, where the boy had his pants down and was crying as the accused was walking away. At the time the grandfather had tried to physically take the boy from Young, saying to his son-in-law "you will only interfere with him." Finally, there was evidence of another man, Lee, who was with Young and the child at the time of the offence (but did not observe it). Lee testified the boy had told him they had fallen behind because "he had been to the lavatory." Justice Gordon thought each of these witnesses corroborated the boy's testimony (*R v Young* [1923] SASR 35, 47). Applying the authority in *Hicks* where, if there was corroboration, there was no need to warn the jury about convicting on the uncorroborated testimony of the child, Justice Gordon had not issued the said warning. Young appealed.

The Court of Appeal found Justice Gordon had erred in failing to give the jury a warning. They did not think the evidence was corroborative, as Justice Gordan had. They found the medical evidence was not sufficiently corroborative to conclude the accused had "misused" the boy. The evidence of the grandfather contradicted the boy's testimony that the accused was in the process of assaulting him when the grandfather arrived on the scene. The grandfather's statement that the accused would interfere with the boy "indicates something he anticipated might be done rather than something he has seen done" (*R v Young* [1923] SASR 35, 47–48). Finally, the testimony of Lee could confirm both the accused's own testimony as well as the boy's and thus could not be treated as corroborative. Referring to the authorities in *Hargan* and *Hicks*, Justice Poole confirmed it was not sufficient for a judge to merely tell a jury that corroboration was not necessary (*R v Young* [1923] SASR 35, 71). Judges also had to warn jurors of the dangers of convicting on the uncorroborated evidence of a child—even though that child had sworn an oath. Justice Poole further confirmed the meaning of the phrase "implicating the accused" was the same whether a court was dealing with a statutory requirement for corroboration or one that fell within "the rule of practice at common law" (*R v Young* [1923] SASR 35, 72).

Justice Gordon also happened to be on the bench for Young's appeal. His judgment was brief but nevertheless clearly reflected his views of the case:

> At the trial…I formed the opinion that the evidence which the prosecution submitted was corroborative, though not strong; was sufficient, if the jury believed it, to confirm the evidence of the boy…Owing, perhaps to a firm belief that the accused was guilty, I have found it difficult to rid my mind of this opinion; but the fact that a contrary view is taken by my learned colleagues convinces me that the question is highly debatable. I therefore agree that the conviction should be quashed. (*R v Young* [1923] SASR 35, 52)

The outcome in *Young* demonstrates the contentious nature of corroboration and its relationship to notions of justice. Justice Gordon acknowledged having been primarily concerned with Young's factual guilt. It appears Gordon had ever-so-slightly tried to bend the law to fit what he thought was the correct verdict. For Chief Justice Murray and Justice Poole, however, justice was the formal application of the law. They made no attempt to bend the law to secure a conviction in circumstances that gave a strong indication, at least, the accused was factually guilty.

It is worth noting Young had been charged with indecent assault but convicted of common assault and whipped in 1905; acquitted of offences against a three-year-old girl in 1915 (*The Express and Telegraph* 1915, 4); convicted of assaulting a five-year-old girl in 1916 and fined £5; convicted of assaulting an eight-year-old boy in 1917 and imprisoned for 12 months; and had a conviction for a serious offence against a male person quashed by the Full Court in November 1922. After the case involving his stepson, Young was convicted of assaulting a five-year-old boy in 1924 and sentenced to two months imprisonment, "the maximum penalty under the section" (*The Register* 1924, 13), and convicted of an attempt to commit a serious offence upon a male, for which he was sentenced to two years and nine months gaol (*News* 1933, 5). Once again before the court in 1933, Young was convicted of assaulting a six-year-old boy (*News* 1933, 5), and another a boy in 1935 (*News* 1935, 2). He was found not guilty of assaulting a girl of "about 11" in 1948 (*News* 1948, 16), and found guilty of indecently assaulting a six-year-old boy and a six-year-old girl in 1950, for which he was sentenced to four and six years' imprisonment, to be served cumulatively (made concurrent on appeal). On this occasion Young was declared incapable of controlling his sexual desires and was to be detained during His Majesty's pleasure after the sentences were served (*The Advertiser* 1950, 10).[3]

The decisions in *Hargan, Hicks* and *Young* provide powerful examples of the common law approach to corroboration in the first half of the twentieth century. They each confirmed corroboration of a child's sworn testimony was not mandatory, as had long been the common law position (see, for example, *R v Paul* (1890) 25 QBD 202). The three cases confirmed the importance of judicial warnings to juries of the dangers of convicting an accused upon the uncorroborated evidence of a child—even if the child had sworn an oath. If this warning had been given, it was nevertheless open to jurors to convict an accused in the absence of corroboration. As per the decision in *Hicks,* where there was corroborative evidence, no warning was required. As the decision in *Young* highlighted, however, the definition of what was and was not corroboration was still unclear, and judges would face considerable difficulty deciding this issue for the purposes of then deciding whether to issue a warning to a jury.

The definition of corroboration continued to be a problem for courts through the next few decades (*R v Kennewell* [1927] SASR 287; *R v Edwards* (1931) 25 QJPR 80; *Baker v Bulley* (1933) 35 WALR 47). Evidence of children, sworn and unsworn, was received but often made redundant by the common law or statutory corroboration rules. It was not until 1944 that the parliament of Western Australia considered reforming the statutory rules. Section 101 of the *Evidence Act 1906* (WA) allowed children to give unsworn testimony regarding any offence but required corroboration of that testimony in "some material particular" before an accused could be convicted (*Evidence Act 1906* (WA) s 101). The suggested reform would give judges "the absolute discretion…to warrant a conviction without any other evidence in corroboration having been called in support of such testimony" (*Parliamentary Debates,* Legislative Assembly, 6 September 1944, 445, Hon N. Keenan). The change was justified on the basis judicial officers were already assessing whether a child could give unsworn testimony, so to have them also assess the child's testimony and convict in the absence of corroboration was well within their capabilities as a judge. The age-old tension between protecting children and preventing wrongful convictions was played out in the parliament. The status quo narrowly won, 12–10 (*Parliamentary Debates,* Legislative Assembly, 6 September 1944, 445–446, Hon N. Keenan; Western Australia, *Parliamentary Debates,* Legislative Assembly, 6 September 1944, 722, Minister for Justice; Western Australia, *Parliamentary Debates,* Legislative Council, 24 October 1944, 1277). Nothing changed.

The interpretation of s 101 of the *Evidence Act 1906* (WA) came before the Western Australian Supreme Court in 1952, some years after this failed attempt at reform (*Scruby v R* (1952) 55 WALR 1). The defendant, Scruby, stood accused of the unlawful assault of a girl under thirteen years of age. The allegations were in relation to two girls, twelve and eleven years old. The trial only dealt with charges against the younger child, with the other indictment being suspended until the first matter had been resolved. The girls both gave unsworn evidence at Scruby's trial. They gave evidence they had been at Scruby's home when the assault took place. Both girls testified the defendant had given them money and described other events that had taken place on the day. Scruby denied the offence. He said he had invited the girls to his home to play with his own daughter (*Mirror* 1952, 3). Justice Wolff allowed the matter to go to the jury, who found Scruby guilty. Unsure of the corroboration point, though, Wolff reserved the matter for the consideration of the Court of

Criminal Appeal. Justice Wolff asked the appellate court two questions. First, whether the unsworn testimony of the older girl could corroborate the unsworn testimony of the younger girl to satisfy the requirement in s 101(2); and second, if the evidence that Scruby had given the child a coin, as admitted by Scruby himself, constituted corroborative evidence within the meaning of the same section (*Scruby v R* (1952) 55 WALR 1).

The court found in the negative on both questions. According to Justice Virtue, the complainant's evidence was corroborated "in fact if not in law" (*Scruby v R* (1952) 55 WALR 1, 2). That is, the evidence of the complainant's friend confirmed the *facts* of the complainant's evidence, but it did not meet the threshold for it to be corroborative in *law*. Applying the English cases of *R v Manser* ((1934) 25 Cr App R 18) and *R v Baskerville* ((1916) 2 KB 658), as well as the authority in *Croft* (*Croft v The King* (1917) 19 WALR 49), the Court reaffirmed the rule that the unsworn evidence of one child could not corroborate the unsworn evidence of another (*Scruby v R* (1952) 55 WALR 1, 4, applying *R v Manser* (1934) 25 Cr App R 18). The accused's admission regarding the coin corroborated a particular of the girl's story, but not a *material* particular, in that it did not directly implicate him in the commission of the offence as charged (*Scruby v R* (1952) 55 WALR 1, 7). Scruby's conviction was quashed (*Prosecution Project,* Trial ID #16303, Henry Scruby, 1952). The decision in *Scruby* represented a confirmation of the strict application of the statute where the unsworn testimony of children was concerned. The attempt at reform in 1944 had been long forgotten. Indeed, the desire for corroborative evidence may have been stronger than ever.

In 1955, South Australia passed the *Evidence Act Amendment Act 1955* (SA) which, on the one hand, represented a relaxation of the state's laws regarding unsworn testimony of children, but, on the other, introduced more stringent and complex corroboration requirements (*Evidence Act Amendment Act 1955* (SA) s 3). Prior to this reform, the state's legislative corroboration provisions were restricted to procuration and prostitution offences. Section 12 of the *Evidence Act* provided only children under ten were permitted to give unsworn testimony (*Evidence Act 1929* (SA) s 12). Other than this, there was no reference in statute to the need for corroboration of a child's unsworn testimony, and the ordinary common law approach applied. Thus, children over ten years could give evidence on oath and judges would need to warn juries of the danger of convicting if the evidence was uncorroborated.

At the time of the 1955 amendment, s 13 of the *Evidence Act 1929* stipulated the weight and credibility to be given to unsworn testimony of a child under ten years would be "as ought to be attached to evidence given without the sanction of an oath" (*Evidence Act 1929* (SA) s 13). The 1955 amendment added to s 13 by providing:

> Where the evidence of a child admitted by virtue of Section 12 of this Act is given on behalf of the prosecution, and the accused denies the offence on oath, the accused shall not be convicted of the offence unless the evidence of the child is corroborated in some material particular by evidence implicating him. (*Evidence Amendment Act 1955* (SA) s 3, amending *Evidence Act 1929* (SA) s 13)

Debating this proposed amendment in parliament, the Attorney-General noted South Australia had been one of the first British communities to provide for the receipt of unsworn testimony of children (*Criminal Law Consolidation Act 1876* (SA) ss 377–378). The recent case of *R v Williams* had highlighted South Australia's unsworn testimony provisions, which had not been amended since being introduced in 1876 (*R v Williams* [1954] SASR 216). In 1876, such a provision was revolutionary, but it was now out of date because, unlike most other states, it did not require unsworn testimony of children to be corroborated. Such an assessment of the proposed amendment demonstrates the thinking that was still dominant within political and legal—and even social—attitudes in 1955. To allow children to give unsworn testimony about any offence was viewed as a great service to justice for offences against children. The Attorney-General noted many children were unable to swear an oath, meaning vital evidence that might convict an accused was often not brought before the court. He continued, referring again to *R v Williams*. Williams had been convicted upon the unsworn and uncorroborated testimony of a six-year-old girl. At trial, however, doubts had been raised about the child's testimony and the unrealistic time frame in which the accused was alleged to have committed the offence. The jury had convicted, notwithstanding this apparent issue with the evidence (*R v Williams* [1954] SASR 216). The Attorney-General noted if South Australia had the same corroboration requirements as other states, this verdict would not have been sustained. It was, he believed, "desirable in the interests of justice that corroboration of such evidence should be required where the accused denies the offences on oath" (*Parliamentary Debates*, Legislative Council, 28 September, 1955, 896–897, The Hon C D Rowe, Attorney-General). The amendment was passed without any further debate.

A rare display of criticism of corroboration rules during the middle of the century is found in the Victorian Court of Appeal decision of *R v Tripodi* in 1961 (*R v Tripodi* [1961] VR 186, 191–193). The Victorian court criticised the High Court's 1924 decision in *R v Eade*. *Tripodi* was concerned with corroboration of an alleged accomplice's testimony, and not a child witness. But, for the first time since the failed attempt at reform in Western Australia in 1944, there was a suggestion, at least, of some unease about the corroboration rules. The Victorian court thought the High Court's reasoning in *Eade* nearly forty years earlier was "not without difficulty" and had the potential "to lead to somewhat remarkable results" (*R v Tripodi* [1961] VR 186, 193). In *Eade*, the High Court indicated denials made by the accused when the police interviewed him could be corroborative of the child's evidence if the jury believed they were lies (*Eade v R* (1924) 34 CLR 154, 159). The Court of Appeal in *Tripodi* thought the High Court in *Eade* had drawn an illogical distinction between denials made by an accused before his or her trial and denials made during a trial, but noted if the distinction had not been drawn, the result would be "the surprising position that an accused person who went into the box to deny a charge brought against him and was not believed by the jury was in a worse situation than an accused who does not give evidence" because denying the offence, even in court, may corroborate the child's testimony and, thus, an accused would always be better off choosing not to give evidence in court (*R v Tripodi* [1961] VR 186, 193). Being a High Court decision, the Victorian court was bound to follow the High Court precedent, but despite their reservations about the lack of logic in the Eade decision, the Victorian court nevertheless agreed that denials could potentially corroborate evidence of another witness, but it would be a matter for each trial judge to determine whether the denials were potentially corroborative and for the jury to determine if, in fact, they did provide corroborative evidence.

In 1965, Queensland's Parliament introduced corroboration reforms via the *Children's Services Act 1965* (Qld). Section 146 introduced a general corroboration provision for "any proceeding" for an offence under that Act where a child witness gave unsworn testimony (*Children's Services Act 1965* (Qld) s 146). The introduction of this provision supplemented the state's existing corroboration requirements, referred to earlier in this chapter. The new provisions were restricted, though. They did not include sexual offences or other criminal offences, other than those contained within the Act that dealt with offences of child abuse or neglect.

Three quarters of the way through the twentieth century, corroboration of children's testimony was still causing problems for courtrooms around the country. In 1974, in *Paine v R*, Paine appealed to the Tasmanian Court of Appeal against his conviction for attempted murder on the ground, *inter alia*, that the trial judge had failed to warn the jury of the dangers of convicting him on the uncorroborated evidence of the complainant, a fifteen-year-old girl (*Paine v R* [1974] Tas SR (NC) N14). The state's statutory corroboration provisions did not apply in this case. Thus, the question for the court was whether the common law approach to corroboration required judges to warn juries *in every case* of the danger of convicting upon the uncorroborated sworn evidence of a child. The Court found, aside from the various legislative provisions that required corroboration in relation to particular offences, at common law corroboration was otherwise a general rule of practice and therefore such warnings were a matter for a trial judge's discretion. Referring to the New Zealand case of *R v Parker* [1968] NZLR 325, Chief Justice Green thought it was "a matter of prudence" for judges to advise juries "to pay particular attention to, or to scrutinise with special care, the evidence of young children, and to explain the tendencies of infants to invention or distortion" (*Paine v R* [1974] Tas SR (NC) N14). Justices Chambers and Nettlefold found a "judge might well be under the duty" to warn juries where the child witness is "young" and where, consequently, "there is a doubt with regard to the reliability of the witness" (*Paine v R* [1974] Tas SR (NC) N14). In this case the court found there was "no reason to think that it would be unsafe to act upon the uncorroborated evidence of the complainant," and the appeal was dismissed. The Court's observations about the reliability of child witnesses generally, however, suggest the Tasmanian court was at least contemplating extending the requirement for judicial warnings to all cases involving the testimony of very young children.

In *Kelleher v R*, also in 1974, the High Court reaffirmed the reasoning of both the *Hargan* and *Hicks* decisions (131 CLR 534). The case did not involve the testimony of a child, but the various decisions of the judges refer to children and relevant case law. Chief Justice Barwick repeated Hale's argument that rape allegations were easily made and hard to disprove (131 CLR 534, 543). According to Chief Justice Barwick, however, the corroboration rule was related to Hale's fears of wrongful convictions and therefore a warning was not required "where those reasons have no play" (131 CLR 534, 543). In other words, those reasons would have no play where there was no risk of a wrongful conviction. Similarly, Justice Gibbs confirmed the "well established" need for a judge to warn a jury of the dangers of convicting on uncorroborated evidence was still "a matter of practice," although it was not required by legislation (131 CLR 534, 553). Justice Jacobs (dissenting) said:

> I will concede that the rule requiring warning in the case of sexual offences remains well based in modern times despite the changes in social conditions and in the status and education of women over the centuries...I must confess that I am puzzled why there is a greater need for corroboration of identification of an alleged rapist or indecent assaulter than of a murder attempter. (131 CLR 534, 568)

Justice Jacobs' reference to the changing status and education of women signalled the potential for a change in the approach to corroboration.

1975 to 2000—the Not-so-Sudden Demise of Corroboration

The doubts voiced by Justice Jacobs in *Kelleher,* as cautious as they were, began to find their way into much of the law reform literature published from 1975 onwards. In 1975 Queensland's Law Reform Commission, for example, concluded the corroboration rules drew "an unnecessary distinction" between sworn and unsworn testimony (*The Law Relating to Evidence* (Report No 19, November 1975) par 9). They recommended abolishing the general, common law warnings, while retaining the statutory provisions regarding corroboration in relation to certain offences in the *Criminal Code.* Unwilling to adopt such recommendations, Queensland introduced a provision in the *Evidence Act 1977* (Qld) requiring judges to warn juries of the dangers of acting on unsworn testimony "unless they find that it is corroborated in some material particular by other evidence implicating that person" (s 9(2)). The Act did, however, expressly prohibit the rule against mutual corroboration confirmed years earlier in *Scruby* and *Croft* and only relatively recently confirmed in the United Kingdom in *DPP v Hester* [1973] AC 296, by allowing unsworn testimony of a child to corroborate unsworn testimony of another child (*Evidence Act 1977* (Qld) s 9(3); *Scruby v R* (1952) 55 WALR 1; *Croft v The King* (1917) 19 WALR 49).

The report of the Commonwealth-appointed *Royal Commission on Human Relationships* was also published in 1977 (Commonwealth of Australia 1978, 215). Reviewing the criminal justice process in the context of sexual offences, the Commission invoked the words of Hale, claiming "it is easy to allege rape but difficult to refute it." Reiterating the traditional view of corroboration as a safeguard for innocent men against the potentially fraudulent allegations made by women and children, the Commission surmised "men need special protection" (Commonwealth of Australia 1978, 195). Like the Queensland Law Reform Commission, they doubted, however, the utility of the common law corroboration warning, concluding:

> [i]f we considered that it gave any real protection to the accused, we would be uneasy about recommending its abolition. However, since the

> warning exhorts the jury to do precisely what it is bound to do in any case, it appears to lack any real substance at all. Its retention would conflict with our general aim to equate sexual and non-sexual cases as much as possible. (Commonwealth of Australia 1978, 196)

The Commission recommended the abolition of judicial warnings in all sexual offence cases. From the 1980s onwards, requirements for the evidence of children to be corroborated soon began to crumble across all Australian jurisdictions, albeit in a haphazard and inconsistent fashion. Reports produced by the New South Wales Law Reform Commission in 1988 (Report No 56, pt 6, div 5), the Law Reform Commission of Tasmania in 1990 (Report No 62), the Western Australian Law Reform Commission of Western Australia in 1991 (Project No 87, 26) and the Australian Law Reform Commission in 1997 (Report No 84, par. 14.67-14.73), each called for reform of the rules regarding corroboration. Table 7.1 on the following page sets out the legislative amendments for these reforms and the time frame in which they took place.

Table 7.1 reveals the slow pace of these reforms, taking place over a period of fifteen years between 1980 and 1995.

After these reforms, an additional line of judicial authority was developed that impacted—and continues to impact—upon the testimony of child witnesses (Australian Law Reform Commission 2005). The courts in the cases of *Longman v The Queen, Crampton v The Queen* and *Doggett v The Queen* confirmed judges could no longer warn juries of the inherent unreliability of children as a class of witnesses (*Longman v The Queen* (1989) 168 CLR 79; *Crampton v R* (2000) 206 CLR 161; *Doggett v R* (2001) 208 CLR 343). They were, however, permitted to warn juries in relation to features of the evidence of the child in the case over which they were presiding. It was—and remains—the case that the uncorroborated testimony of a child can be raised by judges where it "is necessary to avoid a perceptible risk of miscarriage of justice arising from the particular circumstances of the case" to warn the jury to scrutinise the evidence carefully before finding a defendant guilty (*Longman v The Queen* (1989) 168 CLR 79, 86). The risk that inexperienced jurors may interpret warnings as directions by the judge as to what the verdict ought to be has been raised in various circumstances and suggests the testimony

Table 7.1 Reforming corroboration rules and requirements

	NSW	Qld	Vic	WA	SA	Tas
Judge not required to warn re. uncorrob. evidence of unsworn testimony	*Evidence (Children) Amendment Act* 1985s 3	*Criminal Law Amendment Act* 1996s 113	*Crimes (Sexual Offences) Act* 1980s 62(3)	*Criminal Law Amendment Act* 1988s 42	*Evidence (Misc.) Amendment Act* 1993s 3	*Criminal Code Amendment (Sexual Offences) Act* 1987s 17
Judges must not warn re. uncorrob. testimony	*Evidence Act* 1995s 164.	judges can warn re. individual: s 632(2) but must not warn re. unreliability of class of witness: *Criminal Code* s 632(3)	*Crimes (Sexual Offences) Act* 1991s 8	*Acts Amendment (Evidence of Children and Others) Act* 1992s 8	judges still able to warn in certain cases: *Evidence Act* 1929s 12A.	*Evidence Amendment (Children and Special Witnesses) Act* 1995s 122D(2)

(continued)

Table 7.1 (continued)

	NSW	Qld	Vic	WA	SA	Tas
Statutory requirement for corrob. abolished	*Crimes (Child Assault) Amendment* 1985	*Criminal Code, Evidence Act and Other Acts Amendment Act* 1989	*Crimes (Sexual Offences) Act* 1991	*Criminal Law Amendment Act 1988* re. specific offences General provision in s 101 *Evidence Act* 1906 repealed by *Acts Amendment (Evidence of Children and Others) Act* 1992	*Evidence (Misc.) Amendment Act* 1999	*Evidence Amendment (Children and Special Witnesses) Act* 1995

of children may still be assessed based on whether it is corroborated or not (Wood 2003, par 21).

Conclusion

Whether corroboration was a rule of law or a matter of practice, for most of the twentieth century it is clear the testimony of child witnesses was significantly limited by the corroboration rules. Corroboration as envisaged by Hale and Blackstone in the sixteenth and seventeenth centuries was not overly complicated. By the start of the twentieth century, however, the law comprised a complex set of rules and practices with the potential to cause grave injustices for the accused and the victim.

While state statutory frameworks were responsible for many of the rules of corroboration, this chapter demonstrates the impact of the corroboration rules was equally attributable to judicial interpretations of the rules and the complexity that developed around them. The practice of bending the law resulted in considerable inconsistency and confusion. Recognising this, the states deliberately and decisively wrote corroboration out of child witness law in the 1980s and 1990s, only for it to be more or less reintroduced via the alternative route of warnings of the risks of injustice. While Hale and Blackstone, as well as the various state legislatures and members of the judiciary, were motivated by a desire to avoid the conviction of innocent people, this chapter has demonstrated corroboration likely led to many miscarriages of justice for child victims.

Notes

1. Following the passing of the *Criminal Law Amendment Act 1885* (UK), New South Wales, Victoria, Tasmania and Western Australia introduced legislation requiring such testimony to be corroborated. *Criminal Law Amendment Act 1883* (NSW) ss 41–44, 59, 60, as amended by *Criminal Law and Evidence Amendment Act 1891 (NSW)*—sexual offences committed against girls u14 (ss 41–44) and buggery (s 59), indecent assault on male (s

60); applied to those of "tender years;" unsworn, material evidence implicating accused. *Crimes Act 1891 (Vic)*—rape, unlawful, carnal knowledge (and attempt) against girls (s 33(2)); applied to those of "tender years;" unsworn, material evidence implicating accused. *Criminal Law Amendment Act 1892 (WA)*—defilement of girl u12 (and attempt); girl 12–14 yrs (s 4); applied to those of "tender years;" unsworn, material evidence implicating accused. *Prevention of Cruelty to, and Better Protection of, Children Act 1895 (Tas)*—offences under that Act (s 8); applied to those of "tender years;" unsworn, material evidence implicating accused. In Queensland, there were unsworn testimony provisions, but the evidence of children still had to be corroborated for a number of offences (*Criminal Code Act 1899* (Qld) accomplice (s 632); defile girls u12 (s 212); u14 and idiots (s 215); procuring (s217 and s 218). In South Australia there were no specific legislative provisions with respect to the corroboration of the testimony of children, although there were some general corroboration requirements (*Criminal Law Consolidation Amendment Act 1885* (SA) s 14).

2. On defining corroboration see also: *R v O'Brien* [1912] VLR 133; *Sullivan v R* (1913) 15 WAR 23; Backhouse 2001, 297).
3. Pursuant to the *Criminal Law Consolidation Act 1935* (SA), a person could be detained at His Majesty's pleasure "where there is reason to suspect that the mental condition of such person is such that he is incapable of exercising proper control over his sexual instincts" (*Criminal Law Consolidation Act 1935* (SA) s 77(1)(b)).

References

The Advertiser (Adelaide, SA: 1931–1954). "Supreme." November 15, 1950.

The Age (Melbourne, Vic: 1854–1954). "News Of The Day." May 26, 1892.

Australian Law Reform Commission and Australian Human Rights and Equal Opportunity Commission, *Seen and Heard: Priority for Children in the Legal Process* (Report No. 84, November 1997).

Australian Law Reform Commission, *Uniform Evidence Law* (Report No. 102, December 2005).

Backhouse, Constance. 2000. "Skewering the Credibility of Women: A Reappraisal of Corroboration in Australian Legal History." *University of Western Australia Law Review* 29 (1): 79–107.

Backhouse, Constance. 2001. "The Doctrine of Corroboration in Sexual Assault Trials in Early Twentieth-Century Canada and Australia." *Queen's Law Journal* 26 (2): 297–338.

Baker v Bulley (1933) 35 WALR 47.

Blackstone, William. *Commentaries on the Laws of England*, vol. 4 (1765–1769, The Avalon Project, 2008): 214, cited in Louise A. Jackson. 2000. *Child Sexual Abuse in Victorian England*. New York: Routledge.

Blewer, Robyn. 2020. "Testing the Law and Testing a Child's Evidence: Nineteenth-Century Corroboration Reforms and Child Witness Testimony." *Australian Historical Studies* 51 (3): 266–281. https://doi.org/10.1080/1031461x.2019.1697304.

Bronitt, Simon. 1991. "Baskerville Revisited: The Definition of Corroboration Reconsidered Criminal Law Review." *Criminal Law Review*: 30–37.

Children's Services Act 1965 (Qld).

Commonwealth of Australia, *Royal Commission into Institutional Responses to Child Sexual Abuse* (Criminal Justice Report, 2017), I–X.

Commonwealth of Australia, *Royal Commission on Human Relationships* (Final Report, 1978), vol. 5.

Crampton v R (2000) 206 CLR 161.

Crimes Act 1900 (NSW).

Crimes Act 1891 (Vic).

Criminal Code Act 1899 (Qld).

Criminal Code Act 1902 (WA).

Criminal Law and Evidence Amendment Act 1891 (NSW).

Criminal Law Amendment Act 1883 (NSW).

Criminal Law Amendment Act 1885 (UK).

Criminal Law Amendment Act 1892 (WA).

Criminal Law Consolidation Act 1876 (SA).

Criminal Law Consolidation Act 1935 (SA).

Criminal Law Consolidation Amendment Act 1885 (SA).

Croft v The King (1917) 19 WALR 49.

The Daily News (Perth, WA: 1882–1950). "Alleged Criminal Offence." June 8, 1905.

Doggett v R (2001) 208 CLR 343.

Eade v R (1924) 34 CLR 154.

Eather v R (1914) 19 CLR 409.

Evening News (Sydney, NSW: 1869–1931). “Assault on a Child.” July 28, 1921.
Evidence Act 1977 (Qld).
Evidence Act 1929 (SA).
Evidence Act 1906 (WA).
Evidence Act Amendment Act 1955 (SA).
The Express and Telegraph (Adelaide, SA: 1867–1922). “Child Assaulted.” December 20, 1915.
Hale, Matthew. 1736. *Historia Placitorum Coronæ: The History of the Pleas of the Crown*: 634–635, cited in T. D. Lyon and R. Lamagna. 2007. “The History of Children's Hearsay: From Old Bailey to Post-Davis.” *Indiana Law Journal* 82 (4): 1034.
Hargan v The King (1919) 27 CLR 13.
Hicks v R (1920) 28 CLR 36.
Kelleher v R (1974) 4 ALR 450.
Langbein, John H. 2005. *The Origins of Adversary Criminal Trial*. Oxford: Oxford University Press.
Law Reform Commissioner of Tasmania, *Child Witnesses* (Report No. 62, 1990).
The Law Reform Commission of Western Australia, *Evidence of Children and other Vulnerable Witnesses* (Project No. 87, April 1991), 26.
Longman v The Queen (1989) 168 CLR 79.
The Maitland Daily Mercury (NSW: 1894–1939). “Execution of Joseph Campbell.” December 20, 1901.
The Maitland Daily Mercury (NSW: 1894– 1939). “A Re-Trial.” June 13, 1924.
The Mildura Cultivator (Vic: 1888–1920). “Telegrams.” December 14, 1901.
Mirror (Perth, WA: 1921–1956). “Collapses in Dock When Found Guilty.” October 18, 1952.
Myers, John E. B., Susan E. Diedrich, Devon Lee, Kelly Fincher, and Rachel M. Stern. 2002. “Prosecution of Child Sexual Abuse in the United States.” In *Critical Issues in Child Sexual Abuse: Historical, Legal and Psychological Perspectives*, edited by Jon R. Conte, 27–70. Thousand Oaks, CA: Sage.
Naylor, Bronwyn. 1989. “The Child in the Witness Box.” *Australian and New Zealand Journal of Criminology* 22 (2): 82–94.
News (Adelaide, SA: 1923–1954). “Convicted Man Examined by Doctors.” October 3, 1935.
News (Adelaide, SA: 1923–1954). “Found Guilty of Serious Crime.” February 7, 1933.
News (Adelaide, SA: 1923–1954). “Found Not Guilty of Assault Charge.” December 8, 1948.

New South Wales Law Reform Commission, *Evidence* (Report No. 56, 1988).
The North Western Courier (Narrabri, NSW: 1913–1955). "Quarter Sessions." February 24, 1919.
The Northam Advertiser. "A Serious Offence." May 6, 1905.
Oakleigh Leader (*North Brighton, Vic: 1888–1902*). "Justice to All." December 7, 1901.
Paine v R [1974] Tas SR (NC) N14.
Pigot, Thomas, Great Britain Home Office, and Great Britain Advisory Group on Video-Recorded Evidence. 1989. *Report of the Advisory Group on Video-Recorded Evidence.* London: Home Office, United Kingdom.
Prevention of Cruelty to, and Better Protection of, Children Act 1895 (Tas).
The Prosecution Project Database [PP], https://prosecutionproject.griffith.edu.au/prosecutions (version 1, 17 July 2016), Trial ID # 559765, Victorian Supreme Court [VICSC], Edmund Gregg, 1892.
The Prosecution Project Database [PP], https://prosecutionproject.griffith.edu.au/prosecutions (version 1, 17 July 2016), Trial ID #16303, West Australian Supreme Court [WASC], Henry Scruby, 1952. Conviction quashed. *Nolle prosequi* entered on charges relating to the other child.
The Prosecution Project Database [PP], https://prosecutionproject.griffith.edu.au/prosecutions (version 1, 17 July 2016), Trial ID #12096, Western Australia Supreme Court [WASC], John Joseph Croft, 1916.
Queensland Law Reform Commission, *The Law Relating to Evidence* (Report No. 19, November 1975).
Recorder (Port Pirie, SA: 1919–1954). "You Low-Down Skunk." October 19, 1935.
The Register (Adelaide, SA: 1901–1929). "Assault on Little Boy." June 7, 1924.
R v Baskerville (1916) 2 KB 658.
R v Brasier (1779) 1 Leach 199.
R v Brown (1910) 6 Cr App R 24.
R v Carroll (1906) 6 SR (NSW) 258.
R v Eade (1923) 24 SR (NSW) 117.
R v Eather (1914) 14 SR (NSW) 280.
R v Edwards (1931) 25 QJPR 80.
R v Graham (1910) 4 Cr App R.
R v Gregg (1892) 18 VLR 218.
R v Hargan (1919) 19 SR (NSW) 257.
R v Kennewell [1927] SASR 287.
R v Manser (1934) 25 Cr App R 18.
R v O'Brien [1912] VLR 133.

R v Paul (1890) 25 QBD 202.
R v Pitts (1912) 8 Cr App R.
R v Severo Dossi (1918) 13 Cr App R.
R v Smith (1901) 26 VLR 683.
R v Tripodi [1961] VR 186.
R v Walsh (1905) 7 WALR 263.
R v Warren (1919) 14 Cr App R.
R v Williams [1954] SASR 216.
Scruby v R (1952) 55 WALR 1.
South Australia, *Parliamentary Debates,* Legislative Council, 28 September, 1955, 896–897 (The Hon C. D. Rowe, Attorney-General).
Stephen, James Fitzjames. 1914. *A Digest of the Law of Evidence*. London: Macmillan and Company.
Sullivan v R (1913) 15 WAR 23.
Truth (Perth, WA: 1903–1931). "A Uniformed Ruffian." September 9, 1916.
Truth (Perth, WA: 1903–1931). "Baandee Banality." September 2, 1905.
Western Australia, *Parliamentary Debates,* Legislative Council, 24 October 1944, 1277.
Western Australia, *Parliamentary Debates,* Legislative Assembly, 9 August 1906, 939 (Attorney-General).
Western Australia, *Parliamentary Debates,* Legislative Assembly, 6 September 1944, 445 (Hon N. Keenan).
Western Australia, *Parliamentary Debates,* Legislative Council, 4 June 1992, 3397–3398 (Hon Peter Foss).
Western Australia, *Parliamentary Debates,* Legislative Assembly, 6 September 1944, 722 (Minister for Justice).
Wood, Justice James. "Sexual Assault and the Admission of Evidence." Paper, Practice and Prevention: Contemporary Issues in Adult Sexual Assault (University of Technology, Sydney, 12 February 2003).
The Wyalong Advocate and Mining, Agricultural and Pastoral Gazette (NSW: 1900–1928). "Indecent Assault." October 12, 1923.

8

"*The Law Which Professed to Protect … Served to Crush*": Indigenous Child Witnesses

> Aboriginal and Torres Strait Islander readers are advised that this chapter contains names of people who have died.

In 1900, Thomas Tierney was prosecuted in a Sydney courtroom for neglecting his apprentice, a fifteen-year-old Aboriginal girl named Eliza Critchley. Mrs. Eleanor Keele, an inspector under the *State Children Relief Act 1901* (NSW), gave evidence against Mr. Tierney. For over two hours on a bitterly cold, wet and wintry day in July, Keele had watched Eliza working in the back of Mr. Tierney's premises, dressed in an apron and old dress. On closer inspection, Eliza was found to have nothing else on. Mrs. Keele was cross-examined by Mr. Tierney's solicitor, Charles Bull. Didn't she know it was the custom of Aborigines not to wear clothes? No, she did not. But in any event, on such a day, Mrs. Keele surmised, "natives as well as anyone, would wear clothes" (*Truth* 1900, 6). Elizabeth Beaumont and Amy Allen, neighbours of Mr. Tierney's, also gave evidence. They too had seen Eliza in a state of undress on other occasions (*Truth* 1900, 6).

R. Blewer, *Child Witnesses in Twentieth Century Australian Courtrooms*, Palgrave Histories of Policing, Punishment and Justice,
https://doi.org/10.1007/978-3-030-69791-4_8

Eliza was described in the press as "exceedingly well-spoken for a girl of such a tender age" (*Truth* 1900, 6). She denied telling Mrs. Tierney she did not want to wear clothes and gave evidence she was fond of wearing clothes. It was Mr. and Mrs. Tierney who did not let her wear "any of the many clothes she had." The tactic of Mr. Bull's, to argue Eliza voluntarily—and because of her culture—went undressed on a cold winter day, succeeded. Despite the evidence of three witnesses and Eliza herself, Tierney was acquitted—although Eliza was removed from his charge and placed in the care of the state (*Truth* 1900, 6).

This case of Eliza Critchley and Thomas Tierney, and witnesses Eleanor Keele, Elizabeth Beaumont and Amy Allen, demonstrates the marked similarities and significant differences to cases of other child witnesses. Here, like so many others, the testimony of a young girl and other witnesses was rejected in favour of the apparently more persuasive argument of an experienced solicitor and one-time member of NSW Parliament, Charles Bull (*Australian Star* 1906, 4). This is the nature of the adversarial system. Whoever persuades wins.

Eliza's case also raises issues relevant to matters involving Indigenous children. To begin, Eliza was described in the press as "half-caste." In gathering cases for this chapter, no distinction has been made between those described as "full-blood," "half-caste" or otherwise. This decision was made for two reasons: first, this is not quantitative research whereby the description of Aboriginality is a variable.[1] Second, the children in this chapter were dealt with by the criminal justice system on the basis they were Aboriginal. While children may have been described as "half-caste" or even "three-quarter-caste," they do not appear to have been treated any differently on this account, as far as procedure was concerned. For all intents and purposes, they were "Aboriginal." Another issue setting cases like Eliza Critchley's apart is the reference to her cultural background. Notions of Indigenous culture were used to question Eliza's credibility and undermine her testimony. Finally, there were people prepared to stand up in court and fight to protect Aboriginal children.

It was challenging enough to find the two hundred or so cases in this book of male and female children, irrespective of their ethnicities, cultural backgrounds and ages, giving evidence in court, regardless of the offence type. To locate cases involving Aboriginal and Torres Strait

Islander children as witnesses proved a far greater challenge. As recently as 2012, Noongar woman and legal scholar, Dr Hannah McGlade noted Aboriginal and Torres Strait Islander children's "experiences of courts have not been documented" but it is apparent from extant research that "secondary abuse and trauma resulting from the court process is common to all child complainants" (McGlade 2012, 165). Historian Mark Finnane has observed the "relative silence of the historical record on the interactions of Aboriginal people with the criminal justice system" (Finnane 2020, 4). Similarly, historian Libby Connors has noted "Australian colonial historians have been slow to take up the challenge of Aboriginal-centred history" (Connors 2012, 125). Records of First Nations children and the criminal justice process in the post-colonial era reflect the observations of McGlade, Finnane and Connors.

The story underlying the cases described in this chapter is one of the discrimination, abuse, and trauma of Indigenous children at the hands of other Indigenous adults, non-Indigenous adults, and the justice system itself. Despite the temptation to delve further into those broader issues, the focus of this chapter is a narrow one of documenting a number of cases of Indigenous children giving evidence in court as witnesses or complainants in the twentieth century with the objective of considering the similarities and differences in these cases to those considered in previous chapters. In earlier drafts of this book, these cases were woven throughout and appeared alongside the other children. Like the voices of those children, though, the voices of First Nations children in this chapter deserve to be heard but more so, are deserving of a distinct chapter considering how their testimony was received—or not—by criminal courts in the twentieth century because of the unique challenges they may have faced because of their cultural and/or ethnic background (McGlade 2012, 165). Such challenges, furthermore, are linked to "processes of dispossession, colonisation and alienation" (Atkinson 1988 in Tatz 1990, 251). While not representative, the cases canvassed in this chapter illustrate the unique challenges and experiences Indigenous child witnesses experienced as they participated in the criminal justice process over and above those faced by non-indigenous child witnesses in the preceding chapters. The chapter briefly considers the extant literature and research on First Nations children as witnesses in court, followed by a consideration of cases involving Aboriginal children giving evidence and various attempts at reform over the twentieth century specifically in relation to Indigenous child witnesses.

Indigenous Children and the Common Law

Aboriginal and Torres Strait Islanders were subjected to British criminal law in NSW from at least 1836, following the Supreme Court decision in *R v Murrell and Bummaree* ((1836) 1 Legge 72). This case concerned the applicability of English law to two Aboriginal defendants charged with murdering another Aboriginal. Sidney Stephen, counsel acting for Mr. Murrell, made the following submission highlighting how, even in the early days of colonisation, the relationship between Indigenous people and the English criminal justice process was contested:

> The reason why subjects of Great Britain are bound by the laws of their own country is, that they are protected by them; *the natives are not protected by those laws, they are not admitted as witnesses in Courts of Justice,* they cannot claim any civil rights, they cannot obtain recovery of, or compensation for, those lands which have been torn from them, and which they have probably held for centuries. They are not therefore bound by laws which afford them no protection [emphasis added]. (*Sydney Gazette and New South Wales Advertiser* 1836, 3)[2]

The Court disagreed with Mr. Stephen, finding protection was not a necessary precursor to being bound by a law or legal system and therefore, Aboriginal and Torres Strait Islanders were subject to English laws, despite not necessarily having the protection of them (*R v Murrell and Bummaree* (1836) 1 Legge 72; Ford 2010, 196–203; Finnane and Douglas 2012, 37–41; Anthony 2013, 30). This book has revealed a pattern of pragmatism in the practice of common law. Recognising many cases would require the testimony of children, some adjustments to ordinary courtroom practices were made for justice to be served. The same can be said for Indigenous witnesses. Notwithstanding their apparent inability to appear as witnesses per *Murrell and Bummarree*, Indigenous child witnesses did appear in court, albeit rarely.[3] At a broader level, in the years since the decision in *Murrell and Bummarree*, First Nations people have been subjected to the law and "excluded from designing and establishing the legal and political institutions that control and maintain the social structure" (Moreton-Robinson 2015, 66).

Focussing on Indigenous children as witnesses in court, two cases serve as bookends to this chapter. Historian Libby Connors provides a detailed analysis of the case of an Aboriginal boy, Ralph William Barrow, who gave evidence numerous times between 1846 and 1854 in relation to a relentless prosecution of one incident (Connors 2010, 775–787). Ralph witnessed the murders of a white couple by Aboriginal men in the Moreton Bay area in Queensland (at the time northern New South Wales) in the mid-nineteenth century. Ralph's first appearance in court was just days after the offence, when he was ten years old. He was eighteen at the time of his last appearance. Ralph's experience of the adversarial trial process included being imprisoned after his second appearance in court, when he was fifteen. The testimony Ralph had given then differed to the testimony he had given five years earlier. He was cross-examined by both of the defendants and the magistrate and is reported to have started crying on the stand. He was accused of "prevarication" and sentenced to a week in prison. Ralph underwent incredible torment, indeed torture, at the hands of a legal system Connors argues showed itself "surprisingly susceptible to aggressive settler interests on the northern frontier" (2010, 243). As Connors notes, Ralph William Barrow was exploited by the legal system and made a witness "of consequence to a white settler community intent on vengeance" (2010, 231).

One hundred and forty years on, in 1994, a Queensland case was heard in the Brisbane Magistrates Court. Three Indigenous boys, all teenagers, alleged six police officers had abducted them from inner-city Brisbane, taken them out of the city to an industrial area in a suburb known as Pinkenba, and abandoned them at 4am. The boys, aged between thirteen and fifteen years old, were cross-examined at length at the defendants' committal hearing. Indigenous patterns of speech and aspects of culture, such as gratuitous concurrence and silence in deference to elders, were exploited by the barristers who represented the accused officers. Linguist Diana Eades had written a handbook on Aboriginal

English and the law to assist lawyers, and improve the capacity "for the legal system to recognise Aboriginal ways of using English" (2016, 472, referring to Eades 1992). This handbook was subsequently utilised by the barristers for the accused police officers in a way that made "things worse in terms of intercultural communication" (Eades 2012, 484). Of the possibility her work may have been used as an instruction book by barristers to act against the interests of Aboriginal witnesses, Eades said:

> I was assured that the adversarial balance of the common law trial process would ensure that this is not the case. This is probably true for most cases, but the Pinkenba case was both unusual and extreme, because it involved a very serious and highly contested hearing, in which not one, but six police officers were charged with abuse of Aboriginal people, and in which the only evidence against the charged police officers was that of the Aboriginal boys. Further, the case reversed the typical situation in which police officers provide prosecution evidence against accused Aboriginal people. (Eades 2012, 484)

Between Ralph Barrow's case in the mid-nineteenth century and the witness in the Pinkenba Six case at the end of the twentieth century, Aboriginal children appeared infrequently as witnesses in criminal courts. As the following cases demonstrate, however, Ralph's treatment, while a result of frontier conditions as Connors suggested, is also a result of the very structure and nature of a system, the objective of which is to administer justice. Thus, while acknowledging Ralph's experience as a reflection of colonial frontier conditions, this chapter places his case within the context of broader problems inherent in a trial process, the design of which permitted—indeed demanded—the exploitation of this young boy and many other Indigenous child witnesses who came after him. Whether using Ralph to attempt to prosecute an offence repeatedly between 1846 and 1854, or employing tactics in 1994 to stop the prosecution of police officers, the obligation of each side in the adversarial process to fight—and at times to fight dirty—is clear.

Locating Child Witness Cases

Two sources were drawn upon to locate this group of child witnesses. The Trove online database of national newspapers was searched using various terms including "Aboriginal," "Indigenous," and "native," each with and without the addition of "child," "youth," "girl," "boy" and "tender years."[4] The *Prosecution Project Database* was the second source. This is a research database of Australian prosecutions with a public-facing search engine.[5] This database was searched for relevant cases involving "Aboriginal" children. Where Aboriginal children were indicated (either as a victim, witness or in the notes field), or where a matter indicated an Aboriginal victim, additional information was sought in Trove to verify whether an Indigenous child was involved and further, whether they gave evidence in court. Confirmation of *Prosecution Project* data in Trove was also not always possible. In his study of Aboriginal defendants in New South Wales courts between 1850 and 1914, Mark Finnane makes several points about the *Prosecution Project* data that apply equally to the data in this chapter (2020, 5). Analysis of the *Prosecution Project* data indicates the descriptor "Aboriginal" was only entered in court records for one-third of defendants who have since been identified as Aboriginal. Finnane notes police gazettes often provided a valuable source of identifying factors of defendants, including whether a defendant was described as "half-caste." Even then, he suggests "it is generally essential to establish whether there is any reference to Aboriginality in other sources" (Finnane 2020, 5). While these two sources provided a number of cases, the sample is not representative. Detailed archival research may uncover additional cases, as might oral histories.

It may also be the case, however, even where further research is undertaken, that very few cases involving the testimony of Indigenous children were prosecuted. This may be due to racist attitudes of investigators and prosecutors. It may also be because, as Jiman/Bungjalung woman, Emeritus Professor Judy Atkinson noted in 1990, Indigenous women and children had "no faith in the criminal justice system" and that their experience of the system had shown them "it is futile to seek help or protection from the western criminal justice system" (1990, 14). In a 1946 case two Aboriginal defendants, Norminnieorbu and Nundul, were charged with murdering an Aboriginal man at Junction Bay, Arnhem Land. The matter was discontinued after Judge Wells, referring to the Indigenous child witness, stated:

> A mere child who should not have been brought before the court had been brought as a witness and probably, he would get into a lot of trouble when he returned to his tribe. No jury would take the slightest notice of such evidence. (*The Advertiser* 1947, 14)

Why Wells thought the child might "get into a lot of trouble" is not clear. For whatever reason, Wells thought it was not in the child's interests to give evidence, and, even if they had given evidence, he felt certain the jury would have disregarded such testimony. Elizabeth Eggleston wrote of a case in the 1960s where a "young Aboriginal victim of rape" had "less hesitation" in giving evidence when her mother was not in the courtroom than when she was present (1976, 167). Research has suggested Indigenous children are less likely to disclose sexual abuse to police than non-indigenous children. In 1991, the Human Rights and Equal Opportunity Commission noted numerous cases where young Indigenous victims did not report the crime (HREOC 1991; see also Behrendt 2000, 361–362). Further, where Indigenous child victims of sexual abuse do make such allegations, they are less likely to have the matter proceed to prosecution than non-Indigenous children (Bailey et al. 2017, 188). Racist (and sexist) attitudes would likely be a further reason there were so few cases in court, even where the child and/or adults supported such action being taken. In 1940, for example, the employer of a sixteen-year-old girl from NSW wanted to prosecute the child's previous employer:

> This servant, a Koori girl of only 16 at the time the allegations were made public, had been raped by her previous employer. This was confirmed by two subsequent medical examinations. Nevertheless, the Aborigines Protection Board officials to whom the matter was reported "accused the girl of being a "sexual maniac" who had lived with "dozens of men"..." In 1941 this young woman was "committed to Parramatta Mental Hospital where she remained for 21 years until the authorities discharged her as having no reason to remain". No charges were ever laid against her attacker. (Human Rights and Equal Opportunity Commission 1997, 143)

Acknowledging the limits of this data, the cases in this chapter nevertheless provide an important glimpse into how courtroom testimony of Indigenous child witnesses may have been received in the twentieth century. For the cases described below, defendants were described as "Aboriginal" in nine of the twenty-three cases. The child witnesses were described as Aboriginal in ten cases and "half-caste" in thirteen. The children were predominantly female (n19), aged between six and sixteen years of age. Male children appeared in four cases and were aged between approximately ten to fifteen years of age. The offences were primarily sexual offences (n14), with remaining offences being child abuse (n3), child stealing/abduction (n2), assault (n2) and offences involving treatment by police officers (n2). The defendant was convicted in eight cases and found not guilty in nine. The verdict is unknown in two cases and the matter was discontinued (*nolle prosequi*) in three cases.

The Trial Process

Interactions with Police

In Bourke, in 1881, brothers Josiah and Arthur Colless were charged with various offences relating to kidnapping and assault of a child after stealing an Aboriginal boy, Jackey. Jackey gave evidence of being assaulted by Josiah. He told the court how he had screamed as he was taken away by the men in a buggy, and how he had struggled to get away from them. Jackey told the court it was Senior Constable Steele who rescued him, chasing down the buggy as it left town and seizing him from the brothers' hands. The defendants gave evidence Jackey's mother had asked them to take her son and they planned to use him to work on their farm (*The Sydney Mail and New South Wales Advertiser* 1881, 794).[6] The press report notes a "considerable amount of evidence was given by a number of witnesses" who corroborated Jackey's evidence, including Senior Constable Steele, claiming they had seen the brothers take Jackey, heard his screams coming from the vehicle and had seen Steele chase down the vehicle and remove Jackey from it (*The Sydney Mail and New South Wales Advertiser* 1881, 794). The brothers were found not guilty on all counts. It is not clear from this report, but if the charges were brought pursuant to the *Criminal Law Amendment Act 1883* (Imp), s 49, the offence only applied to children under twelve years of age. Reflecting the seriousness of this offence, the penalty if found guilty was ten years' imprisonment. As he stood in court before them, the jury were apparently unsure of Jackey's age. Judge Docker was less than impressed with this outcome. He told the jury the "evidence clearly favoured the boy being under ten years of age"—but if there had been any doubt then "the jury was right to give prisoners the benefit of it." His Honour went on to say though, "anyone who could so ill-use a child, be he black or be he white, deserved a whipping themselves." The brothers were immediately charged with, and tried for, assault. It's not known if Jackey had to give his evidence again. Arthur was acquitted, even though he had held the boy down while Josiah struck him with a whip. Josiah was found guilty and fined £25 (*The Sydney Mail and New South Wales Advertiser* 1881, 794).

With good cops inevitably, it seems, come bad cops. In 1905, the West Australian *Royal Commission on the Conditions of the Natives* noted some of the very worst cops. The Commission report, otherwise known as the Roth Report, detailed a police practice whereby Indigenous children were brought from their communities into town to act as witnesses for the Crown in cattle stealing cases. Witnesses described as "usually young ones" and "little boys of immature age" were rounded up and taken from their homes and families, sometimes in chains, irrespective of whether they had witnessed anything (Western Australia 1905, 14–15; Haebich 2000, 211). Officers would personally pocket the allowances allocated to them for the purpose of looking after said witnesses. The report says, "the larger the number of prisoners and witnesses, the better, pecuniarily, for the police" (Western Australia 1905, 14). The money involved in this enterprise was staggering. A grand total of over £3,000 was taken by officers, and in some cases hundreds of pounds were taken by individual officers. Constable J. A. Caldow received £259 and Constable J. Wilson received more than £462 over a period of eighteen months (Western Australia 1905, 15). Given the scale of this operation, cattle stealing cases would potentially have provided numerous examples of Aboriginal children giving evidence in court—but that was not the case. The children didn't give evidence, most likely because of the number of guilty pleas. In her research from the 1960s and 1970s, Elizabeth Eggleston referred to this police practice described in the Roth Report. While unable to determine whether such a practice had continued, Eggleston noted the "modern practice" of taking Aboriginal witnesses (not necessarily child witnesses) "many hundreds of miles from their home country." (1976, 166).

Competency and Capacity

In Chapter 4, the process for child witnesses to prove their competency to give evidence was considered. Whether swearing an oath, or giving unsworn testimony, this was a task many children appeared able to undertake without any trouble. For many others, it proved an impossible task and their evidence was consequently not received. The situation appears to be no different for Indigenous child witnesses. Jackey gave evidence of his attempted abduction without any concern (reported in the press, at least) over his capacity to do so, despite his young age.

A seven-year-old girl, giving evidence in Melbourne in 1902, clearly impressed those who were observing the proceedings. The defendant was a fifteen-year-old Aboriginal boy, charged with attempting to carnally know the girl. The Chief Justice expressed reservations about allowing the girl to give evidence "for," as the press reported, "she was a tiny little dark-skinned mite, who had to peer through the bars of the witness box, failing to reach to the top" (*Herald* 1902, 1). The child passed the oath test with flying colours:

> "Do you know what will happen to you if you tell a lie?" asked His Honour.
> "Yes…I will go into a big fire."
> "And if you are a good girl and tell the truth what will happen?"
> "I will go to Jesus," was the simple and convincing answer.
> (*Herald* 1902, 1)

The article continued:

> Mr. Shaw, the superintendent of the station, who was present in court, smiled a gratified smile. Here, at least, the work of the teachers had not been wasted. The little child told her story intelligently and readily and was not disconcerted when the prisoner asked her a question. (*Herald* 1902, 1)

Not all children managed to pass the competency test as well as this girl. In 1943, an Aboriginal man, George Cabbage, was charged with indecently assaulting a girl under fourteen. The nine-year-old Aboriginal girl, described as "small," entered the witness box in Broken Hill. "All that could be seen over the top of the witness box was a pair of big brown eyes, framed by a little brown face and dark hair" (*Barrier Daily Truth* 1943, 3). Judge Kinsella asked her "many questions" to determine her "intelligence and to find out whether she should give evidence on oath" (*Barrier Daily Truth* 1943, 3). The girl "appeared to be more interested in the appointments of the courtroom and spoke only in monosyllables which were just audible to the shorthand writer sitting alongside her." In the end, Judge Kinsella said he could not tell if she was "unintelligent or frightened by the surroundings" so he adjourned the matter for the day, resolving to try again in the morning (*Barrier Daily Truth* 1943, 3).

The next day, speaking in a faint voice, the girl said she did not know what a lie was. This is a rare case where press reports of a case conflicted. Judge Kinsella declared neither her evidence nor a statement could be taken because even though she "had intelligence," she did not understand what a lie was (*Barrier Miner* 1943, 3). The *Barrier Daily Truth,* however, reported the child was not permitted to give evidence because "she did not have the intelligence" (*Barrier Daily Truth* 1943, 4). It may be Judge Kinsella had observed the girl was intelligent but not, in his view, *sufficiently* intelligent as per the wording of the unsworn testimony test in statute that were discussed at length in Chapter 4. Cabbage had allegedly confessed to the crime, so the Crown proceeded with the case without the girl's evidence. Cabbage's barrister, however, was able to raise enough doubt for the jury to acquit.

In 1946, an Indigenous man was charged with raping his six-year-old niece. A committal hearing was held at a "special court" at Palm Island, where the defendant was committed to stand trial at Townsville Supreme Court (*The Evening Advocate* 1946a, 3). The Crown alleged the accused had raped the girl, "smacked her across the face and told her to tell her mother that '[another man] had played dirty with her.'" She was hospitalised after the offence on account of her injuries. Police investigations revealed the other man was not in the vicinity at the time of the offence. The girl subsequently told police it was her uncle who had committed the offence, but because she was frightened of him, she had accused another, as she had been told to. A press description of the child suggests the difficulty she had with the process of giving evidence in court: "tongue-tied, dumbfounded and afraid to lift her head" (*The Evening Advocate* 1946b, 2). The girl's "inability to answer the judge's questions" regarding the oath and telling lies was the reason for the "sudden collapse" of the case. Judge Douglas told the prosecutor he had to be satisfied the child understood the meaning of the oath before he could allow her to give evidence. The accused was discharged (*The Evening Advocate* 1946b, 2).

The Courtroom Environment

As previous chapters indicate, charges were often discontinued where a child witness appeared overwhelmed by the courtroom environment. But, as with the other children in this book, there is evidence that in the interests of justice, and in the interests of the child witness, some judges, lawyers, and jurors were willing to do what they could to provide appropriate support to an Indigenous child witness so their testimony could be received. In the 1903 case of Barlow, an Aboriginal girl gave evidence in a Sydney courtroom. Several press reports of the hearing indicate the girl struggled to speak audibly. One reported when

> the task of describing all the details of the horrible outrage perpetrated upon her eventually became so distasteful to [her], Judge Pring invited her—and her mother to sit next to him on the bench. (*Australian Star* 1903, 6)

Seated between the judge and her mother, the child was reported to have shown "less reserve" (*Australian Star* 1903, 6).

Further evidence of concern for an Indigenous child witness is provided in a 1926 West Australian case where, on the application of the Aborigines Department Protector, the court was cleared for thirteen-year-old Grace to give her evidence (*Daily Telegraph and North Murchison and Pilbarra Gazette* 1926, 4). Grace was called to give evidence in relation to a private prosecution run by Mr. Albert Leake, the owner of Prairie Downs cattle station on the border of the Pilbara and Mid-West regions of Western Australia. He brought the action against two Aboriginal defendants, Walgi and Spider, both employees of his. Leake alleged they had entered his house and assaulted him. Grace was called by the defence to give evidence for the two defendants. In doing so, she was cross-examined on the issue of Leake having sexually assaulted her—hence the Protector's application to close the court. It appears Walgi and Spider entered Leake's house with the intention of removing Grace from the premises and returning her to her father. Giving evidence for the two men in relation to their assault charge, thirteen-year-old Grace was effectively forced to give evidence of having been raped by Leake. Leake, under cross-examination, admitted this (*Daily Telegraph and North Murchison and Pilbarra Gazette* 1926, 4). The charges against Walgi and Spider were dismissed. There is no evidence that Leake was subsequently charged with assaulting Grace.

Corroboration

While corroboration was a critical issue for other child witnesses, there was only one case where corroboration of an Indigenous child's testimony was mentioned and, even then, it was only in a peripheral sense. In 1924 in Queensland, station owners Mr. and Mrs. Fredericks were charged with abusing Bella, their fifteen-year-old employee. The defendants gave evidence they had returned Bella to "her people...on account of her laziness, dirty habits, [and] constantly running away from home" (*Truth* 1924, 16). Brisbane's *Truth* reported:

> It was distinctly evident that she had been shamelessly tortured and disgracefully ill-treated by her employers. Hark to her pitiful story! ... Fortunately, ...the child's story was amply borne out. (1924, 16)

In other words, Bella's evidence was corroborated by the medical evidence and another employee of the Fredericks'. The use of "fortunately" suggests an understanding that confirmation of Bella's testimony was desirable before a conviction could be secured. The couple were found guilty and each fined twenty pounds (*Truth* 1924, 16).

Examination and Cross-Examination

A feature of hearings involving Indigenous child witnesses, not found in other chapters of this book, is the use of interpreters. Interpreters featured in three cases. In the matter of William Mills in Queensland in 1892, an interpreter was provided for the child witness, but the press reports suggest his services were required "but little" because there was no cross-examination of the child (*Queensland Times, Ipswich Herald and General Advertiser* 1892, 6).

During the prosecution of John Geraghty, in Western Australia in 1908, the prosecutor, Mr. C. R. Ewing, asked for an interpreter for the examination of the complainant child, a thirteen or fourteen-year-old girl named Mopey (*Geraldton Express* 1908, 4). It appears Mr. Ewing's request was initially refused. Partway through Mopey's evidence, though, Ewing "again urged his Honour that an interpreter should be appointed."

The jury expressed "a similar wish [and] the services of Billo Turner were called into the requisition" (*Geraldton Express* 1908, 4). Mopey continued her evidence through the interpreter and was cross-examined by the accused and further re-examined by Mr. Ewing. Several other Aboriginal witnesses gave evidence for the Crown.

In addressing the jury at the conclusion of the case, Mr. Ewing reminded the jury the other Aboriginal witnesses had effectively corroborated each other's testimony and "that the slight discrepancies which had arisen in the evidence gave a greater verisimilitude to the whole story" (*Geraldton Express* 1908, 4). Geraghty, representing himself, addressed the jury for five minutes, referring to the difficulties of having to defend himself, why he had an alias, and explaining an injury to his hand that other witnesses had referred to when identifying him as the alleged perpetrator. The jury retired for half an hour. They returned to pronounce Geraghty not guilty (*Geraldton Express* 1908, 4).

Another feature of the examination of Indigenous child witnesses was the explicit use of Indigenous culture - or inherently racist notions thereof—to undermine the testimony of Indigenous child witnesses. Eliza Critchley's case, considered at the beginning of this chapter, was one such example. In another, in 1876, John Norman admitted he had tied up his seven-year-old daughter, Emily, with a dog chain, flogged her and left her to sleep on her own with the sheep. Neighbours gave evidence Emily had come to their home, where they had seen "marks" on her body. John Norman claimed he had treated his daughter this way to prevent her from "exercising some of her native proclivities" (*Evening News* 1896, 2). What this meant is not entirely clear, but little Emily had given evidence of repeatedly running away from home and of her mother forcing her to leave. In much the same way Charles Bull had in Eliza's case to defend the actions of Mr. Tierney, Norman used notions of Indigenous cultural practice to argue the child was not running away from him as an abusive father, but rather "going walkabout." He thus had to tie her up and abuse her, he argued, to stop her running away (*Evening News* 1896, 2). In both Eliza and Emily's cases, Indigenous culture was used to cast doubt upon the testimony of the child witness. These were not so much calls for recognition of Indigenous laws as they were strategic methods of exploiting the adversarial process—and the child witness.

Recognition of Indigenous laws and practices, though, has been a concern of the common law in varying degrees since the arrival of Europeans. As Finnane and Douglas suggest, questions about the role of "introduced criminal law in addressing victimisation of Indigenous people against one another...have been asked for over two centuries" (Finnane and Douglas 2012, 1). In Perth in 1910, a charge of rape was defended on the basis the alleged assaults were a part of the child's culture and a traditional marriage ceremony. Tunney Morden, an Aboriginal man of twenty-one years of age, had been charged with raping a teenage girl by the name of Jeffrey. There was conflicting evidence as to Jeffrey's age. Morden's mother gave evidence Jeffrey was seventeen years old, but a police officer and both Jeffrey's parents gave evidence she was fourteen years old. The trial centred on whether the events were part of an accepted marriage ritual within the parties' culture. Another witness, Grace Hart, gave evidence Tunney had pulled Jeffrey "out of bed, twisted her arm, kicked her, lifted her on his horse and cantered off with her." Tunney's defence barrister, Mr. J. B. Mills, interjected: "That's an Aboriginal wooing." Grace continued, informing the court Jeffrey did not seem to want to go with Tunney, saying "[s]he struggled," disclosing Tunney had threatened to murder Jeffrey if she did not go with him. On cross-examination, Grace admitted her own husband had taken her from her home in the same way (*Evening Star* 1910, 3). Jeffrey's parents both gave evidence they were opposed to Tunney taking their daughter. They disputed the assertion this was a case of traditional marriage custom.

When it came time for Jeffrey to give her evidence, Perth's *Truth* newspaper provided a striking description of Jeffrey sitting on the chair in the witness box "as if she dreaded it exploding or collapsing beneath her, and she firmly clutched the rungs most of the time" (*Truth* 1910, 5). Her examination, as reported in the *Evening Star*, suggests Jeffrey's experience was like many child witnesses trying to answer questions from barristers. Jeffrey's cross-examination and re-examination were set out as follows (Mr. Mills was defence counsel; Mr. Barker, the prosecutor):

Mr Mills (Defence): Did you not send a message to Tunney to come and take you away?
Witness: Yes.
Mr Mills: Did you not know you were engaged to Tunney to get married?
Witness: Eh? No; I no [sic] know.
Mr Barker (Prosecutor): Did you send a message to Tunney to take you away from your father?
Witness: No. I sent a message to my father to come and get me from Tunney.
(*Evening Star* 1910, 3)

The slight, but significant, difference between Mr. Mills' and Mr. Barker's questions is important here. The same question asking whether Jeffrey had sent a message to Tunney elicited quite different answers from her. "Did you *not* send a message" versus "Did you send a message" made a considerable difference to the essence of Jeffrey's testimony. Mr. Barker understood Jeffrey's confusion and rephrased Mr. Mills' question in a way that Jeffrey, or any child witness for that matter, could understand. Once the question was phrased appropriately, Jeffrey was able to give her answer clearly and coherently—disagreeing with the proposition that she had asked Tunney to take her away. Additional evidence was given of a debt owed to Tunney by Jeffrey's father and of Tunney already being married to another Aboriginal woman. It was a complex case. The jury took ten minutes, though, to find Tunney not guilty. Whether Mr. Mills phrased his questions to deliberately confuse Jeffrey is entirely possible. Mr. Barker rephrasing the question may have helped—but may also have contributed to giving Jeffrey's testimony an air of untruthfulness, by making it seem like she was contradicting herself. Same question; different answers. What was the truth? Was anyone thinking about the way the question was framed and re-framed? Or were they thinking Jeffrey was being evasive and acquitted Tunney on this basis?

Somewhat related to these issues with Jeffrey's examination is the linguistic practice known as "gratuitous concurrence," which impacts specifically on Indigenous child witnesses (and Indigenous adults). Gratuitous concurrence refers to the tendency for an Indigenous witness, not understanding the purpose of cross-examination, to agree with whatever suggestion is being put to them so as to please the questioner. It is a practice that has been recognised, from as long ago as the mid-nineteenth century (Eades 2016, 476). In 1934, anthropologist A.P. Elkin wrote of the "absurdity of applying the white man's law, and the white man's court procedure" to Indigenous people and highlighted the tendency for Aboriginal witnesses to agree with their examiners:

> What they do is to endeavour to sense what the judge and questioners would like them to say, and then they answer accordingly. As a result one native, be he an accused, an accuser or a witness, is quite likely to contradict himself. He is not concerned with the consistency of his evidence, or the search for abstract justice, but with satisfying his various interrogators. But if he does contradict himself or another witness, he is denounced by the judge, magistrate or barrister as one whose evidence cannot in any way be relied upon, and so on... yet, once he understands the latter's mission, and grip of the subject he is quite truthful. If, then, he is always proved in court to be untruthful, there must be something wrong about the methods used. (*The Herald (Melbourne)* 1934, 6)

Since Elkin, the problems experienced by Indigenous witnesses generally, including anxiety, shyness, and language issues, all of which can make their oral testimony appear unreliable, have been widely recognised (Eggleston 1976, 167; *R v Anunga* (1975) 11 ALR 412; Coldrey 1987, 90). These challenges, including the practice of gratuitous concurrence, were evident in the testimony of three Aboriginal boys, twelve, thirteen and fourteen years of age, who gave evidence as witnesses for the prosecution in a high-profile case in 1995. On 10 May 1994, six Brisbane police officers took three Aboriginal boys from the city and drove fourteen kilometres to an industrial area in the suburb of Pinkenba where they left the boys at 4am to find their own way home. The boys were not suspected of, nor even being questioned, in relation to any alleged offence. The officers said the boys simply agreed to go with them—and, apparently, to be left in an isolated part of Brisbane in the middle of the night without any money or means of getting home. The Queensland Criminal Justice Commission investigated the case. Five months later, in October 1994, pursuant to a recommendation of the Chief Superintendent of the Queensland Police Professional Standards Unit, the officers were charged with deprivation of liberty pursuant to s 355 of the *Criminal Code* (Qld) (Kerr 1996, 12).

A committal hearing took place in February 1995 to determine whether the officers should stand trial. The three boys were cross-examined "at length" during this hearing. By the end of their evidence, the boys had agreed with the defence barristers' suggestions they had gone willingly with the officers. Between them, two barristers represented the six accused officers. When one of the barristers raised his voice when cross-examining the boys, they would stop answering. In response, the barrister said: "we have to take your silence as 'no'" and "your silence probably answers [the] question." Both comments, taking a child's silence as a "no" answer and silence as an answer to the question, had a negative effect on the credibility of the child witnesses (Eades 2008, 111–114). The magistrate took the evidence of the boys literally and concluded they were unreliable witnesses because they had contradicted themselves (Eades 1995, 11). He found because the boys had agreed with defence propositions that they had gone willingly with the officers. There was not enough evidence to establish the boys were taken against their will and thus not enough evidence to try the officers. A representative of the Aboriginal Child Care Agency called the cross-examination of the boys "wilful child abuse" (*The Canberra Times* 1995, 6). Sam Watson, of the Aboriginal and Islander Legal Service, said "It's the children who were on trial here" (*The Canberra Times* 1995, 6).[7]

The Pinkenba Six case came shortly after another controversial decision not to prosecute a different group of Queensland police officers based on the evidence of Indigenous child witnesses. The case involved the death of a young Aboriginal man, Daniel Yock, who died while in police custody in Brisbane on the night of 7 November 1993. Daniel, just eighteen at the time, was unconscious by 6.27 pm when he arrived at the Brisbane watch-house in the back of a police wagon. That evening he had been in the company of a number of other Indigenous boys aged between fifteen and eighteen years of age. These boys were called to give evidence to the subsequent inquiry about the incident. The Queensland Criminal Justice Commission report details the procedure used for interviews to be conducted with the boys and for them to give evidence at the inquiry. The Aboriginal Legal Service facilitated the Commission's interviews with the boys. Each of the boys was interviewed with a support person "with whom the witness felt comfortable"

(Criminal Justice Commission (Qld) 1994, 7). The interviews were tape recorded, transcribed and signed after the witnesses had discussed their statement with Aboriginal Legal Service employees. Following a request from the Aboriginal Legal Service and counsel appearing for the boys, the Commission received a report from Dr Diana Eades (whose observations of the Pinkenba Six case were noted above). Eades thought the boys "would be disadvantaged were information to be sought from them by the usual interview or cross-examination procedure of a court or hearing." She further recommended the boys give their evidence in an "Aboriginal space" (Criminal Justice Commission (Qld) 1994, 10).

Commissioner Lew Wyvill QC declined to have the hearing held in an alternative location. He gave several directions with respect to the procedure for receiving the boys' testimony, however. Namely, the statements taken with a support person present would form the evidence-in-chief of the boys "in lieu of their being required to give oral evidence"; witnesses could have someone of their choice sit with them in the witness box; no uniformed police officers would be in the hearing room while the boys gave evidence; counsel appearing would be directed to pay regard to Dr Eades' report regarding their style of questioning and effective communication; he (Wyvill) would evaluate the testimony of each witness, bearing in mind the manner of questioning and cultural condition or background of the witness, and evaluate his response to the questions accordingly; and prior to the youths giving evidence, their solicitor would indicate to them the name and role of each person in the hearing (Criminal Justice Commission (Qld) 1994, 10–11). On the weekend before the hearing, the boys attended the hearing room with their solicitors to familiarise themselves with the room, including being allowed to sit in the witness box (Criminal Justice Commission (Qld) 1994, 11).

The boys giving evidence ranged in age from fifteen to seventeen years. They gave evidence of having seen Mr. Yock being tackled by police and Daniel's face hitting a rock as he fell to the ground; a male police officer putting his knee on Mr. Yock's neck while handcuffing him; Mr. Yock struggling to stand up when a policewoman "kicked him in the head saying, 'stay down.'" One boy was unable to say precisely where the policewoman's kicks connected with Yock: "I saw the lady copper kicking

Danny. I don't know how many times. She was putting her whole body into it" (*Canberra Times* 1993, 4). The youngest boy who was with Mr. Yock in the back of the police wagon claimed he had repeatedly tried to alert officers to Mr. Yock's condition (*Canberra Times* 1993, 12). He gave evidence "police ignored him and [the female police officer] lit a cigarette and grinned" (Criminal Justice Commission (Qld) 1994, 49).

Counsel for the police officers argued the boys must have colluded in preparing their evidence, given the consistency of their statements and testimony (Criminal Justice Commission (Qld) 1994, 97–98). The Commissioner rejected this submission. He found there was insufficient "evidence of deliberate untruthfulness." He concluded, however, that the boys had discussed the events that evening in ways that may have "filled gaps in their individual recollections and completed a picture of events which, unfortunately, was completely erroneous" (Criminal Justice Commission (Qld) 1994, 97–98). It is worth noting the Commissioner criticised the police for holding a debriefing session after Daniel had died which had involved "all relevant police officers, as a group, discussing not only their feelings but also the events in question" (Criminal Justice Commission (Qld) 1994, 103). While the Commissioner was critical of the "unreliable" and inconsistent evidence of some police officers involved, he found no evidence to support charges being laid against any of them (Criminal Justice Commission (Qld) 1994, 97).

Reform

In the aftermath of the Pinkenba case, Queensland's Criminal Justice Commission released its *Aboriginal Witnesses in Queensland's Criminal Courts* report in 1996. The report appreciated that the problems experienced by Indigenous people giving evidence in court went far beyond what had happened during the Pinkenba case. The focus of the report, however, was on adults as witnesses. Indigenous child witnesses were not considered, although they were at the centre of the Pinkenba case. The only reference made in the report to young people is an acknowledgement that in 1993/94, Aboriginal and Torres Strait Islander children made up 3.6% of the juvenile population of the country, but 34% of court appearances by children, and 56% of detention orders made with respect to children (Criminal Justice Commission (Qld) 1996, 5). The report notes "[t]he very low number of contested matters is at least partly attributable to shortcomings in ways in which the system currently deals with Aboriginal witnesses" (Criminal Justice Commission (Qld) 1996, xi–xii).[8]

Recommended changes or alterations to the trial process made in this report included witnesses giving evidence-in-chief in narrative form (i.e. allowing the witness to speak freely rather than in short question and answer form), increased judicial control of court proceedings, and the use of interpreters (Criminal Justice Commission (Qld) 1996, xix–xx). Similar to the findings made throughout this book, the accepted recommendations were those that focussed on measures that would support witnesses within the existing process, rather than changing the process itself. Such recommendations included, for example, the provision of additional support for witnesses, and cultural awareness training for practitioners and judges. Critiquing these recommendations, Susan C. Kerr said:

> Improving cultural awareness will not effect the kinds of procedural changes that are necessary in ensuring that culturally disadvantaged witnesses receive the justice that is their due. (Kerr 1996, 13)

In a subsequent article analysing the *Aboriginal Witnesses in Queensland's Criminal Courts* report, Kerr observed "the overall conclusion, that language and cultural barriers militate against Aboriginal witnesses in a way that often results in injustice, is unlikely to surprise many readers" (Kerr 1996, 12). In contrast to Kerr's views and, instead, echoing the Commission's recommendations Northern Territory Supreme Court judge, Justice Mildren, advocated for changes to the system that were so straightforward they would not even require legislative reform. Specifically, his Honour said:

> The purpose of this article is not to suggest radical change to the present criminal justice system, but to examine the present system and to see what can be done by police, advocates and judges to improve upon it, especially where no legislative change is necessary. (Mildren 1997, 8)

An appendix to the article sets out Mildren J's model judicial directions for juries. The directions cover issues such as "Aboriginal English," "ways of communicating" and "hearing problems" (Mildren 1997, 21–22). Again, notwithstanding it was children involved in the Pinkenba case who initiated this focus on the evidence of Indigenous witnesses, the article makes no mention of children or young people as witnesses.

The reticence to invoke radical change in the late twentieth century is at odds with calls from the Christian Women's Temperance Union in 1934 to introduce specialist courts for the purpose of prosecuting crimes committed against Indigenous women and children. Mrs. Jessie Reid, superintendent of the Union, gave evidence at the Moseley Commission, officially called the Royal Commission Appointed to Investigate, Report and Advise Upon Matters in Relation to the Condition and Treatment of Aborigines (Western Australia 1935). This was yet another West Australian inquiry into the treatment of Aboriginal people following the 1905 Roth inquiry referred to earlier in this chapter. While most calls for specialist courts ordinarily have defendants as their main concern, the Christian Women's Temperance Union called for better protection in courts for Aboriginal women and children, particularly young girls who were, according to the Union, often "lent" to white men in return for flour and tobacco. The primary concern for the Union was that existing court processes prevented the evidence of Indigenous women and children being received in court in a way that maximised opportunities for justice. Mrs. Reid argued, on behalf of her organisation, Aboriginal women and children had the right to sanctity in their own bodies and "Australian women have a part to play in securing human rights for their dark sisters" (*Daily News (Perth)* 1934, 5). The Union argued for the creation of specialist courts, separate to ordinary courts, claiming "[t]he law which professed to protect the Aborigines in most instances served to crush them" (*Daily News (Perth)* 1934, 5). As with all the calls for reform of child witness procedures made by various women's philanthropic groups documented throughout this book, the calls of the Christian Women's Temperance Union were ignored. Instead, the Royal Commission recommended the establishment of "a different tribunal," which focussed on defendants—"one that will really enable the native to understand what is going on and the proceedings of which can be listened to and understood by others of the tribe" (Western Australia 1935, 19).

In the 1970s and 1980s, various events, cases and reports raised awareness of the impact of the criminal justice process on Indigenous peoples but again, none relate specifically to the evidence of Indigenous child witnesses. The matter of *R v Anunga,* heard in Northern Territory in 1976, did not involve child witnesses but did concern the issue of police interrogation of Aboriginal defendants. The Court set out guidelines for police interrogation of Indigenous people. In 1979, the Aboriginal Child Survival Seminar was held in Melbourne. The outcome of this seminar was the creation, in 1981, of the Secretariat of National Aboriginal and Islander Child Care. In 1986 the Australian Law Reform Commission released its report: *Recognition of Aboriginal Customary Laws* (Report 31). This report covered a variety of issues relevant to court procedures such as juries, interpreters, police interrogations, unsworn statements by accused persons and the like. There is discussion of linguistic challenges Indigenous people face in court, but none address children or young people as witnesses specifically.

In 1990, Judy Atkinson echoed the calls of the Christian Women's Temperance Union 1934 for reform of courts to provide better protection to Indigenous women and children, saying

> Within the Anglo-Australian court system power has been abused and the truth has been distorted...Lawyers blame police, police blame lawyers. As white males, both have been instrumental in facilitating and legitimating acts of violence towards women and children, either by their attitudes, inactions or presentations in court. (Atkinson 1990, 15)

In 1991, the Human Rights and Equal Opportunity Commission *Report of the National Inquiry into Racist Violence* highlighted the importance of the judicial system being "beyond reproach" in addressing racist violence (1991, 302). The report claimed:

> We cannot afford to have a ... judiciary system that upholds racial discrimination for whatever reason and we certainly [cannot] tolerate magistrates or court judges to be racist or [impose] sentences based on racial discrimination. (HREOC 1991, 302–303)

This report was delivered three years before Daniel Yock's death and the Pinkenba Six case. There is no specific discussion of Indigenous children giving evidence in court but there is considerable discussion of cases of young Indigenous people, for example, declining to report assaults committed upon them, including many committed by police officers (HREOC 1991, 300–332).

In August 1997, the *Bringing them Home* report of the Human Rights and Equal Opportunity Commission National Inquiry into the Separation of Aboriginal and Torres Strait Islander Children from Their Families (also known as the Stolen Generations report) was released (HREOC 1997). This report details the circumstances and effects of the removal of Indigenous children from their families and includes details of the extensive sexual assault and physical abuse of these children in institutions, foster families, adoptive families, and places of employment (HREOC 1997, 194–195). The report does not refer to court cases or instances of children giving evidence in court. Indigenous children were clearly, frequently, victims of crime—but rarely, if ever, given a voice or heard with respect to their victimisation: "These vulnerable children had no-one to turn to for protection or comfort. They were rarely believed if they disclosed the abuse" (HREOC 1997, 195).

Conclusion

One hundred and sixty years after Ralph Barrow was traumatised by his experience of giving evidence, the Northern Territory's *Little Children are Sacred* report was published in 2007. The report, prepared by the Northern Territory Board of Inquiry into the Protection of Aboriginal Children from Sexual Abuse, acknowledged court procedures were potentially "extraordinarily traumatic" for Indigenous child witnesses and recommended the implementation of vulnerable witness provisions, and for prosecutors to make use of these provisions (Northern Territory 2007, 113). This is just one report of a number to have been published since the turn of the twenty-first century resulting in recommendations for reform of legal procedure to improve the capacity for the criminal justice system to hear the evidence of Indigenous child witnesses.

In the cases described in this chapter, the child witnesses were put on trial just as much as the defendants. They were called "tarts," "little criminals," "liars" and "sexual maniacs." Their voices were dismissed because they failed to comply with a centuries-old English procedure requiring them to swear an oath—or at least speak in a way the process demanded. Defendants and defence counsel undermined the testimony of witnesses by suggesting the child's behaviour was related to their culture, not their abuse. Communication practices like gratuitous concurrence were identified and understood early in the twentieth century. The deliberate and strategic exploitation of such knowledge was used at the end of the century to extract responses from children to make them appear evasive, at best, and untruthful at worst. Gomeroi law scholar, Alison Whittaker, notes the long-term application of "soft law," comprised of "Royal Commissions, parliamentary inquiries, and coronial hearings," to "the contemporary experience of Australian Indigeneity" (2018, 26). The picture painted in this chapter illustrates Whittaker's point as far as Indigenous child witnesses are concerned. The soft law of the Roth Commission in 1905, the Moseley Commission in 1935, the Criminal Justice Commission reports following Daniel Yock's death, the Pinkenba Six case, purported to engage in much-needed reflection and reform, but, achieved little of either as far as Indigenous child witnesses were concerned. Calls for radical reform were resisted in favour of solutions that skirted around the centuries-old problem of the capacity for the adversarial process to administer justice in these cases. Undoubtedly, the law that should have protected these child witnesses well and truly crushed them.

Notes

1. Alison Whittaker has noted the significance of the question of defining Aboriginality at law (2017). See Finnane 2020 on problems of identifying defendants as "Aboriginal" in court records and press reports.
2. For further information on this case, see Australasian Legal Information Institute, http://www.austlii.edu.au/cgi-bin/viewdoc/au/cases/nsw/NSWSupC/1836/35.html?context=1;query=Murrell%20;mask_path=. See also Australian Law Reform Commission Report 31, para 40.
3. Only three years after *R v Murrell and Bummarree*, the *Aboriginals Competent Witnesses Act 1939* (NSW) was passed. This Act allowed Indigenous witnesses to "make an affirmation or declaration to tell the truth" where it was "found expedient and necessary for the purposes of Justice and the more effectual prosecution of crimes and misdemeanours" (*Aboriginals Competent Witnesses Act 1939,* Preamble).
4. See https://trove.nla.gov.au/.
5. See https://prosecutionproject.griffith.edu.au/.
6. Given what is known of the widespread abduction of Aboriginal children from the very early nineteenth century (Haebich 2000, 79), this is most likely to be a case of abduction rather than a contractual arrangement between an Indigenous mother and two white men for them to take custody of her young son for him to work their farm.
7. See Hannah McGlade's analysis of three case studies where similar observations are made about child victims being "made to feel guilty" (2012, 166).
8. Ten years later, academic Nigel Stobbs criticised the Queensland criminal justice system for its continued failure to deal appropriately with Indigenous witnesses and complainant following the release of the CJC report in 1996 (Stobbs 2007).

References

Aboriginals Competent Witnesses Act 1939 (NSW).
The Advertiser (Adelaide, SA: 1931–1954). "Charges Fail Against Natives." March 26, 1947.

Anthony, Thalia. 2013. *Indigenous People, Crime and Punishment*. New York: Routledge.

Atkinson, Judy. 1990. "Violence Against Aboriginal Women: Reconstitution of Community Law—The Way Forward." *Aboriginal Law Bulletin* 2 (46) (October): 6–9.

Australian Law Reform Commission, *Recognition of Aboriginal Customary Laws* (Report No 31, 1986).

The Australian Star (Sydney, NSW: 1887–1909). "Death of Mr. Charles Bull." May 15, 1906.

The Australian Star (Sydney, NSW: 1887–1909). "Sentenced to Death." November 24, 1903.

Bailey, Cate, Martine Powell, and Sonja P. Brubacher. 2017. "The Attrition of Indigenous and Non-Indigenous Child Sexual Abuse Cases in Two Australian Jurisdictions." *Psychology, Public Policy, and Law* 23 (2): 178–190.

Barrier Daily Truth. "Aboriginal on Serious Charge." May 27, 1943.

Barrier Miner (Broken Hill, NSW: 1888–1954). "Aboriginal Found Not Guilty on Charge of Assault On Girl." May 26, 1943.

Behrendt, Larissa. 2000. "Consent in a (Neo)Colonial Society: Aboriginal Women as Sexual and Legal 'Other'." *Australian Feminist Studies* 15 (33): 353–367.

The Canberra Times. "Police Cleared of Kidnapping Three Boys." December 25, 1995.

The Canberra Times. "Police Laughed While Yock Lay Dying: Witness." December 3, 1993.

The Canberra Times. "Policewoman Kicked Yock in Head." November 30, 1993.

Coldrey, John. 1987. "Aboriginals and the Criminal Courts." In *Ivory Scales: Black Australia and the Law*, edited by Kayleen Hazlehurst. Kensington: New South Wales University Press in Association with the Australian Institute of Criminology.

Connors, Libby. 2010. "A Wiradjuri Child at Moreton Bay." *Queensland History Journal* 20 (13): 775–787.

Connors, Libby. 2012. "Women, Children and Violence in Aboriginal Law: Some Perspectives from the Southeast Queensland Frontier." In *Past Law, Present Histories*, edited by Diane Kirkby. Canberra: ANU Press.

Criminal Justice Commission (Queensland), *Aboriginal Witnesses in Queensland's Criminal Courts* (Report, June 1996).

Criminal Justice Commission (Queensland), *A Report of the Investigation into the Arrest and Death of Daniel Yock* (Investigative Report, 5 April 1994).

Criminal Law Amendment Act 1883 (Imp).

Daily News (Perth, WA: 1882–1950). "Suggestions for Native Welfare Progress." April 6, 1934.

Daily Telegraph and North Murchison and Pilbarra Gazette (WA: 1920–1947). "Aboriginal Assault Case." February 3, 1926.

Eades, Diana. 1992. *Aboriginal English and the Law: Communicating with Aboriginal English Speaking Clients: A Handbook for Legal Practitioners.* Brisbane: Queensland Law Society.

Eades, Diana. 1995. *Language in Evidence: Issues Confronting Aboriginal and Multicultural Australia.* Sydney: UNSW Press.

Eades, Diana. 2008. *Courtroom Talk and Neocolonial Control*. New York: Mouton de Gruyter.

Eades, Diana. 2012. "Communication with Aboriginal Speakers of English in the Legal Process." *Australian Journal of Linguistics* 32 (4): 473–489.

Eades, Diana. 2016. "Judicial Understandings of Aboriginality and Language Use." *The Judicial Review* 12: 471–490.

Eggleston, Elizabeth. 1976. *Fear, Favour or Affection: Aborigines and the Criminal Law in Victoria, South Australia and Western Australia.* Canberra: Australian National University Press.

The Evening Advocate (Innisfail, Qld: 1941–1954). "Aboriginal for Trial on Serious Charge." April 9, 1946a.

The Evening Advocate. "Six Year Old Aboriginal Girl Unable To Testify Against Uncle." May 27, 1946b.

Evening News (Sydney, NSW: 1869–1931). "Ill-treating a Child." January 17, 1896.

The Evening Star (Boulder, WA: 1898–1921). "Native Ways: Question of Aboriginal Customs." September 10, 1910.

Finnane, Mark. 2020. "'They Were Subject to Our Laws': Aboriginal Defendants in NSW Courts 1850–1914." *History Australia* 17 (3): 448–470.

Finnane, Mark, and Heather Douglas. 2012. *Indigenous Crime and Settler Law–White Sovereignty After Empire*. London: Palgrave MacMillan Socio-Legal Studies.

Ford, Lisa. 2010. *Settler Sovereignty: Jurisdiction and Indigenous People in America and Australia, 1788–1836*. Cambridge, MA: Harvard University Press.

The Geraldton Express (WA: 1906–1928). "Alleged Offence on a Native Child: Trial and Acquittal of John Gerahty." January 3, 1908.

Haebich, Anna. 2000. *Broken Circles: Fragmenting Indigenous Families 1800–2000.* North Fremantle: Fremantle Press.

The Herald (Melbourne, Vic: 1861–1954). "Aboriginal Charged." December 10, 1902.

The Herald (Melbourne, Vic: 1861–1954). "Black Men & White Law." May 11, 1934.

Human Rights and Equal Opportunity Commission. 1991. *Racist Violence: Report of the National Inquiry into Racist Violence in Australia.* Canberra: Australian Govt. Pub. Service.

Human Rights and Equal Opportunity Commission. 1997. *Bringing Them Home: Report of the National Inquiry into the Separation of Aboriginal and Torres Strait Islander Children from Their Families.* Sydney: Human Rights and Equal Opportunity Commission.

Kerr, Susan. 1996. "Gratuitous Justice: A Review of the Queensland Criminal Justice Commission's Report into Aboriginal Witnesses in Criminal Courts." *Aboriginal Law Bulletin* 3 (84): 12–15.

McGlade, Hannah. 2012. *Our Greatest Challenge: Aboriginal Children and Human Rights.* Canberra: Aboriginal Studies Press.

Mildren, Dean. 1997. "Redressing the Imbalance Against Aboriginals in the Criminal Justice System." *Criminal Law Journal* 21 (1): 7–21.

Moreton-Robinson, Aileen. 2015. *The White Possessive: Property, Power, and Indigenous Sovereignty.* Minneapolis: University of Minnesota Press.

Northern Territory Board of Inquiry into the Protection of Aboriginal Children from Sexual Abuse, Rex Wild, and Pat Anderson. 2007. *Little Children Are Sacred: Report of the Northern Territory Board of Inquiry into the Protection of Aboriginal Children from Sexual Abuse* (Report, 2007).

Queensland Times, Ipswich Herald and General Advertiser. "The Boulia Aboriginal Abduction Case." July 5, 1892.

R v Anunga (1975) 11 ALR 412.

R v Murrell and Bummaree (1836) 1 Legge 72.

State Children Relief Act 1901 (NSW).

Stobbs, Nigel. 2007. "An Adversarial Quagmire: The Continued Inability of the Queensland Criminal Justice System to Cater for Indigenous Witnesses and Complainants." *Indigenous Law Bulletin* 6 (30): 15–18.

Tatz, Colin. 1990. "Aboriginal Violence: A Return to Pessimism." *Australian Journal of Social Issues* 25 (4) (November): 245–260.

The Riverine Herald (Echuca, Vic: Moama, NSW: 1869–1954). "The Riverine Herald." September 27, 1881.

The Sydney Gazette and New South Wales Advertiser (NSW: 1803–1842). "Supreme Court." February 23, 1836.

The Sydney Mail and New South Wales Advertiser (NSW: 1871–1912). "Bourke." November 5, 1881.

Truth (Brisbane, Qld: 1900–1954). "A State Child." October 14, 1900.
Truth (Brisbane, Qld: 1900–1954). "Little Aboriginal Girl's Excruciating Experiences." September 7, 1924.
Truth (Perth, WA: 1903–1931). "A Half-Caste Helen: Tunney Tries to Trap a Tart." September 10, 1910.
Western Australia, *Royal Commission on the Condition of the Natives* (Report, 1905).
Western Australia, *Report of the Royal Commissioner Appointed to Investigate, Report and Advise Upon Matters in Relation to the Condition and Treatment of Aborigines* (Report, 1935).
Whittaker, Alison. 2017. "White Law, Blak Arbiters, Grey Legal Subjects: Deep Colonisation's Role and Impact in Defining Aboriginality at Law." *Australian Indigenous Law Review* 20: 4–47.
Whittaker, Alison. 2018. "The Unbearable Witness, Seeing: A Case for Indigenous Methodologies in Australian Soft Law." *Pandora's Box*: 23–35.

9

"Changes in Law Were Full of Danger": Conclusion

Legal scholar, Roscoe Pound, made a controversial proposition in 1910. He dared to suggest the "law in action" often differed from the "law in books" (Pound 1910, 12). He appears to have been arguing that what happened in courts and legal practice did not always reflect what would be expected according to the law found in judicial decisions and legislation. Pound drew on a passage from Mark Twain's 1884 novel, '*The Adventures of Huckleberry Finn*' to advance his argument. Tom Sawyer and Huck Finn were debating which tool to use to dig their friend Jim out of a hole. Should it be a case knife or pickaxe? A case knife was the right tool, but Tom thought a pickaxe would be more efficient and effective. He suggested a way to get around the problem:

> It ain't right and it ain't moral, and I wouldn't like it to get out – but there ain't only just the one way; we got to dig him out with the picks and *let on* it's case-knives. (Twain 1884 [2009], 317–318)

R. Blewer, *Child Witnesses in Twentieth Century Australian Courtrooms*, Palgrave Histories of Policing, Punishment and Justice,
https://doi.org/10.1007/978-3-030-69791-4_9

Pound compared this scene to the common law. He argued the law "…has always managed to get a pickaxe in its hands, though it steadfastly demanded a case-knife, and to wield it in the virtuous belief that it was using the approved instrument" (Pound 1910, 12–13).

While Pound's realist theory of law was not universally endorsed (Hull 1989; Halperin 2011, 46), it has been "widely acknowledged" (Goodman-Delahunty et al. 2019, 504) and is evident throughout this book. There are numerous examples of the law wielding a pickaxe to administer criminal justice, while letting on it was a case knife. In 1892, Chief Justice Higinbotham (and others) explicitly referred to the "means, independent of the statute" through which child witnesses were taught how to pass the oath test before they went into court (*R v Gregg* 1892, 221). Courts were closed in contravention of the principle of open justice but, if the judicial officer framed it as an order in the interests of justice, rather than the interests of the child witness, it was acceptable (*R v Hamilton* 1930). Interpretations of rules of evidence were inconsistent and, at times, illogical but appear to have been made to fit the desired outcome (whether to convict or acquit). In *R v Walsh,* the child being in the defendant's home was not corroborative of the child's testimony ((1905) 7 WALR 263) but in *R v Carroll,* the boots Carroll wore in court that "curiously" matched the prints at the scene were corroborative (1906) 6 SR (NSW) 258). The case of Mary Ryan, in 1901, demonstrated an extreme level of pragmatism as the evidence of her daughters was manipulated, first so she would be committed to stand trial for murdering her newborn (when it appeared she had demanded her daughter burn the baby), and then again at her trial so she would be acquitted and free to continue to care for her four daughters.

Cases where the law was strictly applied indicate why courts may have frequently chosen the more pragmatic path. Close adherence to the law resulted in many cases being discontinued where the circumstances suggested a strong likelihood a guilty person would get away with their crime. A grandfather's knowledge his son-in-law would rape his grandson was not enough to corroborate the child's testimony; nor was a child having the same sexually transmitted disease as a defendant. If children could not swear an oath, their testimony was not received. If they could not stand in a courtroom and speak audibly in front of a room full of strangers, their testimony was not received; if they did not understand the cross-examination process, they were accused of being unreliable and untruthful. Cases were discontinued, defendants acquitted.

At the start of the century, children were often placed in what would now be recognised as inherently vulnerable positions like, for example, having to touch a suspect in a line-up or being cross-examined by an accused or sitting in a crowded courtroom full of strangers. By the end of the twentieth century, however, children were generally presumed competent, the oath test had been replaced with strict legislative provisions, corroboration rules no longer applied, warnings about the inherent unreliability of the evidence of children were prohibited, and technological advances meant children were rarely physically present in the courtroom. We might look at contemporary procedure that uses remote video recordings, pre-recordings of evidence and prohibits cross-examination by an accused and assume the process is infinitely better today than at the start of the twentieth century.

Were such an assumption based on the law in books, it would be correct. For most of the century, there was little case law or legislation indicating or regulating supportive measures for children. The law in action, however, was often sympathetic to the child's plight and often supported them using a variety of "common sense" measures like allowing them to sit at the judge's bench while giving evidence, holding a toy, or having a support person near them when sitting in the witness box, even giving evidence as a witness for the Crown while sitting on their mother's knee—when the mother was the accused. Cases were found where children participated in a dress rehearsal or the courtroom was closed to the public. This view of the courtroom suggests a legal process more mindful of the difficulties that children experienced in court and more supportive of children than otherwise assumed.

One of the objectives of this book was to explore such assumptions and uncover important junctures of change. Examining attempts to resolve contradictions and inconsistencies in the law revealed not only how reforms changed the black letter of the law, but also what forces shaped such change. Periods of significant reform are evident. The first wave of feminism, the social purity and child protection movements of the late nineteenth century led to the unsworn testimony reforms in the early twentieth century. Similarly, the second wave of feminism and social changes of the 1960s and 1970s, as well as technological advancements, human rights and victims' rights movements, credible child witness research and the evolution of the mass media in the 1980s each played a part in reforming a process widely understood to be difficult, if not harmful, for child witnesses. The law reforms of the twentieth century can only be fully understood when these factors are considered (Hay 1984).

An overwhelming feature of this book and the process of law reform is the presence of women's groups. The National Council of Women, the Australian Federation of Women Voters, the Women's Service Guild, the Country Women's Association, the League of Women Voters, and the Christian Women's Temperance Union all highlighted problems with various aspects of child witness policy and procedure. More importantly, they made suggestions for reforms such as the appointment of women police officers, witness intermediaries and specialist courts to hear matters dealing with offences against children or those involving Indigenous women and children. The calls these groups made for change were ignored at the time only to be implemented in some form in the decades following.

Women continued to play a role in law reform in the latter part of the century. The second wave feminist movement of the 1960s and 1970s was largely responsible for the increased awareness of victims of crime leading, in turn, to the victims' rights movement (Logan 2008, 140). This rights movement was derived from the human rights movement which, as a concept, has been traced to ancient times. The modern human rights movement developed in earnest following the Second World War. The United Nations General Assembly's Declaration of the Rights of the Child in 1959 was reflected a re-conception of children and childhood. Through the second half of the twentieth century, there was a growing recognition of the rights of humans, victims, women and children which impacted upon the law reforms of the latter part of the century. From the human rights movement, the victim rights movement emerged in the 1970s (Kirchengast 2006, 163; Ryan 2003, 111–112). The rights of children drew more attention following the United Nations Convention on the Rights of the Child in 1989. Rights discourse found its way into legislation as was discussed in Chapter 5 where the *Evidence (Children) Act 1997* (NSW), for example, gave children the right to give evidence by closed-circuit television, the right to alternative arrangements where such technology was not available and the right to have a support person with them when giving evidence (*The Evidence (Children) Act 1997* (NSW), s18, s24 and s27).

The calls for child witness reform that women's groups made throughout the twentieth century were predominantly in the context of prosecuting sexual offences. The media played an important part in disseminating these calls. The Mr. Bubbles case in Australia, and other high-profile investigations and cases in the United Kingdom and United States were all subjects of intense media attention in the 1980s and 1990s. Such attention forced a genuine problem into the spotlight (Garland 2008, 13) and provided an important space for "feminist analysis to enter into wider discourse" and for demands for change to be made (Swain 2015, 293). The power of the media to generate interest and prompt "official enquiries, policy responses and action" in relation to child sexual abuse is undeniable (Adrian 2019, 90). A great deal of the research in this book relies on the reports of the behaviour of children in court—whether being upset, precocious or appearing like a character in a fairy tale. These images informed the public of what courtrooms were like. The capacity for the media to influence reform of child witness procedure was reduced following the legislative reforms of the 1980s and 1990s which closed courtrooms to the public and media and thus removed the ability for journalists to report details of what had happened in court. These reforms were made in the best interests of the child witnesses but, at the same time, they have removed a powerful method of informing the public of the nature of the trial process. Instead, the public is largely privy only to quaint little stories like the one where an orphaned joey (baby kangaroo) attended the Charleville District Court in Queensland to provide support to a child witness (*Women's Weekly* 2020, 10).

With the capacity for the media to observe and report on these cases being reduced at the end of the twentieth century, the work of researchers and academics has become the only source of knowledge about what was happening in court and whether change was needed. In the 1970s, women began studying and practising law and becoming law professors in substantial numbers (Myers et al. 1999, 206–207). This had a marked effect on the nature of legal practice and on the issues researchers and academics turned their attention to. Decades earlier, in 1935 legal scholar John Wigmore had argued it would be inappropriate for the law to listen to expert psychologists (cited in Ceci and Bruck 1993, 407). Half a century later though, it was inappropriate for the law *not* to listen. Irrespective of an awareness of children's rights, or the influence of the mass media or a social, cultural and political willingness for law reform there is a chance none of the reforms of the late twentieth century would have been possible without the research on children, child psychology, criminology, victimology, history and law conducted in the 1970s, 1980s and 1990s that looked at old questions in new ways and created new questions to examine the potentially damaging effects giving evidence in court might have on a child. The need for reform could not be ignored when credible, robust psychological research like that of Gail Goodman and her colleagues, as well as Mark Brennan and Roslin E. Brennan, in the 1980s, Judy Cashmore, Stephen Ceci and Maggie Bruck, John Myers and colleagues in the 1990s began to prove what others, like the women's groups and some members of the judiciary had long suspected. Because of research undertaken in this specific area of law we know, as Justice Brennan surmised in 1936, it could harm a child for life to come into an adversarial court. We know the examination process could be difficult for children, as the Federation of Women Voters argued in 1931. We know children, as Blackstone had thought two centuries beforehand, could be truthful and credible witnesses.

Researchers in the latter years of the twentieth century were able to take advantage of technological advances to implement their research findings. Audio-visual recording technology invented in the second half of the century gave the legal system the alternative options to bringing children into court that Justice Brennan had longed for in 1936. This technology transformed the way police interviews were carried out by enabling a permanent and accurate recording of what was said. Similarly, pre-recording of child witness testimony prior to a trial reduced potential issues with delays in running a trial and for courts to receive a child's testimony. The technology also allowed the evidence of children to be received by courts without children ever having to enter the courtroom. The adoption of such procedures was not without debate, as noted in Chapter 5.

Judges and legal practitioners exercised considerable caution where a supportive measure, such as closing a courtroom or pre-recording evidence, compromised common law principles of open justice and the accused's entitlement to a fair trial. Reflecting on, and thinking critically about the reforms noted in this book, and how they were executed, highlights how the role of judicial officers changed over the course of the twentieth century. The preceding chapters on competency, corroboration, the courtroom and examination all point to the pivotal role of the judicial officer as a decision-maker, courtroom manager and authority on the law. While they may otherwise have been relegated to a more passive role of referee (Mack and Roach Anleu 2007, 342), judges had considerable control over how child witness cases were conducted in the first half of the century. Judicial officers examined children on their understanding of the oath, decided whether their testimony would be received, decided whether evidence was corroborative and warned juries of the inherent dangers of convicting on a child's uncorroborated testimony. They moved child witnesses around the courtroom so the child could be heard and often took personal responsibility for comforting distressed children. While there are many examples of judges relying on erroneous, stereotypical views of children in their decision-making, judges and magistrates were among the most vocal opponents of practices in relation to police, competency procedures, the courtroom environment, the cross-examination of children and corroboration rules. The reforms of the late twentieth century, however, effectively removed much of the capacity judges had previously had to decide if, and how, a child witness's testimony should be received.

While child witness reforms were introduced with a view to improving procedures for the receipt of child witness testimony, they had a marked effect on the work of magistrates and judges. In their preparedness to wield pickaxes as if they were case knives, were judicial officers unfairly blamed for being unsupportive of children and for maintaining outdated legal rules and principles? The refining of the concept of the fair trial by the High Court in the cases of *Dietrich v The Queen* ((1992) 177 CLR 292) and *Jago v District Court (NSW)* ((1989) 168 CLR 23) confirmed an accused's expectation of a fair trial had to be balanced with the interests of others, like child witnesses. The evidence uncovered in this research suggests many judicial officers had been doing this balancing act throughout the century. It was simply that the law in books did not reflect this. Judicial officers were often found to have pushed limits of the law in the interests of child witnesses and in the interests of justice. Defence barristers pushed back, appealing against the receipt of hearsay evidence as they did in *R v Brasier*; appealing against judicial interpretations of corroboration rules, and opposing closed courtrooms.

By the end of the twentieth century, opportunities for judges to wield pickaxes were reduced in the face of an increased political will of state legislatures to address issues of crime and child protection. The failed attempt at reforming corroboration laws in Western Australia in 1944 demonstrated the complex nature of political debate around child witness policy and criminal justice. On that occasion, the rights of the accused won out as politicians prioritised the need to protect innocent men from wrongful convictions. Three decades later "law and order," previously a bi-partisan issue, had become a political vote-winning tool (Garland 2008, 10). Sex offences were identified alongside anti-social behaviour as issues of concern for the general population and thus issues politicians had an obligation to address (Ryan 2003, 124).

The reforms of the late twentieth century are due to a complex web of relationships between various stakeholders and circumstance. Before celebrating the common law system as one that had great capacity for change, it is worth reflecting on what really changed in the one hundred years from 1900 to 2000? The conclusions drawn in each chapter of this book were remarkably similar even though each addressed a discrete aspect of the prosecution process. The pattern that emerged was one in which the child witness's journey remained constant. At the start of the century, there was a standard police investigation process followed by a committal, trial, issues of competency, courtroom environments, examination and cross-examination and the application of rules of evidence. The situation was effectively the same one hundred years later. The law remained remarkably impervious to change despite repeated calls for change in all aspects of child witness testimony. In 1910, "[c]hanges in law were," as Roscoe Pound put it, "full of danger" (Pound 1910, 12). It seems they were still full of danger a century later. This was acceptable if procedure could be circumvented while giving the appearance it was being applied. The experience of the law throughout the twentieth century, though, is effectively summed up in the following observation:

> The tragic results of the entrenched failure of our criminal justice process to protect vulnerable people from abuse and bring their abusers to justice demonstrates that we have been too tentative in implementing measures to improve their situation, too wary of fundamental change, and that we have delayed too long in making recommended difficult reforms. (Bowden et al. 2014, 544)

This book has drawn on the stories of hundreds of child witnesses who gave evidence in Australian criminal courts in the twentieth century and in so doing, has told a much bigger story about the common law, criminal justice and the adversarial trial. A century of children giving evidence in court demonstrates that twentieth-century innovations like unsworn testimony, intermediaries, specialist courts and ground rules hearings were too long in coming but, when implemented, did not result in significant changes to this process. For all the reforms detailed in this book, the process looks much like it always has. Juries are reminded to consider uncorroborated testimony carefully. Children are still effectively forced to demonstrate their credibility as witnesses. Children are still cross-examined. They still cry. Many continue to suffer secondary trauma at the hands of this system that remains constrained by centuries-old principles and approaches to the administration of justice. Historians Dorothy Scott and Shurlee Swain have argued "[j]ourneys across time can put a different light on the pathways of the present as well as those of the past. Perhaps it is even possible for a journey across time to illuminate new pathways that may take us in a different direction in the future" (Scott and Swain 2002, 188). If criminal justice systems are to take the well-being of child witnesses seriously, and ensure that courts have the best evidence before them, then perhaps this journey across time tells us it is time to consider entirely new pathways for child witnesses in Australia.

Notes

1. See, for example *Criminal Law Consolidation (Child Sexual Abuse) Amendment Act 1994* (SA), s 3.
2. *McKinney v The Queen* (1991) 171 CLR 468 at 478, *Jago v District Court* (NSW) (1989) 168 CLR 23 at 56, *Dietrich v The Queen* (1992) 177 CLR 292 at 299, 326. See discussion of changing conception of the fair trial in James Spiegelman, "The Truth Can Cost Too Much: The Principle of a Fair Trial," *Australian Law Journal* 78 (2004): 30.

References

Adrian, Bingham, (2019). 'It Would be Better for the Newspapers to Call a Spade a Spade': The British Press and Child Sexual Abuse, c. 1918–90. *History Workshop Journal*.

Bowden Pheobe, Terese Henning, and David Plater. 2014. "Balancing Fairness to Victims, Society and Defendants in the Cross-examination of Vulnerable Witnesses: An Impossible Triangulation." *Melbourne University Law Review* 37 (2): 539–584.

Ceci, Stephen J., and Maggie Bruck. 1993. "Suggestibility of the Child Witness: A Historical Review and Synthesis." *Psychological Bulletin* 113 (3): 403–439.

Crampton v R (2000) 176 ALR 369.

Criminal Law Consolidation (Child Sexual Abuse) Amendment Act 1994 (SA).

Daily Herald (Adelaide, SA: 1910–1924). "Stepmother Totally Unfit," January 28, 1918.

Dietrich v The Queen (1992) 177 CLR 292 at 299.

Doggett v R (2001) 208 CLR 343.

Garland, David. 2008. "On the Concept of Moral Panic." *Crime, Media, Culture* 4 (1): 9–30.

Goodman-Delahunty, Jane, Natalie Martschuk, Martine Powell, and Nina Westera. 2019. "Special Measures for Children in Court: Law in Action in a Multi-agency Committee." *Australian Social Work* 72 (4): 503–516.

Halpérin, Jean-Louis. 2011. "Law in Books and Law in Action: The Problem of Legal Change." *Maine Law Review* 64 (1): 46–76.

Hay, Douglas. 1984. "The Criminal Prosecution in England and its Historians." *The Modern Law Review* 47 (1): 1–29.

Hull. N.E.H. 1989. "Reconstructing the Origins of Realistic Jurisprudence: A Prequel to the Llewellyn-Pound Exchange Over Legal Realism." *Duke Law Journal* 5: 1302–1334.

Jago v District Court (NSW) (1989) 168 CLR 23.

Kirchengast, Tyrone 2006. *The Victim in Criminal Law and Justice*. New York and Houndmills: Palgrave Macmillan.

Logan, Anne. 2008. *Feminism and Criminal Justice: A Historical Perspective.* London, UK: Springer Nature.

Longman v The Queen (1989) 168 CLR 79.

Mack, Kathy, and Sharyn Roach Anleu. 2007. "Getting Through the List: Judgecraft and Legitimacy in the Lower Courts." *Social & Legal Studies* 16 (3): 341–361.

McKinney v The Queen (1991) 171 CLR 468.

Myers, John E.B., Susan Diedrich, Devon Lee, Kelly McClanahan Fincher and Rachel Stern. 1999. "Professional Writing on Child Sexual Abuse from 1900 to 1975: Dominant Themes and Impact on Prosecution." *Child Maltreatment* 4 (3): 201–216.

Pound, Roscoe. 1910. "Law in Books and Law in Action." *American Law Review* 44: 12–36.

R v Baskerville (1916) 2 KB 658.
R v Brasier (1779) 168 E.R 202.
R v Carroll (1906) 6 SR (NSW) 258.
R v Gregg 1892 VLR 218, 221.
R v Hamilton (1930) 30 SR (NSW) 277.
R v Young [1923] SASR 35.
R v Walsh (1905) 7 WALR 263.
Ryan, Mike. 2003. *Penal Policy and Political Culture in England and Wales: Four Essays on Policy and Process.* Hook: Waterside Press.
Scott, Dorothy, and Shurlee Swain. 2002. *Confronting Cruelty—Historical Perspectives on Child Protection in Australia.* Melbourne: Melbourne University Press.
Spiegelman, James. 2004. "The Truth Can Cost Too Much: The Principle of a Fair Trial." *Australian Law Journal* 78: 29–49.
Swain, Shurlee. 2015. "Giving Voice to Narratives of Institutional Sex Abuse." *The Australian Feminist Law Journal 41*(2): 289–304.
The Evidence (Children) Act 1997 (NSW).
Twain, Mark. 2009. *The Adventures of Huckleberry Finn.* Melbourne: Penguin Group (Australia).
Western Australia, *Parliamentary Debates*, Legislative Council, 6 April 1992 (Hon Peter Foss), 3397.
Women's Weekly. "In Brief." December 2020.

Index

A

Aboriginal and Torres Strait Islander 209, 211, 212, 230, 234
Aboriginal English 232
abuse v, 3, 4, 6, 19, 35, 53, 211, 214, 224, 233, 235, 249
  child abuse 23, 26, 51, 52, 197, 217
  sexual abuse 4, 20, 22, 24–26, 43–45, 54
adversarial trial 2, 7, 9, 14, 24, 63, 110, 139, 142–144, 149, 150, 156, 213, 249
age of consent 20, 66
Atkinson, Judy 211, 215, 233
Australian Federation of Women Voters 124, 140, 159, 160, 244
Australian Law Reform Commission (ALRC) xi, 3, 42–45, 53, 56, 97, 100, 108, 123, 127, 128, 131, 132, 148, 163, 200, 233
  Children's Evidence: Report 63 128
  Issues Paper 131
  Recognition of Aboriginal Customary Laws 233
  Seen and Heard: Priority for Children in the Legal Process 97, 108, 148, 163

B

Backhouse, Constance 3, 18, 173, 204
Baginsky, Adolf 21
battered child syndrome 4, 23. *See also* Kempe, Henry
Bentham, Jeremy 18, 117, 141
Bialestock, Dora. *See* failure to thrive

R. Blewer, *Child Witnesses in Twentieth Century Australian Courtrooms*, Palgrave Histories of Policing, Punishment and Justice,
https://doi.org/10.1007/978-3-030-69791-4

Binet, Alfred 21
Birrell, John and Robert 23
Blackstone's ratio. *See* Blackstone, William
Blackstone, William 18, 21, 117, 173, 174, 189, 203, 246
Boe, Andrew 9
Brennan, Mark 23, 160, 246. *See also* Brennan, Roslin E.
Brennan, Roslin E. 23, 160, 246
Brennan, Frank 15, 107–109, 128, 131, 143–144, 247
Brewer, Holly 17–19, 126
Bruck, Maggie 3, 21–23, 25, 49, 246. *See also* Ceci, Stephen J.
Burnside, Robert 94
Bussau, Albert 94

C

Campbell, Joseph 40, 41, 43, 44, 157, 176
Carroll, William 42, 179–180, 242
case law. *See* common law
Cashmore, Judy 3, 24, 122, 124, 156, 160, 246
Ceci, Stephen J. 3, 21–23, 25, 48, 51, 246. *See also* Bruck, Maggie
Chamberlain, Aidan 1
Chamberlain, Azaria 1
Chamberlain, Lindy 1, 3
Chamberlain v. The Queen (No.2) (1984) 1
Cheers v Porter (1931) 46 CLR 521 64, 69, 78, 79, 82
childhood 3, 5, 17–20, 244
child protection 19, 21, 23, 24, 244, 248
Christian Women's Temperance Union 232, 233
closing courtrooms to hear children's testimony 119–120
  found improper 120
  in Camera 119, 121, 125, 161
  open justice 120, 247
collusion 161
common law 2, 4, 5, 7, 8, 14–17, 19, 44, 63, 64, 66, 69, 73, 76, 86, 109, 117, 118, 140, 141, 171–174, 184–188, 190–193, 195, 197, 199, 212, 214, 225, 242, 247, 249
  doctrine of *doli incapax* 19
  doctrine of precedent 15
  oath test. *See* oath test
  origins of 15
  overview of features 15
  principle of open justice 117–118, 120
communication aid 163. *See also* intermediary schemes
competence 63, 82
competency 4, 6, 8, 16, 21, 63, 64, 69, 72, 74, 84, 94, 95, 97, 98, 100, 115, 128, 140, 219–220, 247, 249. *See also* oath test
  common law procedure for a child to demonstrate 16
  reforms 95
confront accused 24, 41, 55, 118, 122, 127. *See also* police

corroboration 4, 8, 16, 22, 26, 67, 81, 87, 171–203, 223, 243, 247, 248
  barrier to conviction in sexual assaults against children 89
  of a child's testimony in common law 16
  common law preference for 64
  implicating accused 204
  statutory requirement for 177, 181, 191, 202
  sworn testimony 171, 174, 177, 178, 184, 187, 188, 192
  unsworn testimony 171, 174, 177, 181–183, 193–195, 197, 199, 201
credibility 8, 66, 142, 143, 149, 150, 156, 160, 164, 171, 173, 175, 189, 195, 210, 228, 250
Criminal Justice Commission (Qld) 227–231
Criminal Law Amendment Act 1885 (UK) 66–68, 184, 203
Croft, John 44, 181, 182
cross-examination v, 3, 7, 8, 47, 56, 101, 109, 116, 128, 133, 139–165, 171, 187, 223, 225, 226, 228, 229, 243, 247, 249
  bullying 149
  child abuse 228
  of child by accused 157–159
  harassing 155
  illegitimate advantage 150
  intervene in the cross-examination 154–156, 162
  restrictions on 142
Cossins, Anne/Annie 132, 139, 140, 149, 150

D

defence barristers 77, 91, 146, 148, 150–152, 155, 156, 225, 228, 248
denials made by an accused 183, 196
discretionary powers
  of judges 84, 108, 182, 183, 199, 222, 247
  of judges and magistrates 77, 91, 108, 227, 233, 247, 248
  of judicial officers 4, 75, 83, 116, 118, 124, 141, 148, 156, 161, 193, 242, 247, 248
  of judiciary 75, 108, 203, 246
  of police 36, 37, 112, 139, 150, 214, 233
Dupré, Ernest 21

E

Eade v R (1924) 34 CLR 343 84, 87, 155, 182, 183, 196
Eades, Diana 143, 213, 214, 227–229
Eastwood, Christine 24
Evil Angels 2
Evidence-in-chief 6, 7, 33, 54, 55, 139, 148, 149, 153, 158, 229, 231

F

failure to thrive 4, 23. *See also* Bialestock, Dora
fairness to the accused 90, 143, 188, 189

fair trial 109, 117, 126, 143, 247, 248, 250
fantasise vi, 151
Finnane, Mark vi, 34, 35, 38, 211, 212, 215, 225, 236
Fisher, William 79, 80, 115, 116
Fitzjames Stephen, James 14
Flin, Rhona 109, 140
Franklin, Benjamin 18
fraudulent allegations 199

G

gender assumptions
  about competency of male and female child witnesses 80
  about male police officers' capacity to handle child witnesses 36, 38, 229
  about reliability of witnesses 197–198
  in police interviews 51
Gibbens, T. 161
Goodman, Gail 2–5, 21, 23, 24, 53, 246
ground rules hearing 127, 162, 249
guilty plea 87, 147, 157, 219

H

Hale, Matthew 18, 21, 73, 117, 172–174, 189, 198, 199, 203
Hargan v The King (1919) 27 CLR 13 186–188, 191, 192, 198
High Court of Australia
  role in Australia's criminal justice system 16–17
Higinbotham, George 88, 174–176, 242
hostile witness 112, 145–147, 164
Human Rights and Equal Opportunity Commission 3, 97, 108, 216, 217, 233, 234

I

identification parade (line up) 35, 42, 43, 45, 53
implicating the accused 67, 175, 178–181, 184, 185, 191, 204
inconsistencies 54, 77, 79, 86, 143, 150–154, 161, 184, 185, 203, 244
Indigenous child witnesses 8, 9, 86, 163, 210–219, 222–224, 226, 228, 230, 233–235
  cross-examination 223
  custom 209, 225
  Daniel Yock 228, 234, 235
  eye-contact 220
  gratuitous concurrence 226, 227, 235
  Pinkenba 213, 230
  recognition of Indigenous laws 224, 225
  silence 228
  specialist courts 232, 244
  swearing oath 243
  traditional marriage 225
Inquest into the death of Azaria Chantel Loren Chamberlain 2012 1–2
intermediaries 159, 244, 249
intermediary schemes 140. *See also* communication aid

interpreters 223, 224, 231, 233
interrogation by suspect 6, 41. *See also* confront accused
Irvine, William 111

J

judicial warnings 184, 192, 198, 200
Jackson, Louise 19, 37, 38, 49, 174

K

Kempe, Henry 23
Kaladelfos, A vi, 20, 143

L

Langbein, John 14, 64, 65, 73, 141, 142, 149, 173
leading 48, 122, 150, 151, 244
lead the witness 145
legislation 4, 15–17, 25, 34, 40, 45, 64, 68–70, 73, 78, 79, 81–84, 87, 91, 97, 100, 101, 108–111, 118, 121, 123, 124, 128, 131, 142, 161–163, 174, 177, 198, 243, 245
  allowing unsworn testimony of children 94, 97, 219
  defining age of consent 96, 217
  mandating closed courtrooms in sexual offence cases involving child witnesses 219
  regarding corroboration of the evidence of children 22
  requiring corroboration of a child's unsworn testimony 4, 82–83, 177, 183, 194
  to allow unsworn evidence from child witnesses 16, 194. *See also* unsworn evidence legislation
Longman v The Queen (1989) 168 CLR 79 200

M

McGlade, Hannah 211, 236
McGough, Lucy 2–4, 25, 26
media
  newspapers 110–111
  The Maiden Tribute to Modern Babylon series 66, 67
Mertin, Peter 24
Moreton-Robinson, Aileen 213
Mr Bubbles case 25, 96. *See also* Seabeach Kindergarten Investigation
Myers, John E.B. 22, 116, 117, 173, 246

N

nolle prosequi 108, 217
New South Wales Royal Commission into the New South Wales Police Service (Wood Royal Commission) 25
New South Wales Law Reform Commission 45, 200

O

oath
  kiss the book 146
  legislation 40, 68
  religious knowledge 68–69

oath test 65, 69, 73, 74, 77, 79–82, 87–89, 91, 93, 94, 97, 100, 101, 144, 220, 242, 243
difficulties for children 65–66
failure of 77, 79, 157
links to religious knowledge and beliefs 68
opposition to it being administered to children 91–94
preparation and training for 108, 118
responses to questions 76, 235
oral testimony 7, 139, 141, 164, 185, 227
reliance on 109
oral tradition 139, 141–144. *See also* oral testimony

P

Pear, T.H. 21. *See also* Wyatt, Stanley
police v, 5–7, 25, 33–40, 42–55, 63, 76, 86, 93, 146, 150, 158, 161, 164, 179, 183, 196, 213–219, 221, 225, 227–231, 233, 247, 249
confronting the suspect 35, 40–42, 53, 146
identifying suspects 35, 42–45
by touch 42, 55
and Indigenous child witnesses 163, 211, 230, 232–234
line-up/identification parade 35, 42–45, 53, 55, 65
police cooperating with other services or disciplines 35
police interviews with child witnesses 35–36, 50–51, 54
techniques for greater success 34, 35
women police officers 36–39, 46, 123, 244
Pound, Roscoe 9, 241–242, 249
Prince, J. 161
Prosecution Project vi, 56, 111, 151, 176, 194, 215
prosecutors 63, 109, 139, 140, 142, 144–148, 164, 215, 234
psychological impact on child witnesses
of confronting the accused in court 24
of courtroom environment 109
of cross-examination 7
of direct contact with the accused 35, 40–42, 53, 55
of giving evidence in court 2, 3, 24, 114
of identifying the suspect 42–49
of multiple interviews 26, 52, 55
of police interviews 51, 53
of public hearings of sexual assault cases 131

Q

Queanbeyan Outrage. *See* Campbell, Joseph
Queensland Law Reform Commission 94, 199
Queensland Criminal Justice Commission
Aboriginal Witnesses in Queensland's Criminal Courts report 230–231

Queensland Committee of Inquiry Regarding Sexual Offences (1944) 126, 161

R

Ramsay's Bush Outrage. *See* Campbell, Joseph
recognition of Indigenous laws 224, 225
reforms 3–7, 9, 24, 35, 51, 52, 55, 65, 67, 88, 124, 125, 128, 139, 43, 159, 161, 163, 171, 174, 175, 184, 197, 200, 244–249
  of police interviews with child witnesses 53
  to competency of child witnesses legislation 98, 100
  to legislation allowing unsworn evidence of children 85
  to legislation in response to the child protection movement 19
  to legislation regarding children swearing an oath 92
  to legislation to protect children from the impact of the adversarial trial process 24
reliability 3, 24, 40, 51, 96, 128, 198
  in identifying suspects 42
  in police interviews 51, 53, 54
  perceptions of the 23, 34, 46
  suggestibility 21, 48
  testimony 18
  views against 22
rights of children 245
right to cross-examine 141, 157, 159
Royal Commission into Institutional Responses to Child Sexual Abuse 3, 132
Royal Commission on Human Relationships 126–128, 143, 161, 162, 199
R v Baskerville (1916) 2 KB 658 184–186, 189, 194
R v Brasier (1779) 1 Leach 199 2, 65, 66, 74, 248
R v Grills (1910) 11 CLR 400 41, 42
R v Sparkman (1930) 31 SR (NSW) 80 49, 50, 81
R v Smellie (1919) 14 Cr App R 128 109, 122
R v Gregg (1892) 18 VLR 218 88–91, 174–176, 242
Ryan, Mary 46–49, 112, 114, 242

S

Scott v Scott (1913) AC 417 109, 118, 120, 122
Seabeach Kindergarten Investigation 25, 95. *See also* Mr Bubbles case
Seen and Heard: Priority for Children in the Legal Process 97, 108, 148, 163
self-represented defendants 158, 159
Slape, Myrtle 38, 151–154
Smaal, Yorick vi, 20
Snelling, Harold 51
South Australian Law Reform Commission 123
specialist courts 124–126, 132, 232, 244, 249
Spencer, John 109, 140, 149, 160

sufficient intelligence test 6, 63, 67, 71, 83–87, 98, 101, 221. *See also* competency
legislation 81–84
test, failure of 79
suggestibility 21, 48
supportive measures 7, 109, 117, 131, 132, 154, 243
ground rules hearings 127, 162, 249
Letters Patent 114
objections to 117
swearing an oath 6, 64, 76, 92, 219. *See also* competency; sworn testimony
swearing and oath alternatives 81
sworn testimony 64, 65, 69, 72, 74, 77, 78, 81, 87, 95, 100, 171, 174, 177, 178, 187, 188, 192
superiority of 87

T

tears 2, 14, 46, 47, 49, 107, 111, 112, 147, 155, 164, 190, 213
tender years 20, 37, 67, 69, 70, 73–77, 83, 85, 88, 99, 164, 174, 177, 181, 187, 204, 215
Tobin, John 20
Tomison, Adam 24
traditional marriage 225

U

Uniform Evidence Law 97, 100
United Nations Convention on the Rights of the Child 20, 131, 245
unsworn evidence 4, 16, 41, 63, 65–70, 73, 78, 79, 81–88, 90, 91, 94, 97–99, 101, 171, 174, 176, 177, 180–183, 193–197, 199, 201, 204, 219, 221, 244, 249
inferiority of a child's 66, 83, 89
sufficient intelligence test 67, 83–86
unsworn evidence legislation 81

V

van Krieken, Robert 19
Varendonck, Julien 4, 5, 21
video 7, 24, 45, 53, 54, 100, 128, 148, 243
Victorian Statute Law Reform Committee 6, 132

W

Walsh, John 177
warnings 8, 144, 174, 184–190, 192, 197–200, 243
Western Australia *Royal Commission on the Conditions of the Natives* (Roth Commission), 1905 218
Whittaker, Alison 235, 236
Wigmore, John Henry 22, 140, 149, 246
Women's organisations 124, 131
Australian Federation of Women Voters 124, 140, 159, 160, 244

Christian Women's Temperance Union 232, 233
Country Women's Association 125, 244
League of Women Voters 126, 244
National Council of Women 37, 124, 125, 244
Women Justices Association 123
Women's Services Guild 131
Wyatt, Stanley 21. *See also* Pear, T.H.
Wood Royal Commission. *See* New South Wales Royal Commission into the New South Wales Police Service

Y

youth examiners 51, 162. *See also* intermediaries
Yock, Daniel 228–230, 234, 235

The manufacturer's authorised representative in the EU is Springer Nature Customer Service Centre GmbH, Europaplatz 3, 69115 Heidelberg, Germany. If you have any concerns regarding our products, please contact ProductSafety@springernature.com

Printed and bound by CPI Group (UK) Ltd, Croydon, CR0 4YY
30/09/2026
02225327-0007